Teaching English
So It Matters

Teaching English
So It Matters

*Creating Curriculum For and
With High School Students*

Deborah Stern

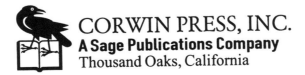

CORWIN PRESS, INC.
A Sage Publications Company
Thousand Oaks, California

For information address:

Corwin Press, Inc.
A Sage Publications Company
2455 Teller Road
Thousand Oaks, California 91320
E-mail: order@corwin.sagepub.com

SAGE Publications Ltd.
6 Bonhill Street
London EC2A 4PU
United Kingdom

SAGE Publications India Pvt. Ltd.
M-32 Market
Greater Kailash I
New Delhi 110 048 India

Printed in the United States of America

Library of Congress Cataloging-in-Publication Data

Stern, Deborah, 1963-
    Teaching English so it matters: creating curriculum for and with high school students / Deborah Stern.
        p.   cm.
    Includes bibliographical references and index.
    ISBN 0-8039-6183-9 (alk. paper)
    1. English language—Study and teaching (Secondary)—United States. 2. Popular education—United States. 3. Teacher-student relationships—United States. 4. Classroom management—United States. 5. Curriculum planning—United States. I. Title.
LB1631.S735 1995
428'.0071'273—dc20

94-3465·

This book is printed on acid-free paper.

00 01 02 03 04 10 9 8 7 6 5 4 3 2

Production Editor: Yvonne Könneker
Typesetter: Andrea D. Swanson

⠿ Contents

Part II. Thematic Instructional Units   **79**

▓ List of Figures

❖ Foreword

William Ayers

Every child—somewhere, sometime—must connect with a caring adult. In order to grow up whole, each of us needs to find someone who can see us fully—our minds as well as our hearts; our concerns, fears, and needs; but perhaps more important, our skills, our abilities, our hopes, our dreams, and our aspirations. In order to become a person of values each of us requires another who values us. Each of us would benefit from an encounter with someone such as Deborah Stern, a teacher who struggles intensely to connect with her students as fellow human beings.

Deborah Stern shows teachers a way to see youngsters more fully, to take them more seriously, to value their humanity, and to tap into their experiences more wholeheartedly. In *Teaching English So It Matters,* she opens a pathway to the energy and vitality that students bring with them to school. Stern is an idealist in the best sense—she posits a hopeful vision of a humane classroom toward which to work. There is, however, nothing in her ideal that is romantic, abstract, or unattainable. She is faithful to her own experience and grounded in the lived situations of her flesh-and-blood students.

Schools are organized typically with the idea of aggregating youngsters, normalizing them, sorting them into winners and losers. As a recent newspaper editorial put it, schools function to instill values and habits that employers find desirable: punctuality, deference, unquestioning acceptance of rules and procedures. When teachers think there is more to it than this, when they struggle toward a shared project or a collective inquiry or some common purpose with their students, they confront the everyday banality of schools as prisons of the mind.

All the machinery of schooling—the class schedule, the press of time, the organization of subject matter, the bells, the grades—is in the service of this straightforward but difficult task: to coerce consciousness. The deepest lessons of school are about hierarchy and your place in it, obedience, conformity, passivity, and provisional self-esteem. Much of the rest is merely decoration.

One of the commonplaces of modern schooling is sorting and labeling, and labeling is something each of us has experienced in and out of school. Many years ago as a graduate student at Teachers College, Columbia University, I was asked to introduce a renowned scholar to a college symposium. It was a steamy July day, and everyone dressed casually in gym shoes, shorts, and light shirts. I did my job, he gave his talk, and later, while being chauffeured to the airport by another student, the scholar—referring to me—asked my colleague, "Who's the guy with the tattoos?"

We had a laugh about it later. I never had thought of myself as "the guy with the tattoos" before. It reminded me of a time many years before that when I spent an afternoon playing pickup basketball on a playground in the Bronx. Choosing new teams for what seemed like the hundredth time, the two best players went down the list: this one, that one, this one, that one, until finally one said, "I'll take the old white guy." Again it was me; again I was surprised; again I had been categorized in a way that was both true and yet somehow overdetermining. Just the thought of being tagged or numbered or labeled makes each of us, I think, want to rebel; the poisonous impact of casual categorization (at least when applied to ourselves) causes us to recoil.

And yet the lingua franca of most schools is casual categorization. This one is special ed, that one is behavior disordered, the other one is emotionally mentally handicapped. Everyone is "at risk." Although the explanatory power of these labels is suspect at best, their repeated use gives them a type of power nonetheless.

The challenge is for teachers to see every student as unique. The moral demand is to know that each child or youth is induplicable—the one and only who will ever walk the earth. This means that when connections are missed, opportunities lost, and failures registered, we recognize our own shortcomings and are not so quick to blame. It also means that we struggle to move beyond the arid view permeating our schools that sees kids only as obstacles and problems, collections of deficits and encumbrances.

Teachers need to question the common sense—to break the rules, to become political and activist in concert with the kids. This is true heroism, an authentic act of courage. We need to take seriously the experiences of youngsters, their sense-making, their knowledge, and their dreams. In particular, we must question the structures that kids are rejecting. In other words, we must assume an intelligence in youngsters, assume that they are acting sensibly and are deriving meaning from situations that are difficult and often dreadful— and certainly, not of their own making. In finding common cause with youngsters, we also may find our own salvation as teachers. This book provides a practical powerful alternative.

⠿ Foreword

Mark Perry

Leanne says that the thing you should not do is put your name up on the board the first day of class. You'll lose the students for the whole semester. Salvador says that his goal is to be alive by his senior year. Naomi says that the best thing about school is cutting class to be with her friends. She goes on to say that her English teacher threw her jacket in the garbage so Naomi picked up some scissors and threw them at her. Daniel says his science teacher called him a wetback so he called the teacher a honky. The teacher grabbed Daniel so he hit him. Louisa says she hated all of her teachers. They put her down and called her names. Fernando says teachers think they have power over you. He thinks it would be better if teachers and students worked together.

Deborah Stern poses a challenge to all teachers, most especially teachers in urban, inner-city classrooms. Are we willing to listen to our students? Are we willing and capable of sharing the classroom, developing a student-centered environment in which we model democracy, trust, fairness, and cooperation?

Once we leave our teacher education programs we're on our own. What a setup. If we're lucky we have supportive principals. Most likely, the older teachers will look down on our energy and enthusiasm, and the other teachers with whom we want to talk and share our questions are too busy fighting for their own survival. Ultimately, we face the students. Rule number one: Don't write our names on the board. They don't teach this in education school. Rule number two, according to Leanne: Be yourself.

The cocreative classroom is a joint proposition, a room within a room—a sanctuary in which the teacher-centered teacher can become a student-centered teacher and the students can feel safe and respected as learners. What Stern proposes is much more difficult than traditional teaching and class management, a prescribed curriculum handed down by a central office or a department head.

In her first three chapters, Stern develops the cocreative classroom framework. She explains the rationale for student-centered teaching and helps teachers and students studying to become teachers ask questions of themselves. Be forewarned. It's not for every teacher—only those who are willing to take a risk, the risk being the challenge of becoming a self-reflective and effective teacher capable of motivating students to become empowered learners.

One of the essences of self-reflective teaching is listening to and learning with the students. The cocreative classroom is an opportunity to do this. It is a risk, as Stern explains, but a risk well worth taking. It is also a process that does not happen overnight, is continually evolving, and never ends. That is what is so powerful.

The question I am asked most by new teachers and teachers wanting to be more student-centered in their teaching is "tell me the method." I nearly always respond with an answer that is frustrating, but it is the only answer that I feel is honest. There is no *one* method, no *one* approach that will work in the classroom. What is unique about *Teaching English So It Matters* is that it is an invaluable resource for both new and experienced teachers. The duality between structure and freedom, between content and critical inquiry, can be processed only through practice. Stern's lesson plans present not a formula but a road map to explore with the students as we walk together through the journey of learning.

The ultimate responsibility for learning falls on the teacher. Deborah Stern shows us how the process of cocreation and student-centered teaching can be fun, fulfilling, and effective. It is now up to us to add our own ideas to Stern's framework. Fasten your seat belts and get ready to listen, learn, and explore new horizons with your students.

⠿ Acknowledgments

I would first like to thank my coauthors, without whom this book could not exist: Sharon, Deon, Ray, Gina, Missy, Sharond, Brenda, Phalla, Claudia, Guy, Soraida, Ilia, Jennifer, Alex, Ximena, Nathan, Jackie, Doris, Nancy, Jay, Joel, Carmen, Vanna, Frances, Verna, Denise, Richard, Tammy, Terri, Vanessa, Kevin, Gene, Sherri, Indira, Lisa, Aziz, Kim, Antoine, Dave, Manuel, Sorn, Dinh, LaTrece, Arlene, Geri, John, Danielle, Maurice, Eric, Aaron, Lanford, Rebecca, Eson, Mike, Lloyd, Andre, Pierre, Arennia, Cynthia, Gail, Janet, James, Roger, Kevin, Barnabas, Yolanda, Chris, Anthony, Homer, Tonya, Berenice, Will, Curtis, Sherri, Liz, Lakivia, Larita, Ceci, Marla, Gabrielle, Lawanda, Keith, Sergio, Tamara, Kenny, Utarus, Bernie, Terry, Hussain, Ron, Vashonda, Bernard, Angela, Len, Stephanie, George, Winter, Tina, Tony, Becky, Rich, Herb, Amanda, Brian, Lela, Leithzy, Ed, Tracy, Juan, Adam, Bebe, Paul, Andy, Kwame, Joyce, Laura, Angie, Keizier, Atavia, Candy, Toni, Latanya, Kat, Valerie, Don, Keke, Latosha, Nettie, Demont, Lawrence, Lila, Mario, Burnett, Danny, Sarina, Leticia, Millie, Valerie, Frank, Roman, Charles, Lenise, Eddie, Lettan, Mema, Tennille, Norman, Rotosha, Sandra, Justin, Paloma, Jessica, Liza, Jamale, Holly, Erica, Damiso, Rob, Irene, Sharonda, Keith, Janice, Kris, Juan, Evernell, Heather, Angel, Migdalia, Charles, Cassandra, Tito, Yolanda, Mario, Evelyn, Tameka, Dahnetta, Valarie, Marsha, Darvin, Mark, Vikkiey, Moises, Julio, Sam, and Rosie.

I thank my friends and colleagues who will recognize their ideas and their own hard work in this book: For a million suggestions, debates, "The Hero" unit, and her example of high intellectual expectations for herself and her students, I cannot thank Ann Goethals enough. I am indebted to Dorothea Anagnastopoulos for the Foucault adaptation, suggestions for materials, the creative scenarios, and for reminding me that a teacher's most important asset is a sense of humor.

I appreciate the assistance given me in locating authors and securing copyright information by Adele Tuchler at Washington University, Michelle at *LA Weekly*, Faith Barbato at HarperCollins, Mimi Ross at Henry Holt, Hilda Hinojosa and Dr. Nicholas Canellos at Arte Publico Press, Nancy Bereano at Firebrand Books, Sondra Robinson Gatewood at Acme Features Syndicate, A. J. Benson at Cherry Lane Music, Julia Kent at the *Village Voice*, Eileen Papain at the Wallace Literary Agency, Laine Dougherty at *Common Sense*, Steve Bing at the Massachusetts Advocacy Center, Ellen Reeves at *The New Press*, and William at the Chase Manhattan Bank in New York.

I am grateful especially to all the artists, writers, and educators who generously have allowed me to reprint their works: Marge Piercy, Ivan Illich, Adrian LeBlanc, Dr. Robert L. Williams, Léon Bing, and Don Sabo.

I also appreciate the advice, inspiration, and examples set by George Hillocks, Sara Manewith, Carol DeMoll, Bill Ouellette, Paul Pajeau, Christine Wedam-Rosario and Nancy Green at the Chicago Teachers' Center, Pa Joof, Dale Russel, Matt-Yanny-Tillar, Ruth Hinz, and all interviewed teachers and students.

I thank Alice Foster and everyone else at Corwin Press.

❖ About the Author

Deborah Stern teaches at DuSable High School in Chicago. She has worked as a curriculum consultant with Northeastern University's Chicago Teachers' Center, with the Alternative Schools Network, and has involved urban and suburban students together in interscholastic educational projects. The English program she developed for and with students at Prologue Alternative High School was named in 1990 by the National Council of Teachers of English as one of four National Centers of Excellence in North America for serving students at risk. In addition to teaching secondary students how to implement their own English curriculum, she has taught children of all ages to produce their own dance, theater, and music programs. She holds a master of arts degree in teaching from the University of Chicago and continues to work on curricular reform in and out of the classroom.

This book is dedicated to my parents,
the best teachers I know,
and
to Bob, who makes it all possible

PART I

The Cocreative Classroom

1

▓ Teaching With—
Instead of To—
  Students

This is a book for high school teachers, written by one teacher and 350 students. We have been working together on it for five years, although none of my students knew they were collaborating authors. They thought they were just going to English class—a class that they recognized as being different from any other they had taken in high school. I teach *with*, not *to* my students; together, we create assignments, activities, and curriculum.

My students come from various secondary schools in the city of Chicago. Officially, they are all drop outs—part of the 50% that have given up, have been expelled, or have been otherwise unable to graduate from Chicago public high schools. Their careers in school have been marked by high absenteeism, pregnancy, gang involvement, drug and alcohol abuse, and extreme disaffection. They are classified as "students at risk." What we do together in English class is create curriculum that treats their experiences as resources, not liabilities. This book gives testimony to the efficacy of this strategy. It outlines the process that evolved through one teacher's cooperation with her students. It details activities, tested in the urban classroom, that can be adapted to work in other environments.

My students are African American, Asian, Latino, Native American, and White male and female teens. The units of instruction provided here represent some of their interests and concerns over the last five years. These are the lessons and activities that my students and I created together as we read, wrote, discussed, argued, and learned about literature and real-life experience.

Not all of these units will interest all students everywhere. An all-female class in Miami or a suburban class in Kansas, for example, may have different problems and different fears, and may want to study different topics. Teachers must solicit student opinion before embarking on a unit of study with them. Although it is true that all teenagers share some of the same concerns, they must be given opportunities to make decisions about their own education. They need to feel a sense of ownership. It is their right. Alienation from this process is one of the factors that puts a student at risk.

This book is for teachers who want to reach their students by teaching them how to examine their world critically. It is especially for teachers working in urban classrooms in which high school students' experiences so often go beyond the "normal" watersheds of adolescence.

Teachers working with other populations also can use the affective, high-interest, student-centered activities and assignments in this book. They can teach cocreatively with their students. This technique shows students that education is of immediate and paramount relevance. It validates and allows students to reflect on their own realities. It teaches them to learn from each other. All students—urban, suburban, or rural; apathetic or college-bound—can benefit from this approach.

The best way for teachers use the book is *selectively*. The first three chapters discuss the cocreative, student-centered approach and give instructions, descriptions, and accounts of its implementation. Each chapter ends with "applications for teachers": a series of reflective questions for educators. These questions ask teachers to consider the viability and application of the student-centered approach in their own classrooms. Chapter 4 offers instructors' notes and student handouts that provide guidelines applicable to various lessons. Chapters 5 through 9 contain complete units of instruction that teachers can adopt and modify with their own students.

Any instructional methodology must be taken as an option, not a prescription. Every lesson described in this book will not successfully engage every student. As teachers know, what works one day will not work the next. And frankly, we must acknowledge several realities. First, we are adults—outside the family and outside the core of these students' lives. Sometimes it seems as if we do not inhabit the same world as our students. We live in a different place, we are often of another culture, and we do not always share the same socioeconomic conditions. Even if these factors did not put us outside the sphere of direct influence, there is still another factor that distances us from our students and their lives.

We are teachers. Our job, no matter how involved we may get with individual students, is to educate kids. We are not counselors, social workers, police officers, surrogate parents, or baby-sitters—although it would be difficult to find a teacher who has not worn all these hats at one time or another. The job is a flexible one, requiring interpersonal talents of the most exhaustive and creative nature. But no matter how sensitive or caring or "in touch" teachers may be with students, we must know when to stop. Every teacher must recognize the limited range of their human power: We can't save their lives, can't help all students all the time. This is the larger truth. It can be profoundly sad and humbling. Sometimes these teenagers are dealing with problems of such enormity that all the well-intentioned, responsive, empathetic instruction in the world cannot help them out of their dilemmas.

This is not to say that the task is hopeless. The grim reality gives us choices. We can settle for less, or we can search for new avenues, new ways to reach out. If there is anyone who can reach a 17-year-old in discussion of the issues that challenge us all—sexuality, substance use and abuse, family relationships, making a living—it is another 17-year-old. No, not always, and certainly not automatically. Some teenagers seem to have a talent for giving each other the worst advice imaginable (I remember the time I heard one girl telling another to get back at her cheating boyfriend by sleeping with all his friends). I am not suggesting that we encourage the blind to lead the blind or that English classes turn into peer counseling sessions.

The trick is to educate those peers. Give them information and tools so that they can ask each other the right questions. Raise some consciousnesses, and let students challenge each other. Provide them with opportunities to share the insight they might get from parents, other role models, characters in literature, or their teachers. In the process, they will bring to class their greatest strength: the ability to teach one another.

Teachers who want to use this book and this approach must be willing to do one thing: make informed, responsive choices. Teachers must select and implement only those lessons that have instructional potential for their students. They must be willing to reject those ideas that do not inspire creativity in their students.

This is not a limitation; it is, in fact, the point. The cocreative approach suggests that teachers look closely and listen even more carefully to individual students in their classes. Teachers must expect to make changes as they go along. When students take an active role in their own education, unpredictable variables always enter the classroom equation. Teachers must be willing to accommodate these variables. They must work with their students to create their own process of cocreation. This is the true spirit of this approach and its only pedagogical goal.

Classroom reality is also the reason for this particular format. The book is laid out for busy teachers; all handouts are ready to be copied and distributed to students. Teachers can use this book in any way they find useful. They can follow and use whole units, or individual lessons can be used out of order and assigned as separate critical thinking and writing exercises.

This book aims to show teachers one way to blend their agendas with their students' concerns. Teachers and students can work together to encourage good work habits, improve language and study skills, read great literature, focus on important issues, and develop critical thinking skills that will enrich students' lives when they leave the classroom. The key to success with these students is to expand the scope and the extent of actual student participation in planning, implementing, and evaluating their courses of study.

DEVELOPMENT OF THE COCREATIVE APPROACH

This approach has evolved organically. I never "decided" to start letting my students teach each other. What happened was that my students began to contribute to class in unexpected ways. I merely encouraged and worked with their contributions.

When I began teaching in the city I had some teaching experience (one year in a suburban middle school) and a master's degree in teaching. I was, however, in no way prepared for my urban students' poor skills, frustration, boredom, and sense of hopelessness. No one teaches teachers how to deal with these realities. Together, my students and I have worked our way out of my naïveté and their hopelessness.

I started with thematic units of instruction, which had proved successful in my previous experience. Well-structured, conceptual units, as explained in George Hillocks's *Dynamics of English Instruction 7-12* (1971), provide an effective way for teachers to organize instruction and give students unifying themes to explore as they study literature. Hillocks delineated an invaluable framework, one that provides the essential construction of all the units here. As a colleague has said, my students and I have "taken Hillocks to the streets."

In designing a first unit of instruction for my students, I tried to choose a topic that I thought they would find interesting: power. Over the course of the academic quarter, my students did respond positively to both the unit's ideas and materials. At the end of the quarter, one of them, Ray, asked if he could bring in a song about power to play for the class. Why not? I thought. Students had just finished their final unit test, and I wasn't exactly sure what I was going to do in class the next day, anyway. Ray warned me that the song was an explicit rap. This was 1988, and I had not really listened to any rap music closely—so I was a bit concerned. But Ray was a reflective kid, a good student, and I was curious. I let Ray play his tape the next day, after asking him to copy and distribute the lyrics to the class. That class was the turning point of my teaching.

We analyzed Ray's contribution—Ice T's song "Power"—using the same terminology and rigor that we had applied to the literary works I had assigned. Students in the class were far more responsive to the song than they had been to any of my materials. The song was dissected, praised, mocked, and dragged over the coals by the class. Here was the energy I had wanted them to apply to Orwell's *Animal Farm!* Here was the passion I had hoped to find in their essays! Here was the critical analysis I had wished they could apply to their own lives. Ray's song brought about a "merging of critical thought with daily life" (Shor & Freire, 1987, p. 3).

Obviously, we were on to something here. After class, several students came up to me and asked if they could bring in songs. Their choices helped us determine, as a class, that the next concept we would study would be "success." We did make this our next unit of study; students' contributions to class were exciting and provocative, and expanded the scope of the unit far beyond my expectations. Parts of our curriculum had come from the students' world, and that made all the difference.

Over the next five years, I continued to develop units of instruction with my students, using their suggestions for unit concepts and materials. As I got more comfortable with this cooperation, I had students give presentations, create discussion questions, quiz each other, edit their peers' work, and most important, evaluate the effectiveness of the unit we all had developed together, cocreatively.

Students do see the difference in the cocreative approach. At one time or another, every teacher has faced students asking, "Why do we have to learn this?" It is one of the many frustrating moments of a teacher's day. Teachers may pull a power trip when faced with this question ("Because I said so"). We might discredit the student's ability to judge value ("You don't realize that this is necessary or beneficial yet, as we adults do. That's why"). What we are likely to do, if we are in the middle of a million things (as we usually are), is to perceive this question as a hostile challenge to our authority.

The temptation to dismiss the question must be overcome. No matter how it is posed, it is a legitimate question and one whose answer students need to know. The more adolescent students know about the place and the point of an exercise, the more potential that exercise has to increase their understanding meaningfully. Sometimes the question is sincere. On the other hand, it is entirely possible that the student asking the question may be seeking to undermine a teacher's control and derail the class.

Teachers cannot play into that process—and this is exactly what ignoring the issue accomplishes. When a teacher treats a legitimate question about the reason for an activity or a subject as a distraction, that teacher devalues students' role in the process of learning. This naturally makes students draw back from their involvement in that work (Pauly, 1991).

I am not suggesting that teachers need to justify every assignment. Some students might play with teachers' good intentions; teachers might find themselves explaining the same things over and over. The key is to make the answer to that question obvious or at least within the students' reflective grasp. Teachers should not have to answer it—students should. And they will be able to, once they begin to be involved with the genesis and the objectives of the lesson. When daily activities and long-range goals revolve around expression and clarification of issues that students deal with every day, the point of daily lessons becomes clear. They "have to learn this" because it is what they want to know, what they believe they need an education in.

And where does literature fit into this? How can students' real-life issues and more academic interests be served simultaneously in the classroom? The key is to develop tools with students that work with situations in their lives and situations in literature. This tool may be a theory, an analytical procedure, a list of criteria, or a reading.

One class studying "Life on the Streets" generated a list of rules that they and their peers followed on the streets. This list became the analytical yardstick that we applied to characters in books, articles, poetry, and videos.

The class read Piri Thomas's *Down These Mean Streets* (1967/1991) and excerpts from Richard Price's *Clockers* (1992). One student, Keke, began her final essay with an analysis of the characters' actions according to the class's criteria:

> There are three rules that you have to follow to survive on the streets: respect the people who are there already, have guts, and don't think too much about what you're doing. Piri Thomas follows all these rules, because even though he is hipped to street life, he is not hipped to himself. He goes along with things, sometimes, that he shouldn't, because he's too wrapped up in it all. Thumper in Clockers starts out playing by street rules. He sees the thing as you either smoke or you get smoked. He starts to get into trouble when he starts thinking too much.

Her paper continues with quoted evidence and further explication of life on the streets for these characters. For Keke, what mattered was the analysis of street protocol and the application of these rules to lives not too different from hers and those of her peers. Keke's academic progress was demonstrated by her much-improved ability to generate claims and substantiate them with warranted evidence; this was one of my goals.

In addition to giving students a chance to get some insight into their own lives, I was pleased that this unit of instruction was able to keep students interested so that they actually read the books and wrote longer essays with original theses and textual citations. Sometimes getting a student to complete his work is the most realistic and most valuable academic achievement. Kwame confessed:

> I never finished a whole book in school before. I never saw the point. Even if it was good, I had better things to do with my time.

Lakivia said:

> I used to hate writing, but now I love it, especially about things I already know.

Students shared stories, experiences, and perspectives. As Tanya wrote:

> This class has given me a chance to see how people can share the same problems I have. It has shown me that I can listen, be listened to, and be open about certain things. Also this class has taught me about myself.

The whole class learned from each other. We pooled our knowledge, and all came away enriched.

CURRICULUM INNOVATION

When we review regular high school curriculum and the forces that instituted it, we get some perspective on cocreative teaching's value for today's students. Since the mid-19th century, teachers in this country have been given a mission: to facilitate the Americanization of immigrant children. Toward that task, administrators specified materials, guidelines, and standards—skills and facts every educated American should know (Pauly, 1991).

One hundred and fifty years later, our schools still run on the same model. The current drive to institute national school reform and the debate over what shape this reform should take still are seen in terms of maintaining the national standard. The overall decline in student performance is blamed on students' inability to assimilate, teachers' inability to teach, and other failings within the school.

We are misguided to blame teachers and students for this trend. We should focus our attention, rather, on the potential in every classroom and on the realities of our students' lives. In our efforts to figure out how to "fix" public education, we have neglected to consult the people who know best what is working, what is "broken," and what is not going to make any difference anyway. These people are teachers and students.

Traditional high school English curriculum, mandated by district or department, is out of touch with many students' cultural backgrounds. Mexican or Asian students can go through 12 years of education without ever reading a work by a Mexican or an Asian. No, it is not necessary to abandon any and all literature written by White males. But it is essential that we try to engage students with some readings and works that will reflect their experience, or at least their dreams.

That is one reason teenagers would rather sit in front of the TV than read school assignments. These videos, songs, and movies are up-to-date, and they speak to certain fantasies or fears, or with humor to which students can relate. When teachers ask students to read in school, we often are asking them to cross-identify with people and situations completely out of their experience. Yes, that is one of the joys and benefits of reading—but it is a skill, one that takes time to master.

Traditional high school curriculum requires students to make another stretch, one concerning prior knowledge. When students like mine are assigned a reading from *Julius Caesar*, for example, the teacher must supply considerable background information about imperial Rome, about Shakespeare, about drama in general. These are students who have not studied ancient history—or if they have, it hasn't "sunk in." They have heard of Shakespeare—but that's all: They've heard of him, period. Most have never seen a play.

That's a lot of blanks to fill in. Of course, teachers can just go ahead and plunge into works that are far removed from their students' lives—but to what end? To cover the material? That is a goal that often is fulfilled at the expense of the student and one that needs to be rethought.

Tradition also says that students need to be graded by the teacher, held up to a standard level of achievement. This model crumbles under scrutiny, too.

We are taught, as teachers, to be comfortable only with classrooms in which we hold the reins. But this is not always what is best for our students. I was taught to select academic tasks for my students and then to determine the appropriate nature and structure of these tasks. I learned that for formal collaborative exercises, I should divide students into groups to ensure the most efficient and beneficial arrangements. I was taught also how to evaluate student performance and how to determine the criteria by which student achievement should be judged.

In recent research, Roger L. Collins (1992) has given this set of conditions a name: the high-resolution classroom. Students in high-resolution classrooms, all performing the same tasks, can and do judge themselves according to each other's performances.

My experience supports the value of the low-resolution classroom in which students play more of an active role in selecting, determining, and evaluating their tasks. They feel empowered and make gains in self-esteem. Individual students are given opportunities to decide what they need to work on and with whom they would like to work. Groups of students decide by consensus how to judge each other's work. Because they are not all doing the same thing at the same time, students cannot compare grades. Because of this, students who once had received the lowest scores in the class are less likely to "live down" to their poor grades. This may look like chaos to the teacher or administrator used to classrooms in which everyone is doing the same thing and is being graded by the teacher. But it is, I have found, what works best for my students.

It is not, however, what most school reformers recommend. As a solution to the current school crisis, many reformers propose a national set of standards and curriculum, including increased testing of students.[1] This is ironic, because it will not give students what they really need to make them want to achieve, meet standards, and score higher on tests: the certain knowledge that high school is relevant and valuable to them.

Any systemic solutions to the problem will miss the point. Students and teachers are the ones who ultimately will determine the efficacy or failure of any program. Whatever program is instituted officially, a great many students will not benefit from it. They will slip through the cracks, as they are doing now. All the high standards and mandated multicultural curriculum in the world will not bring a student to school, will not develop life skills students can use for the rest of their lives, will not engender the feeling Tanya described:

This class is great because it's taught me that what I think matters. Sometimes I just sit and listen, but then I can take in that information and decide with myself. I think that's what education ought to be.

TEENAGERS "AT RISK"

Recently there has been a lot of talk about the causes, signs, and problems of the student at risk. Teachers know that forces from within the home, within the school, within the student, and within society all serve to put a student at risk. For what are they at risk? Failure in school? Certainly. Failure to become a productive member of the community? Possibly. Failure as human being? This is our worst fear. But what does that failure mean? What does that failure mean to a teenager? And what can teachers do about it?

The term itself is problematical. Unintentionally but actually patronizing, it speaks of deficiencies instead of potential and serves to reinforce negative stereotypes about poor children, children of color, and children in the inner city. On every front, these kids are dealing with a world that treats them as problems, not as future leaders or even as potential average citizens. Teens of color in the city regularly see themselves stereotyped and vilified on TV. Many become cynical and begin to embrace this self-fulfilling prophecy ("Everyone already thinks I'm such a bad person. Why shouldn't I make them happy?" asks Tito, a 19-year-old student who has been labeled "at risk"). Of course, bright students such as Tito recognize the apprehension they inspire. What are they at risk for, except realization of society's worst fears?

Ask any observant high school teacher if he or she has students who fit into any of these categories as characterized by the American Association of School Administrators (AASA): "abused, failing, suicidal, alienated, delinquent, overchallenged, underchallenged, alcohol/drug abusers, English-deficient, poverty-stricken, latch-key, neglected, pregnant, minority, or truant." The teacher will say, "Of course." By this broad definition, more teenagers are at risk than are not. And the ranks are swelling. Former NEA president Mary Hatwood Futrell recognized that this classification will describe more and more of our high school students in years to come. She said, "No teacher will escape teaching at-risk youth in the future" (AASA, 1989, p. 54).

The AASA recommends lots of strategies for helping the student at risk. These children need to be identified and referred to support services. They need to be in classes in which teachers keep the workload appropriate, improve student self-esteem, vary teaching and learning styles, and create a supportive classroom community.

It is hard to conceive of a student who would not be helped by such a program. Of course, teens who lack the support of a stable home or who are surrounded by negative role models have the most to gain by this personal and responsive approach.

It is frustrating to work with these students, to say the least. These are the teenagers who bounce around city schools, getting into fights, getting expelled, barely learning how to read, or reading at (or well above) grade level but still wholly uninterested in passing classes. If only they would come to school more regularly, focus their energies a bit, do their work. All we want them to do is think about where they would like to be in five years and act accordingly. If we, as teachers, could just scare these students into recognizing that it is their own lives they are playing with . . .

They know this. But there are two factors that complicate the situation—that in fact distort it beyond recognition. One is teenagers' inability to conceptualize and plan for the passage of time. It is maddening, but it is developmentally appropriate. The younger a child is, the less formed is his or her concept of future time. To an impatient three-year-old, five minutes is a year, and asking ten-year-olds to wait two months for a new video game is like asking them to wait an eternity. The older we get, the faster time goes and the easier it is for us to imagine ourselves six months, a year, five years from now.

Teenagers can imagine a few months down the road, at most. But the "future"? To most teens, this is a time as distant and as unreal as a hundred years in the past.

It is the end of September, and one of my students, Joel, already has had trouble getting to school. He is unable to ride the train to school for fear of being accosted by rival gang members. He asks me, "Why should I worry about how I'm going to get to school this semester, when I know I can almost always get a ride from my homie?" What can I say to him? He is 16 years old and has gotten to school *today*. That's enough. Why worry about the future? he asks—especially when he is talking about his world, not my world.

This leads to the second, far more disturbing factor in the equation, the one that does put students decisively and literally at risk. Many of my students think that they will never get a good job, live a violence-free life, and establish a functional relationship with society—not today, not in the future. These things always will be impossible. Tragically, quite a few of the boys do not expect to be alive ten years from now.

They encounter hassles at school, on the street, at home, at their jobs. They are unable to make connections between these environments, do not see that one could have any impact on the other. They see school as being the least likely place where they could learn something meaningful.

They still believe that a diploma will help them get a better job, but they regard it only as a credential that you get when you "play the game." It is a sign of achievement but not of learning. As research is confirming, "fewer and fewer of America's youth believe that conventionally legitimate means to success, such as schooling, are still viable methods for securing their futures" (Johnston & Borman, 1992, p. ix). This is not a new conclusion; it was first named the "articulation hypothesis" in 1964. Students continue to see little benefit to be gained from commitment to school or a diploma because there is no relationship between these things and material success and/or securing a good job (Natrillo, McDill, & Pallas, 1990).

Or as Martin, an 18-year-old trying to graduate (but still unable to earn credit), put it succinctly: "What's the point of school when I could be outside taking care of business? Everything I really need to know, I learn on the street."

We cannot persuade students to pay attention in class by asking them to consider their "futures." As Martin said, many students see no connection between school and real life. Furthermore, there are too many obstacles between them and any future that they would want.

So, here we are in a room together for 50 minutes a day, teacher and students, each of us with his or her own agenda, each of us frustrated. Joel fears for his life on the train that takes him to school. Martin has a baby to take care of and is engaging in the only lucrative business that he knows—drug dealing.

As a teacher, what can I do about these situations? I could give these kids quiet seat work, grammar exercises, stories and reading comprehension questions. With this program, I could hope that their skills would improve and they would experience a measure of success in a supportive, stable classroom. That is something.

But that doesn't help Joel get home safely or change Martin's life. A supportive teacher in a consistently safe classroom can give some stability to these kids' lives, but that is not going to help Soraida with her baby, nor will it give Kim any resources to deal with her abusive boyfriend.

If they trust their teachers, students will tell them what they need. A teacher can help students in direct, personal ways, but we all would burn out fast if we spent our days giving kids rides, job applications, lunch money, and self-defense lessons. The best we can do is offer them a curriculum that is life enriching, that will teach them to listen to and work with each other, that will trust them with responsibility and test them by letting them fulfill those responsibilities. These students need a curriculum that gives them skills and practice in helping a friend in trouble or helping themselves—one that teaches them to examine and make inferences about people's intentions and motives, one that gives them a measure of self-determination and empowerment.

TEACHERS' USE OF THE COCREATIVE, STUDENT-CENTERED APPROACH

The public blames teachers for falling test scores and an overall decline in student performance. Teachers want their students to succeed but always are negotiating external pressures that interfere with students' success. These pressures vary but can include students' troubled lives outside of school, overcrowded classrooms, inadequate teaching materials and classroom conditions, unsupportive administrations, and unrealistic expectations of student achievement. This is not to say that all teachers work under these pressures. There are many schools, even city schools, in which teachers work with caring, effective administrators to create functional classrooms.

Such environments, however, require vision, creativity, and funding. These three assets are not always found in our public school systems. Nowhere is the perceived problem in the schools greater than in cities, and nowhere do teachers receive more censure. What most critics seem to have forgotten is that teachers are at the bottom of the pyramid, second only to students in their voicelessness.

Teachers know what works and what does not work in their classrooms. And realistically, when they close the door, they will teach what they choose to teach. This book has been written for teachers to use behind those closed doors, if they have to. It presents five units of study created for and with urban teenagers, all of which were taught at least twice to at least two different sets of students with different problems and different skill levels. The book also intends to provide teachers with simple instructions about how to design new units of study with their students.

This may not change public education as we know it. Administrators and curriculum designers may reject the basic thesis of this work: that students need to be given the tools to take charge of their own education. But as we know, no matter what curriculum is prescribed for teenagers in the 1990s, they still will have to face considerable odds. These odds are compounded for urban teens, some of whom are facing life on the streets, a job market unsuited to their qualifications, and the challenge of raising their own young children.

Isolated assignments based on ideas in this book or adoption of whole units of study can allow teachers to use a student-centered approach to address these realities. If students can have classroom experiences that allow them to consider their own choices and give them the tools to make future choices critically, school will have been real, life affirming, and important to them. This is, of course, a desirable goal for all educators, but it also sounds a bit risky. Am I suggesting that teachers abdicate all power to the students? How could this work? Wouldn't teachers lose all authority? Wouldn't we be foolish to delegate our professional responsibilities to our teenaged students? These questions and others are answered in the next chapter.

APPLICATIONS FOR TEACHERS

1. What do you think your students need to survive and succeed?

2. What do you think your students expect to learn in your classroom? Are they satisfied with what they learn?

3. What do you expect your students to learn in your classroom? Are you satisfied with these lessons?

4. What limits your students' effectiveness as learners?

5. What limits your effectiveness as a teacher?

NOTE

1. It is gratifying to note that some academics working in curricular reform see the need for "more instructional strategies formulated to involve students in the learning process, to link new information to prior knowledge" (Fly Jones, 1988, p. 82).

2

⠿ Teachers' Concerns

Although they may seem apathetic or unwilling at first, I fully expect my students to come to care about their own education. Based on experience, I feel confident that they will learn to value their rights and handle their responsibilities appropriately. I know not all teachers have confidence in their students' abilities to care, to focus, and to follow through. I appreciate teachers' doubts and concerns about depending on students in this new way. Furthermore, teachers may have considerable reservations about abandoning a more traditional English curriculum in favor of one that centers around student issues.

In presenting aspects of the student-centered approach at various teachers' conferences, I have faced all types of questions from teachers and administrators alike. What follows is a sampling of these questions. Responses to these questions come from experience. I have been compelled to view classroom issues of control and power in a new way and now question some basic pedagogical assumptions. Some of the concerns expressed by teachers here reflect the conflicts between teacher training and classroom experience. I also have recorded student reactions to teachers' concerns. This chapter closes with questions teachers might ask themselves as they consider cocreative teaching.

Ten concerns crop up, in one form or another, when I talk to teachers about using the cocreative, student-centered approach in an English classroom. They say:

1. "Students don't care enough to get involved."

2. "Teachers need to hold on to power in the classroom."
3. "If given the opportunity, students would turn the classroom into a zoo."
4. "Student suggestions for topics of study would be unusable."
5. "Student contributions to classroom materials wouldn't be substantial enough or would be chosen just to provoke the teacher."
6. "The handouts in these units of instruction look like regular old worksheets: What's so 'student-centered' about this?"
7. "This isn't English! Where's the grammar?"
8. "What can I do if the only materials available are specified textbooks?"
9. "I'm limited by district and departmental requirements."
10. "It's too big a risk."

"STUDENTS DON'T CARE ENOUGH TO GET INVOLVED"

This seems to be the sad truth for some teenagers. After 10 or more years in school, after exposure to unjust conditions in school and society at large, some kids already have given up on their own chances. Some students cannot be roused from their apathy. I've known several. I honestly believe it is better that some students leave school in their teens and get jobs. It is hoped that they will mature enough to recognize the limitations of their choices and will return to school when they are ready to earn GEDs and pursue other careers. This is not to say that we should give up on students who seem to be without motivation. We, as teachers, need to remember that other issues in students' lives sometimes take precedence over school. Most students do care about school—or would like to.

In recent informal interviews, students attending (or recently graduated from) Chicago high schools responded candidly to my question: "What would you do if a teacher gave you power in a classroom?" Sam, 17, said: "If a teacher left me in charge of a class, I'd let them tear that motherfucker up, 'cause I don't care."

Teachers know that some students will be motivated to use power destructively, not constructively. The whole concept seems like a trick to Sam and one for which he is unprepared. No, I don't believe Sam is one of those teenagers who should quit school and get a job simply because he isn't ready to run a class.

I feel he is a prime candidate for participation in a cocreative classroom. Ask Sam what he wants to study. Let him engage in dialogue with his peers about issues that are of real concern to him. Maybe then he will redirect some of his anger and some of his energy. Of course, he might not be ready after all. There is only one way to find out.

Then there are students such as Gwen, 18. She says she already has had teachers who have let students lead the class. Because this idea is not new to her, she treats it with enthusiasm. If she were to lead the class, she says, she would work to ensure that "everyone there could trust everyone else." In concluding that trust is critical to her own learning, Gwen is taking a first step toward self-directed education. She is eager to bring her insight to her peers.

Similarly, Calvin, a recent graduate of 19, says he kept his own classroom experiences in mind when he was given the chance to be the authority in the classroom. He took his position seriously, using humor and empathy to gain his peers' trust. He speaks confidently and modestly about his success as a "teacher." His self-assurance shows the powerful effect responsibility can have on a student's sense of self-esteem.

In my experience, most high school students do care enough to make classes exciting and educational for each other. Even students who have not shown interest in choosing topics of study have come around despite their initial prejudices. They have been able to learn from each other.

Students in one of my recent English classes chose to study AIDS—all except Tony, 18, and Sarina, 17. Tony's first comments were, "No way am I gonna sit and listen to someone who's got it. It ain't my problem. I'll be absent." After a few weeks of reading about and studying the disease, we did bring in speakers who had AIDS. They spoke honestly and openly with the class. Tony did not skip that class after all. After the presentation, Tony wrote:

> At first I didn't think of AIDS. Then the Big News Bullitin came out about Magic Johnson. At first it caught my attention but after a while I just was back to my old self. Now I look at AIDS as a murderer. The youth of the world need to know about this disease. After all the education I got in my brain, and after hearing people in this class be honest about what they do, now that I know about the virus, I will practice more safe sex.

Sarina also reflected at the end of the unit of study. She wrote:

> My attitude change alot. My actions will change because now I don't have anything against someone who got HIV or AIDS because I know they are human beings like we are. I will like to say thank you for asking Ida and the other lady for coming in. I will say thank you to everyone in this class.

The next year Sarina wrote "if there was one thing that would stay with me the rest of my life it would be when Ida was here talking to us about AIDS" as a personal reflection in the yearbook.

Neither student wanted to get involved, much less provide leadership at the beginning of the semester. Eventually, both Tony and Sarina learned quite a lot about AIDS and suggested that the class open up discussions and educate a larger section of the school. Their peers followed the committed, mature example set by these two previously uncooperative students.

Some students have found it a strain to go between classes that are designed around their interests and classes that are not. Students have said they let some of their "walls" down in my classroom. On good days, they lose their inertia, their cynicism, and their distance. In other classes, in which they are much less personally involved with their studies, they have had to reerect those defenses. The adjustment can be a difficult one. The teacher working with student-centered curriculum must be prepared for reactions to this change, both from students and the teacher's own colleagues.

"TEACHERS NEED TO HOLD ON TO POWER IN THE CLASSROOM"

I take issue with the basic assumptions of this statement. Teachers have power in classrooms; so do students. A teacher makes assignments—and students either complete the assignments or resist them. As one teacher interviewed in Edward Pauly's (1991) *The Classroom Crucible* put it, "They [students] make the rules. They have made all the rules in the room. Anything that happens in the room, it's them" (p. 51). Whether or not you agree with this sentiment, we need to ask: What, exactly, is there to fear in a classroom in which teachers acknowledge students' power and teach them to use it in their own best interests?

At the start, teachers can work with students in establishing classroom rules, roles, and assignments. Admittedly, it is easier if teachers set rules themselves. Even if teachers do want to work with students to establish and maintain classroom rules, they may find the process time-consuming and difficult. I myself have been loath to work through these issues with students when we have so much else to do, and there never seems to be enough time to get our other, "real" work done. But what work takes precedence over learning how to coexist? Is time the real issue here?

Herbert Kohl (1967) addressed what he called this "tightness with time" in *36 Children,* his classic account of one year in an urban classroom. He says this constraint is established needlessly by teachers and "has nothing to do with the quantity that must be learned or the children's needs. It represents a teacher's fear of loss of control and is nothing but a weapon used to weaken the solidarity and opposition of the children that too many teachers unconsciously dread" (p. 21). Kohl wrote about elementary school children; perhaps elementary teachers do "unconsciously dread" their students' energy and potential power. Secondary school teachers' fears are quite conscious. We all have heard stories of violence and chaos in high schools. We want to create safe places. One way to do this is to run a tight ship—establish and maintain teacher authority at all costs.

But this is only one model, and it is one that does not always facilitate enthusiasm, curiosity, or participation in the classroom. Can we, as teachers, reorder our priorities so that students can be included in the determination and maintenance of classroom rules and roles? Or is this the "wrong" type of power to give students? What type of power should teachers have in classrooms, and what are its sources?

Mark is a 17-year-old senior (and former dropout) in Chicago. His answer to the question "What would you do if a teacher gave you power in a classroom?" represents what is to me the most intriguing aspect of the cocreative classroom: the students' sense that they could fix what is wrong with their educations, if only they were given the opportunity. Mark says that he would teach what he believed was right but that the teacher most likely would rescind the offer once "things got going." At this point, he says, the class would "have to rebel," because "if you tryin' to keep something away from us, and it's something that we want, we gonna try to take it. What do we want? Power." Mark's teachers might think that he "has an attitude" and therefore represents a destructive—as opposed to constructive—force in the classroom.

When asked to explain what he means by power, Mark and his peers explain, "We need to have the power to contradict something we know isn't true." This seems to be not only a reasonable request but an appropriate one. Mark goes on to talk about Christopher Columbus. He says that a class full of African American and Latino students doesn't want to spend time with stories of Columbus's heroism, which he calls "bullshit indoctrination."

Although Mark's objections to class curriculum may be more sophisticated than that of most students, his sincerity and his desire to make school worthwhile are not unique. Our students deserve the best education we can help them get. Congratulations go to the teenagers who have recognized the subjective nature of recorded history. Let's give these angry, bored kids more to do than regurgitate facts. History (and art and social sciences and English) classes can only benefit from debate and discussion about bias.

Some teachers may consider students' questions to be out of order, might regard them as insubordination. Are students' rejections of standard curriculum challenges to our authority or merely to our pride? Students will say that some teachers cannot stand to be challenged on any point. Julio, 17, sadly recounts his observation: "Most of the time teachers want to be right. Some will shut you up if you just point out a math mistake on the board."

We must encourage our students to think critically if they are going to be able to survive. They need to recognize bias. They need to learn that power comes not from the ability to punish but from the ability to instruct. In order to get our students to care about school, they must be given the opportunities to ask questions. They must be allowed to earn self-respect by bringing their own ideas into the classroom.

"IF GIVEN THE OPPORTUNITY, STUDENTS WOULD TURN THE CLASSROOM INTO A ZOO"

I have a nightmare about trying to get a room full of kids to quiet down. They are talking and yelling. One couple is locked in a passionate embrace in the corner. Some are walking across desktops. Some are throwing each other out the window. Some are trying to throw me out the window . . . or is this just a flashback of my first year teaching? This scene is one that lurks in the subconscious of every teacher. Some teachers believe that this is what would happen if they relax the rules or do not establish and maintain strict classroom control.

We do need organization in the classroom. It is what allows the educational process to work. It is a teacher's responsibility to establish regular order and create a stable environment. This environment must be based on rules that are themselves based on mutual respect. We can establish simple standards and enforce them consistently. We do our students a favor by insisting on codes of behavior. No, it is not all right to walk across desktops. It is not appropriate to curse constantly.

A student-centered, cocreative curriculum and classroom order are not mutually exclusive. Rules do not have to be ordained from above. I determine rules of classroom behavior with my students the first few days of school. We talk about what will be necessary if we are going to work together; our ideas are not so very different. Students will veto each other's more outrageous proposals if properly challenged. Once we get the rules straight, I ask someone in the class to make a poster listing classroom protocol and leave the poster up for the rest of the semester. It is usually bold and bright and looks like graffiti.

Developing rules together establishes immediate student-teacher cooperation and shows students that their opinions are valued. It also sets up a new classroom structure, something many classrooms desperately need. Instead of absolute authority, teachers are able to give students choices. Instead of controlling students, we show them that they can control themselves. By defining behavioral parameters, students are able to become more aware of their own learning preferences. As Nancie Atwell (1987) said, "Freedom of choice doesn't undercut structure. Instead, kids become accountable for developing and refining their own structures" (p. 15).

"STUDENT SUGGESTIONS FOR TOPICS OF STUDY WOULD BE UNUSABLE"

All the best units of study that I have taught over the last five years have been suggested by my students. Student ideas may sound unlikely—too provocative, too disturbing, too mundane—when first proposed. But student requests to study sex and money, for example, can be reshaped into more viable topics of study by instructors, that is, "Gender Roles" and "Success." Teachers can name and give shape to students' inarticulate expressions of personal frustration, offering a unit on "Individuality and Conformity" or "Mainstream Society" when students ask to study "how to go with the society," as mine did.

Some students do propose highly impractical topics. One year I asked my class this straightforward question: "What do you want to know more about?" Mike, 17, named guitars and snakes. I'm sure that we could have taken a closer look at these suggestions and perhaps incorporated both ideas into a unit on "Powerful Symbols." I don't think that is what Mike wanted, though. Teachers must take care not to squeeze the personal relevance out of students' suggestions. Instead of trying to force profundity out of every adolescent utterance, it is better to guide the class toward the substantive issues that matter to them.

Mike's answer was not the only one to catch me off guard; a few of the girls in the class wrote that what they really wanted was information about a few of the boys of the class. They went on to specify that they wanted to know Andre's phone number, what time Len got off work, and whether Kensha had a girlfriend.

I decided to try another tack. The next day I asked the class to tell me what they thought was wrong with the world or what they wanted to make right in their own world. This produced much better results. Students listed "domestic violence, abortions, homelessness, children, gangs, birth control, crime, stress, censorship, rape, AIDS/SIDA, power, religion, magic, myself."

Students at first might seem incapable or unwilling to suggest topics of study. Prompt them with short lists, asking the class to check the topics they find most compelling. Depending on the materials that have been collected and the instructors' academic objectives, this list might start off:

What would you like to read, write, and think about in class this semester? Check as many as you want:

___ Hatred: Why do some people treat others with such viciousness?
___ Love: What is it? Is there such a thing?
___ Racism: Why can't different people live together in harmony?
___ Work: Why do we have to work? Do we need jobs to be happy and
　　　successful?

I like to propose only broad categories of study and leave lots of room for student refinements and suggestions. For additional techniques designed to solicit student input for topics of study, see the section on determining student interests in Chapter 3. See also HANDOUT C: CHOOSING TOPICS OF STUDY; INSTRUCTORS' NOTES D: STARTING OFF: OTHER IDEAS (Chapter 4).

Even in a class full of students who seem to want just to annoy and test the teacher, activities such as these can be highly useful. If students propose totally inappropriate and outrageous topics of study, we have an unlimited number of options. We can try again, as I did with Mike's class. We can ask the class, as a whole, to come to consensus on a topic of study.

If we are comfortable with student suggestions that happen to fall outside regular class curriculum, we can go ahead and try them. If the whole class really wants to study witchcraft or partying and the instructor feels knowledgeable enough to piece together a short unit on either topic, why not give it a try? If no likely theories or thought-provoking questions seem inherent in the unit, teachers can ask students to generate definitions and relevant criteria.

Make sure to do a thorough evaluation after this unit of study and share the responses with the class. If everyone rated the unit as valuable, then it probably was. If there were some students who wanted to concentrate on more regular academic matters, make sure their opinions are voiced. Each subsequent unit of study should accommodate more and more of all students' interests and needs. Students will become better at recognizing and naming those needs, and their suggestions will become more and more penetrating.

"STUDENT CONTRIBUTIONS TO CLASSROOM MATERIALS WOULDN'T BE SUBSTANTIAL ENOUGH OR WOULD BE CHOSEN JUST TO PROVOKE THE TEACHER"

Students generally enjoy bringing in materials for the class to share. There are, however, always some who do not want to bring in anything, who say they have no access to music or other works they feel comfortable sharing with their peers. In this case, a teacher can let those students team up to present a work with a friend. Or the teacher can help the student devise an alternative assignment.

Students need to bring in thought-provoking materials. Help students learn to judge which songs and poems are presentation-worthy. Give them practice comparing meaningful and meaningless messages. Be careful that you don't try this out on student-supplied materials. Students are hurt when their peers dismiss their favorite songs as stupid fluff. Better to bring in two songs or poems yourself and ask the class to analyze both.

I did this with a love song by Peter Gabriel ("In Your Eyes") and a Hallmark valentine. We had five questions that we were ready to apply to all "Love" presentations. We spent 20 minutes on the Peter Gabriel song, trying to understand his symbols and interpreting the metaphors. The Hallmark card took five minutes. The class got an idea about what types of works can and cannot generate a meaningful class discussion. Consequently, when their turns came to make presentations to the class, they contributed works that were relatively substantial. Remember, pop music can speak profundities to teenage ears.

Teachers, too, should share works that they find moving or affecting. Students will find traditional poetry less intimidating if they see it in a context of varied poetic statement right next to work by artists more familiar to them. There are former students of mine who will never hear Nikki Giovanni's or e.e. cummings's work without thinking of pop musicians Bon Jovi and Luther Vandross. All sorts of pleasantly surprising juxtapositions arise from knocking down the walls between English class and the rest of the world.

Teachers can establish their own procedures for student contributions. You can ask students to bring in a lyric sheet so that you can look it over before the students play the song (or read the poem) to the class. Colleagues of mine who have had to talk with students about inappropriate presentations have had no problem persuading their students to present other works. I never have had to forbid a presentation, but teachers who are worried about profanity and obscenity should be careful. There are ways to work around the crudity of some popular materials. Ask students if they think there is a potential problem—some parents are very concerned with the works to which their children are exposed in school. Talk about the possibility of sending class-written notes of warning home with your students. And try not to play the songs too loudly!

Some students have brought in works just to provoke me. The important thing to remember is to leave the criticism up to the class—always. Don't rise to the bait as I did once. For presentations in a unit on "Power," one student, Lloyd, brought in a article disparaging female self-defense classes. Instead of letting the class take Lloyd's article through the series of questions that we had generated to analyze each presentation (questions such as "Who is in power?" "How did they get this power?" "Are they using it well or abusing it?"), I made the mistake of reacting angrily to the article's smug tone and insulting assumptions. Although he admitted later that he had brought in the article to "get a rise out of" me, Lloyd felt personally attacked in class.

From this episode I learned to let students stay in charge during presentations. Teachers must be careful never to criticize a student for the style or contents of the work he or she has chosen to bring in to share with the class. If a student has brought in an obscene or otherwise offensive work merely to annoy the teacher, the class should have the tools to analyze it and find it without merit themselves. If students cannot dismiss the work, then I believe the teacher must recognize that the work has value for them, no matter how offensive it might be.

Student contributions to the class necessarily will extend the scope of the unit and often the teacher's purview. Unless teachers are prepared to deal with the (sometimes ugly) reality of that environment, they will be operating at a disadvantage. Only if we can look honestly at our students' everyday lives can we hope to understand our students and help them make sense of their (sometimes ugly) worlds.

"THE HANDOUTS IN THESE UNITS OF INSTRUCTION LOOK LIKE REGULAR OLD WORKSHEETS: WHAT'S SO 'STUDENT-CENTERED' ABOUT THIS?"

This question gave me pause the first time I heard it. "These aren't just regular old worksheets—are they?" I asked my students. "Of course they are," they said. It made me take an honest look at these assignments and ask myself if the whole approach really was student centered.

I first looked at the unit topics and realized that all the units presented here were created, definitely and decisively, for and by my students. When I considered each of the unit topics, I remembered the particular classroom discussions and arguments they generated. These are the topics my students chose. These are the ideas they felt deserved their energies and their creativity.

The assignments themselves also grew out of students' needs. They are not questions on texts' content or the subject matter. The topics and academic objectives of my English classes never supersede my students' realities; they are in service to them.

When I read over the assignments described in Chapters 5 through 9, I remembered particular students and classes. Although it is true that I created the bulk of these handouts, it is more important to look at the types of student response solicited by each question and each assignment. Some handouts provided in this book ask students to think critically about their lives. Some ask students to express the insights that they have gotten from each other and from daily life and apply them to literary characters.

Our classroom paradigm differs from the traditional model. That model starts with instructional objectives and materials (curriculum) that is selected and processed by teachers before it gets to students. Students' work with the (teacher-processed) curriculum stops with each of them, individually, as shown in Figure 2.1.

The starting point of cocreative teaching is student reality. This determines the curriculum, which then directly addresses student needs and interests. Teachers' decisions about curriculum also are informed by student reality. Students and teacher choose and process materials and determine instructional activities. These reach everyone in the class, compelling group and individual reflection (see Figure 2.2).

CURRICULUM → TEACHER → STUDENTS

Figure 2.1. Traditional Model (Teacher-Processed Curriculum)

STUDENT REALITY → TEACHER

↘   ↙

CURRICULUM

↓

STUDENTS AND TEACHER

Figure 2.2. Cocreative Model (Student-Centered Curriculum)

The handouts in this book differ in intention and in execution from more standard reading comprehension questions and study guides. Even exercises designed to help students practice skills strive to place these skills in practical, familiar contexts.

Teachers who want to make their classes more responsive to student reality can use these lessons as a model. Although teachers still will be distributing worksheets and assignments, the orientation and the purpose of these activities will be changed wholly.

"THIS ISN'T ENGLISH! WHERE'S THE GRAMMAR?"

One teacher, in responding to the ideas in this book, said:

This is fine for younger teachers. But a lot of older teachers were trained to teach material. They thought about teaching their subject matter; they didn't think in terms of students. There's a great distinction there, don't you think? Students can interfere with teaching. These teachers think, "Well, we didn't cover the material!" And they all go racing along. "We have to cover this material!" Well, what does that mean, in the long run?

This made me recall one class I took in high school, when a history teacher tried to fit the entire Renaissance into the two days before Thanksgiving. I do remember her laughing with the class about it. I don't remember much of the material that got truncated—no big surprise there. My teacher's goals were to cover the subject matter.

I see now how counterproductive this is. Of course, no teacher plans to squeeze a historical era into two days: Everything takes longer than you think it will, class schedules get crunched, things just happen. As a student, I probably didn't care much about it. As a teacher, this phenomenon makes me recognize the need for acute curricular reorientation.

We teach kids, not subjects. What is the point of covering material at the expense of students' understanding? Why do we sometimes view students as if they get in the way of the class's progress? If students "slow a class down," it is the teacher's responsibility to figure out why and do something about it.

We do have several options at our disposal. We can attend to students' differing skill levels by having the more advanced students work as tutors. We can let students design their own goals and determine their own deadlines for assignments. If the whole class is not moving as fast as the teacher would like, the teacher must take a good look at the subject matter. Perhaps we can try to reconcile some of the gaps between subject matter and students' lives.

I know there are some caring, insightful teachers out there bringing Chaucer, for example, to kids in the inner city. These kids never would be exposed to the classics, never would get a chance to read this great literature, otherwise. Maybe these students respond positively and with interest to *The Canterbury Tales* because their teacher has shown them how to care about people who lived 700 years ago. Maybe this teacher has created a safe, stable environment for students, even if issues central to their lives are not addressed there.

Students appreciate what this teacher gives them. This teacher probably does a good job with Chaucer. He or she also might be working one-on-one, helping individual students a lot. But I do not think this teacher is maximizing students' ability to listen to, learn from, and help each other. And in the long run, that is what will help these teenagers make the world a better place for themselves and for their children. That is why we must prioritize correctly. No one and no thing is more important in the classroom than our students.

As for grammar and other mechanical skills usually taught in English classes: There is still a place for them in the student-centered classroom. Teens who are planning to take the ACT or SAT need to concentrate on language mechanics and need to be prepared to function in the world of high standards and higher education. Every year that I have asked students what topics they want to study, someone has said, "Verbs."

I don't ignore these requests. I realize that these kids have recognized their own weaknesses as writers, as nonnative English speakers, as students, as future employees. What I know also is that some of these students—70% in some Chicago communities—never will graduate from high school. There is a way to serve both the students who seem to be headed for a dead end and those who are determined to get out of the neighborhood.

Reciting the rules of proper usage for the subjunctive mode is not an essential skill for every student. There are some basic skills and elements of proper usage that all students must know so that they will not be at a disadvantage when taking standardized tests, applying for jobs, and going out in the working world. We need to teach students how to write complete sentences. We should teach them to recognize standard English subject-verb agreement. We can teach them the parts of speech and whatever other formal grammar they will need to know for the standardized tests they must take. But we do not have to teach grammar as an end unto itself.

I do not believe that it is effective to teach language skills outside the context of usage. Teachers can incorporate grammar skills in a conceptual unit (see Chapter 6, "Racism"). As for other language and writing skills, teachers can give students practice quoting textual passages (see Chapter 5, "Sex Roles, Power, and Identity"). In this way, these skills are not practiced and developed in an academic vacuum. Students will see them for what they are: tools that can make expression clear, resonant, and precise.

Recently some researchers have noted an important reality in our public schools: Although they all are intended to serve Americans, the Americans in them have very different needs. "The diversity that exists in disadvantaged populations and the ways these differences relate to formal education calls for policy which permits the creation of local remedies and options" (Johnston & Borman, 1992, p. xii). Some teachers and administrators do make distinctions of a sort within schools and districts. They reserve English literature classes for their more advanced students. Their rationale might go something like this: Grammar and language mechanics are basics. Students whose skills are limited need basics. Literature texts require more from students. Hence, literature is better for college-bound students who already have mastered basic language skills.

This is not "creation of local remedies or options." It is educational bias. Students with poor skills must spend time developing writing skills and other language arts—but we can give them substantial ideas and issues to address in these efforts. Often students who have not been labeled college-bound are trapped in a joyless curriculum of grammar and vocabulary exercises. No stories, no contexts, no juice. Their affective responses never are solicited.

Furthermore, just because a student does not test well does not mean necessarily that he or she does not think well. And if the students in question have not developed powers of critical thinking, what better, more useful skill can we teach them in school? Teachers who struggle to give their students large doses of standard English curriculum (grammar, vocabulary, and excerpted classics for the higher skilled students) are overlooking the greatest resource at their disposal. Expression of students' own experiences and insights into literature must be the English teacher's first concern.

"WHAT CAN I DO IF THE ONLY MATERIALS AVAILABLE ARE SPECIFIED TEXTBOOKS?"

At various presentations and speaking engagements, teachers have taken me aside and said, "This all sounds wonderful. But let's be honest: What sane teacher would abandon a 700-page literature textbook loaded with stories, poetry, and writing assignments in favor of your plan? Especially if the textbook is all she's got to work with?" If you are using a literary anthology or textbook that you believe in and that serves your and your students' needs, do not abandon it. Build on it. If the only material available is grammar or composition texts and you feel they serve your students well, I suggest that you incorporate them into conceptual units.

Many of the English textbooks with which I have been presented, however, have been old and boring and in bad condition. My students can relate to nothing in these books. The vignettes of family life, adolescence, romance, and opportunity in this country are 20 years behind the times and elicit either blank looks of confusion or derision from my streetwise but "culturally deprived" students. Sometimes my students cannot get past the ironies and bygone lifestyles innocently depicted in grammar exercises. When they are asked to correct the punctuation in paragraphs describing a visit to the shopping mall or a county fair, for example, it is almost impossible to go over these exercises without laughing out loud; they regard the paragraphs as a type of science fiction. It is hard enough for them to concentrate on punctuation without such distractions. If teachers in the 1990s have only texts such as these with which to work, they probably already are frustrated and looking for other available resources.

Not all English textbooks in use are ancient. Material in some literature textbooks of the 1970s and 1980s is arranged into "thematic units." There are a few problems with this. First and most significant, the editors already have done the work that teachers and students need to do together: taking a concept apart and figuring out how and why it matters. These ready-made units of instruction are incomplete. Most are merely collections of literature. Sometimes textbook units cover literary terms and genres as opposed to concepts. Even the texts that stress affective response to literature do not engage teachers and students together in a cooperative process. No textbook can serve a class as well as cocreative teaching. None encourages an ongoing, communal project in which tailor-made curriculum is created by students and teachers together.

Furthermore, the individual works in textbooks are chosen according to difficulty, fitting the editors' conception of what is appropriate for readers at different levels. Teachers may not agree with these classifications. I have found great materials in literature textbooks—but I have used these works carefully. As it happens, I never have taken a poem from a ninth grade textbook and used it for a class of ninth graders. Similarly, I never have used a story to represent the concept that textbook editors suggested. For example, I came across Borden Deal's "Anteaus" in a textbook unit on "Conflict"—but my class read and analyzed it when we were studying "Innocence and Experience." I have searched textbooks divided into units on "Theme," "Imagery," and "Drama" and found works to use in units on "Good and Evil," "Paradise," and "Love."

This is the way in which textbooks can be of greatest use to the teacher who wants to try student-centered cocreative teaching. If you have access to a textbook whose works reflect your students' experiences, ethnicity, and interests, use it. But do not just go through it. Textbooks are resources, not curricula. The problem is not textbooks themselves. The problem is uncritical reliance on them.

"I'M LIMITED BY DISTRICT AND DEPARTMENTAL REQUIREMENTS"

Rebecca Killen Hawthorne (1992), in *Curriculum in the Making: Teacher Choice and the Classroom Experience*, says: "State curricular frameworks, textbook adaptations, and mandated testing with incentives and penalties tied to end results conspire to assure educational change by fiat. What to teach and, more frequently, what materials to use are decisions more and more often removed from teacher hands" (p. 1). Especially in districts caught up in the debate about educational reform (and what districts are not caught up currently in this debate?), administrators and curriculum designers feel the pressure to improve education by specifying and standardizing curriculum for teachers.

But do these incentives and penalties reach teachers in individual classrooms? Certainly some teachers follow a prescribed curriculum; if they did not, their students would be unprepared for certain standardized tests or for the next year's instruction. However, no teacher ever has told me that she wanted but was not allowed to refocus curriculum around students. I wondered why—until I asked one teacher. "Do you think teachers will be unable to use this student-centered approach because their curriculum is determined for them by outside agencies?" This teacher laughed. "When I close the classroom door I do what I want," she said. Another veteran added: "I don't care what administrators tell me to do. I go home at the end of the day and think: Did I help that kid survive?"

These teachers are neither arrogant nor dangerous impediments to school reform. They are honest. The people who know what is needed in classrooms—teachers and students—are not being consulted in the current discussion of educational reform. In one sense, this is misguided and silly. In another sense, it is the reality that dooms any and all efforts at reform through regular channels. Innovations in curriculum, textbooks, or testing are not going to make any difference in students' performance if teachers do not choose to use them or do not know how to use them.

Furthermore, different approaches work for different teachers and students. Researching issues in this book, I spent hours talking with teachers and students, alone and in groups, in and out of school. What differences! What varying styles, needs, orientations, attitudes, and experiences. Consequently, what a rich mix of personalities there is inside of every classroom. This is why no single curricular program can hope to work for all schools, all teachers, and all classrooms.

Be that as it may, the people who devise these programs will keep devising them. The debate will continue about whether higher standards or more social services should be the number one priority of the schools. Some classrooms will work. Some will not.

If high school teachers want their classes to be relevant and meaningful to their students, they need to judge carefully the various solutions and prescriptions suggested and mandated by "experts." Then they need to close the door and do the best they can do using all the resources available to them. Included in these resources are required texts and curriculum—used selectively and thoughtfully. Teachers' own experience and talents also constitute a substantial resource. And then, there are the students. Their interests and voices must be included also in teachers' decisions about curriculum and materials.

"IT'S TOO BIG A RISK"

This is one fear expressed by an older teacher. He said that because all teaching is, in a sense, performance, for a teacher to try a new approach is like asking an actor to play a new part without rehearsal. The analogy is useful up to a point.

We are always "on" in the classroom. If a teacher is used to lecturing or is not comfortable facilitating discussions, then a cocreative approach is a big change. If this teacher is interested in incorporating some student concerns in the class curriculum, he or she needs to find some way to do this that doesn't feel unnatural. This teacher need not try cocreative teaching every day in every class. Perhaps this teacher will ask for students' more personal responses to literary works and situations only in written work. Perhaps this teacher will assign a presentation as an alternate or additional activity to a few students every marking period.

The other type of risk I think teachers are concerned with is the risk of trusting students with manifest responsibility for each other's learning. Students will sometimes fail, letting themselves and their peers down. I admit I have trouble letting this happen. When one student forgets to bring in a tape or when another student's absence stalls the whole class, it is all I can do to stop myself from coming down like some instructional *deus ex machina* and improvise, reschedule, and otherwise "fix" things.

Teachers must resist this temptation. Such actions will not do anything except reinforce students' feelings of powerlessness. They will regard their independence as a sham and their responsibilities as token.

Of course, no student should pass or fail a class based on whether a friend has remembered to bring in the group essay. If teachers are going to take the risk of letting students depend on each other, they also need to be flexible. This flexibility must not encourage kids to disregard deadlines and commitments; it should, instead, recognize effort and be reasonable overall. The idea is to foster individual effort and group creativity.

For better or worse, school is a social institution. Students are there to learn skills—academic, personal, and social. Teachers do take a risk in letting students depend on each other. It is much easier (and thinking conventionally, much more fair) to let every student depend on him- or herself alone. But if we can impart feelings of collective responsibility and solidarity, we are giving our students experiences whose value extends beyond the classroom. I believe this is a risk worth taking.

APPLICATIONS FOR TEACHERS

1. Based on your teaching style, what reservations do you have about working with students to develop units of instruction?

2. What external limitations do you expect to encounter?

3. What types of power do you feel students have in your classroom? What types of power do you think they feel they have?

4. What is the worst thing that could happen if you experiment with sharing power and decision making with your students? What is the best thing that could happen?

5. How responsive to your students' lives are the materials you currently use?

3

✪ Developing Student-Centered Curriculum

If teachers are interested in creating meaningful units of instruction for and with their students, the first thing they need to do is ask their students what they want to study. Teachers already will have some preconceptions about appropriate or necessary topics of focus for their students. These ideas will be based on memories of their own adolescence, observation, and popular agreement about kids today. They may or may not jibe with students' actual interests.

Some teachers can remember what it felt like to be 17. Some may be parents of teens or may be privy to parts of teen life that make their observations particularly accurate and insightful. Some teachers read, watch, and listen to the latest "experts" talk about teenagers. Still, even these teachers' best ideas will be lacking—lacking the one critical ingredient that no amount of dedication can supply: genuine student input.

In the cocreative, student-centered classroom, it is the students' job to decide what to study. Even if teachers know what will interest their students,

AUTHOR'S NOTE: Portions of this chapter first appeared as "Structure and Spontaneity: Teaching With the Student at Risk" by Deborah Stern, *English Journal, 81*(6), pp. 49-55. Copyright © 1992 by the National Council of Teachers of English. Used by permission.

they must resist the temptation to impose these ideas on students. Students may want to spite even the best suggestions from the most sincere teacher. Even if they think the suggested topic of study is interesting, still it is the teacher's idea and is, therefore, more of the same. Business as usual. Same old . . . school.

For example, a teacher may want to focus on the hot topics of teen violence and anomie recently highlighted by weekly national news magazines and television shows. Despite this media focus (or perhaps because of it), students may have no interest in studying "Teen Violence in the City" in class. A teacher suggesting this topic of study risks being met with groans and risks being regarded as an intrusive, nosy "bummer." Of course, any suggestion coming from a student also risks rejection. But it will have integrity as an idea among ideas. It is not a pronouncement from above. It can be debated, analyzed, modified, and adapted. And it is a *student's* idea.

When tailoring units of instruction for their students, teachers must be careful not to concentrate exclusively on the grimmer aspects of students' lives. All teenagers, no matter how cynical or how far removed from the conventional trials and tribulations of adolescence, deserve an environment in which they can just be kids for a while. Despite this truth, teachers who see student-centered curriculum as their opportunity to get into nitty-gritty issues with students may be frustrated if their students choose to study a seemingly innocuous topic, such as love or happiness.

If that is what your students want or if that is what they say they want, that is what the topic of study has to be. Doubtless, if the class truly follows a student-centered approach, students' experiences and perspectives will color the unit in unexpected ways. A unit on childhood can twist and transform into a critical reexamination of innocence, initiation, savvy, and betrayal—if the students are allowed to express their experiences honestly. Sometimes the best thing a teacher can do is help create a safe place, one in which teenagers can put aside adult worries they might be facing (i.e., concerns such as money and babies and revenge) and just be teenagers. If such a place is created, students most likely will voice their other, more pressing concerns. No matter what the topic of instruction is, if enough trust and group support have been nurtured in this safe place, students will have ample opportunities to get some critical feedback and reflect on their more adult worries. A teacher can work to establish this environment by listening to students' preferences about topics of study.

DETERMINING STUDENT INTERESTS

There are many ways for teachers to ask students what they are interested in, but teachers will need to experiment to see which is most compatible with their own style. At times the most sincere cooperation between myself and my students has started naturally, almost by accident. Some of the most compelling topics of study in my experience have grown out of an offhand remark or a sarcastic rejoinder. "Racism" was suggested by an African American student who had just interviewed for a job with a White friend. (The friend got the job; my student did not.) "Life on the Streets" was another topic of study that came out of a student's unsolicited wisecrack at the end of one semester.

If such suggestions are not forthcoming, there are more formal ways to begin a joint assessment of genuine student needs and interests. For the students and teachers who normally do not deal with personal issues, it might be a good idea to ask students to reflect individually. Interest inventories and suggestion boxes are good vehicles for this. Typical questions that I include on interest inventories run from the meaningful to the mundane:

1. What is the best thing that happened to you this summer?
2. What do you like to do when you're not in school?
3. Name some things that you hate.
4. What bothers you most about school?
5. What places would you like to visit in the city? Outside the city?
6. What was the best movie you ever saw?
7. What in your opinion is the best thing about living in Chicago? The worst thing?

See HANDOUT A: INTEREST INVENTORY; HANDOUT B: STRENGTHS AND SUCCESSES INVENTORY (Chapter 4) for complete interest inventories.

Teachers should expect that some students might use these questions to test them by being vulgar, profane, or phony. If you would be disturbed by Jonathan's answers (1. I got laid; 2. Fuck; 3. Condoms; 4. The fucking teachers; etc.), ask less provocative questions. It is a risk that I have been willing to take: Jonathan was the exception, and we did do a unit on sexuality that year (although most students expressed their interest in more socially acceptable terms). Student responses typically touch me and give me the sense that no matter how hard-boiled these students seem, they are still children. "What are some things you hate?" I asked 17-year-old Bernard in 1989. "Gang violence and carrots," he wrote.

I make it a point to tell students that they do not have to answer every question, that the inventory is designed to make the class responsive to the individuals within it. I have returned these inventories with supportive comments, with welcoming remarks (this exercise usually is done at the beginning of a marking period), and with no corrections in spelling or mechanics. There will be time to work on these things later. Students need to know that they are not being judged by their experiences and comments.

Another effective way of soliciting student opinion is brainstorming—first writing suggestions on the board and then evaluating all the suggestions in open class discussions. Students in individual classrooms also can take informal polls of each other's most pressing concerns and interests.

At this point, teachers can determine whether the topic merits an entire instructional unit itself or would be more appropriately served as a focus within another unit. In past years I have begun courses with such surveys; I also have asked students to suggest courses of study in June so we can schedule courses for the following year.

It is interesting to note that although students' needs change and vary from year to year, there are certain constants running through their chosen topics of study. Teenagers are concerned with behavior, conformity, and questions of right and wrong. Perennial favorites have been "Power," "Success," "Good and Evil," "Parents and Kids," "Justice," "Self-Destruction," "Growing Up," and "Love."

WORKING WITH REMEDIAL CLASSES

Student self-determination is effective at all levels; it is especially critical at a remedial level. When asked what they genuinely would like to learn about at the beginning of a new quarter, students in one of my remedial reading classes (fifth grade reading level) said, "Sex and drugs and rock and roll." This gave me pause. But then I wondered: Why not? Why couldn't these subjects appropriately serve the course's larger objectives?

This unit of instruction turned out to be a success by anyone's standards. I designed the unit's objectives with my students' poor skills in mind. The topics served as vehicles, providing us with focused ideas to discuss and investigate as we worked our way through more practical tasks.

The quarter's lessons stressed note taking, following tables of contents and indexes, and test-taking strategies, in addition to reading comprehension, essay writing, and creative writing. One student brought in a comic book called *AIDS News* (Rifas & Campos, 1988), which we read and discussed. We pilfered the health teacher's supplies and spent a month struggling through a regular high school-level textbook's chapters on drug and alcohol abuse. We all brought in tapes of different types of music and took extensive notes on those musical qualities that we thought distinguished the different genres.

So often teachers assume that a student whose reading and writing skills are deficient cannot handle abstract reasoning. This is not always the case. The fact that these students have survived life on the streets attests to their own invaluable, highly developed thinking skills. Unfortunately, tests do not measure these types of abilities. Those students who read considerably below grade level often are left with vapid materials and unchallenging assignments. Instead of engaging their abilities, instruction caters to their disabilities.

Courses for these students must stress ideas as well as skills. Teachers, in trying to accommodate a student's social and personal disadvantages, plan with only his or her low reading skills in mind and thus neglect the concomitant struggles engendered by these economic and personal realities. This results in a counterproductive confusion of misguided sympathy, veritable neglect, and nonresponse.

Left to my own devices, without student input, I most likely would have trapped myself and my students in such a cycle. Attending to problems instead of solutions prevents students from reflecting on and determining their own educational agendas, and also effectively guarantees further alienation and failure.

PRELIMINARY PLANNING: UNIT RATIONALE, KEY QUESTIONS, AND GOALS

Once students and teachers work together to determine appropriate and meaningful unit topics, responsibility for planning falls back on the teacher. But it does not rest there exclusively; nor does it stay there permanently. Because the students have asked expressly to study a particular concept, they have taken the first step in designing the unit. I ask students to explain in class, in conversation, or in writing why they want to study this topic. As they struggle to articulate their reasons, they provide a rationale for the unit's inclusion in the curriculum. I usually find my own reasons for teaching a particular unit as well.

For example, when the topic of sex roles was suggested as a possible unit of study, my students expressed real delight at being able to talk about this new business of being men and women. After witnessing various forms of oppression, pressure, and unenlightenment among the student body at large, I also recognized a pressing need to examine sex roles. My concern was about social mores; theirs, perhaps, was about hormones. Both our senses of need were valid. Both provided a strong justification for teaching about sex roles.

From students' efforts to justify their interest also come the key questions of the unit. These questions are the basic analytical building blocks that we apply to various works within the unit. For the unit on sex roles, I thought about the concerns and questions expressed by students and came up with the following key questions:

1. What are sex roles? What are male and female sex roles in our society?
2. What determines the different roles that men and women play in society?
3. What gives a person power in a relationship?
4. How does gender affect identity?

For examples of how these key questions were used in an instructional unit, see Chapter 5, "Sex Roles, Power, and Identity."

In sum, a teacher must first see to the rationale for a unit of study. Next, he or she must delineate the unit's basic analytical framework. Finally, there is only one step that he or she must take before turning at least some of the planning back over to the students. This step is determining the unit's terminal objectives.

Terminal objectives are the larger goals toward which a class is working. It is best to keep these goals straightforward and not too numerous. Because the students I teach need to improve reading and writing skills, my terminal objectives generally are limited to three or four basic goals. Always, one of these goals is to reflect on and/or write about the unit concept. Another one deals with the unit's major literary work, if there is one. My goal regarding this work is usually that the students read and understand it. This may seem insufficient, but when I remember that I am teaching students who seldom read at all, who come from households with no books, I realize this is no puny goal. One of the other terminal objectives stresses some written expression requiring synthesis of different unit materials: either an essay or an essay test. Terminal objectives also can include practical skills students need to develop (e.g., note taking, use of reference works, etc.).

Determining terminal objectives is the teacher's responsibility. Students should be free to state what skills they believe they need to work on, but a teacher is the only one in the classroom with the training necessary to decide how and in what order academic goals should be achieved. These goals must be realistic. It is important that students feel a sense of accomplishment and growth when the unit is over.

Teachers always should add one final terminal objective: Both students and teachers need to reflect on the value and effectiveness of the unit. We need to get student feedback and suggestions for future implementation. In that way we avoid repeating exercises that do not work and can increase students' sense of self-worth.

BACK WITH THE STUDENTS: SEARCHING FOR MATERIALS

Once the unit's validity and objectives have been determined, it is time to plan with the students. Finding appropriate materials is both the teacher's and the students' responsibility. I usually line up the major work for the unit and assemble a small collection of supporting shorter works—films, poems, and short stories. Tailoring materials and exercises to fit a "Violence" unit is (sadly) easier than trying to construct a unit around a theme such as "Satire."

Students' reading level is a constant concern. For a class reading considerably below grade level, I can use shorter classics commonly found in high school storerooms, such as *The Pearl* or *The Little Prince* (both appropriate for a "Success" unit), if I need a major work. If teachers are required to use specified literary works, it is quite possible to work backward and build a student-centered curriculum around these works. What teachers need to do is start thinking about these literary warhorses in a new way. Most classics and young adult favorites are on departmental reading lists for good reasons. But I believe also that some works are wrong for some classes.

Again, use your judgment. Don't assign Conrad Richter's *A Light in the Forest* without first giving students some way they can connect to it. Teens need more than historical background to care about people who lived 200 years ago. They need to feel some connection to the characters and events in the novel. It has to matter to them. Perhaps the book could be a part of a unit on cultural identity in which students also read short, more contemporary works about youths' experiences as Poles, Latinos, Asians, and so forth. Students could write about their own experiences and observations of interracial and intercultural dating. They could read recent newspaper articles about the experiences of families who adopt children of other races. Or they could read excerpts of the book as part of a larger investigation into families in general. The point is that even standard curriculum should and can be made more responsive to student reality and student concerns.

The search for materials outside textbooks or anthologies can intimidate busy teachers. It is not always easy to find good materials. Sometimes all it takes is a rethinking of the works teachers know and enjoy on their own. In this way, a poem sent to me by a friend—Nikki Giovanni's "My House" (1983)—found its way into a unit on love, and one summer's reading—Ivan Illich's (1970) *Deschooling Society*—inspired me to start gathering related materials for an "Education" unit.

The best part about hunting for materials to use in these high-interest units is that everyone you know will have an idea for you. This might help the new teacher who always is struggling to find good materials. Even before soliciting ideas for materials from students, I have gotten great recommendations from friends who do not teach. Not surprisingly, they have been far more forthcoming in suggesting movies and articles dealing with parenting or social injustice than they were when I was searching for materials in a unit on "Metaphor."

I have at times put many of my planned supplementary materials—poems, songs, movies, articles—on hold in favor of student-supplied materials. When a student brings in a work to present, he or she is trying to connect the known with the unknown and is teaching as well as learning. These are powerful combinations. The unit on love is sometimes built exclusively around student contributions. After I start things off by bringing in one poem and one short story, the next few weeks are full of scenes from popular videos, poetry, and an almost constant supply of pop music.

When students bring in taped songs to play in class, it is crucial that they also bring in the words (which I then copy for the whole class) to these songs. This is the only way the song can acquire the status of literature and command the attention and serious consideration of both the teacher and the students. This requirement for transcribed lyrics also gives students with lower reading and listening skills the opportunity to "take dictation" from the music they are presenting, which they always enjoy.

Presentation of a 3-minute pop song generally takes at least 15 minutes, even if the student has the cassette cued and the lyrics have been copied and are ready to be distributed. The presenting student first plays the song and then discusses it according to the predetermined key questions or presentation guidelines established before presentations began.

My colleagues express doubt. "I can't count on my kids to bring in anything," they say. It is true that student contributions cannot always be relied on. As instructors, our first impulse might be to penalize the students who have failed to fulfill their responsibilities—after all, these responsibilities are the foundation of the cocreative classroom.

We need to avoid reacting to the situation and remember to respond, instead, to the student. When students come unprepared, they forfeit a chance to make the learning environment truly reciprocal. They have "blown it," but their peers, too, have missed out. When this happens in my classroom, other students in the class sometimes will rally to rescue their unprepared peers. When legitimate complications (such as lack of funds, sick baby-sitters, and court dates) confound students' most sincere efforts, I may resort to my own backup materials—poetry, music, or articles—and give a day's grace.

On the other hand, there are times when students come to class unprepared due to sheer negligence. In this case, we need to assess the situation and again stress students' responsibilities to each other. At the beginning of every semester in my classroom, a student brings in a taped song to present but "forgets" to write out the lyrics for the class to analyze. I do not reach into my own reserves to play a song or distribute a short, exciting poem. Instead, we spend the day working on some other, relatively mundane assignment. It is usually a long and disappointing class—everybody's favorite tape is just *sitting there* in the unplugged tape player. The presenting student is writing out the lyrics, furiously, for the next day. Students think, "This is what happens when the *teacher* is in charge." No one in that class ever again brings in a song without also bringing in the lyrics.

CONTINUED STUDENT/TEACHER COOPERATION: DAILY LESSON PLANS

Once we collectively have seen to the unit rationale, key questions, terminal objectives, and materials, it is customary to start thinking about daily lesson plans. How will the class accomplish any of the unit's larger goals? What will we do with the materials? Can the students be involved in this part of the process?

Certainly they can. Of course, it is the teacher's job to dissect a larger goal such as "write an essay" into stages and less ambitious, medial objectives. Medial objectives are the smaller, constituent goals within each terminal objective. These medial objectives consist of predetermined and sequential lessons, which are means to an end; their scheduling and exercise calls for varying amounts of student input. Teachers of college-bound students necessarily are concerned with more varied, formal tasks and will need to spend more time guiding the students toward them.

For students who are cocreating their own curriculum, the objectives are more basic: Learn how to look critically at your own reality. Learn how to express your vision and understanding.

Nothing mobilizes a class more than examination and expression of their own lives. One of the terminal objectives for a "Violence" unit is for each student to present one work that teaches them something about violence, that speaks to them about the human capacity to inflict or accept pain. It is not necessary to make a presentation a terminal objective for every unit of study. But it is appropriate for the high-interest topic of violence for two reasons.

First, "Violence" is a broad topic and one that strikes close to home for all my students. Although they can, therefore, all relate to the topic, I do not want to get too mired in the personal or ask students to spill their guts too much. This may appear, at first, at variance with the stated rationale for a student-centered curriculum. Aren't students supposed to share their experiences and learn from them? Yes—but then again, there has to be a limit. We all have heard and they all have experienced enough war stories. Urban teens already are depicted as living lives of savage violence in movies such as *Boyz N the Hood* and *American Me.* I do not want to add to the glamorization of violence on the streets—and I know that that's not what will help my students take a good, hard look at it. It is better to give them the tools with which to analyze aggression and help them practice applying these tools to lives similar to their own.

The other reason I choose to make student presentations a terminal objective for this unit is as a check on my own tendency to preach. When students bring in songs, they are the ones offering commentary and criticism. They are the ones who can and do tell each other that the songwriter is "full of shit" and is just trying to make a buck by pandering to some teenager's sick fantasy. I cannot do it, no matter how much I would like to. Such criticism, if it came from me, would alienate the student who had chosen the work. We would be playing out the familiar, dysfunctional dynamic between teachers and students in the classroom.

Students generally enjoy bringing in songs and other materials for the class to work with. Almost always their examination of these works is more intense, and they are more on task with their own materials than they are with mine. No matter how much they may enjoy reading *Lord of the Flies* or *Johnny Got His Gun* (both major works for a "Violence" unit), they are more excited and more involved in their own and their classmates' presentations.

We prepare for these presentations by determining which key questions presenters ought to consider in choosing and teaching their works. I ask each student to check with me before making the presentation because we are dealing with such a potentially volatile topic: I don't want someone to bring in a song celebrating a particular gang or other affiliation that would make the classroom a dangerous place for all of us.

Always, teachers should stress that students bring in songs and other works that are saying something. There are plenty of songs and films out there that talk to teenagers. Almost nothing matters more universally to American teenagers than their music. Tell them to bring in the stuff whose lyrics hit them in the guts, bang them on the head, really make them think.

One year for a "Violence" unit, a student brought in a gruesome clip from a slasher video and then showed a violent scene from a more intellectual thriller. We discussed the movies' different uses of violence and the cinematographic techniques employed by the filmmakers. Another student brought in a song by the heavy metal group Slayer entitled "Kill Again" (1989). This song raised questions of brutality and intention and caused the class to challenge Slayer's sincerity and sanity. They also reflected on Slayer's fans: What drove them to like this music's message?

Such presentations compel students to bring the same level of analytical rigor to popular culture that they have applied previously only to literary works. Each time I ask the class to contribute materials, I am struck by the consistent effectiveness of this technique. As we continue with presentations, the class becomes more adept at analyzing familiar works, and the presentations become freer and more creative. Some students begin to use mood lighting, incense, or illustrated song lyrics. The rest of the class tends to respond positively ("I can't believe she's letting us do this!") and consequently treat the song, video, or poem with increased attention. Every time we have presentations, students ask, "Can we do this again?"

Student presentations show students that they can be successful in ways that are just as meaningful to them as good grades: They see that they can make good choices about what they want to learn, that they can take responsibility, and that they can demonstrate their insight. Although students have not initiated the idea of the presentation, they have scheduled, determined the format of, and collectively evaluated these presentations. For the teacher, this activity provides several different types of high-interest daily lessons: We analyze each work presented; we sum up, review, and include students' materials on tests. These materials are treated as valid, quotable resources for essays and other writing assignments within the unit.

Student presentations create additional opportunities for teachers who are planning and structuring daily classes. For example, presenting students usually love to quiz the class on their presentations. What works best here, I have found, is to group together three or four students after they have made related presentations and have them create quizzes for the rest of the class. It is important to stress that students ask each other challenging questions which require inference; the student who has written a good question has engaged in serious thought. Furthermore, each team of quiz makers must generate criteria for the answers to questions on their quizzes. They must work to figure out what they are looking for and what constitutes a complete answer.

Students creating quizzes for each other sometimes ask their classmates to make claims and then substantiate those claims by quoting references to song lyrics. They write questions that ask their peers to cite their own experiences to defend or contradict a song's messages. Most students find creating, taking, and evaluating these quizzes to be an empowering experience. (Students can, of course, also create quizzes based on teacher-supplied materials. Students reflect on characters and concepts, determine relationships between ideas, and usually find themselves teaching as well as learning. They spend one day writing questions and one day taking and discussing each other's quizzes. See Chapter 6, "Racism.")

In these ways a single terminal objective—to present one appropriate, educational work—can, depending on class size, generate whole weeks of meaningful daily activities. Some of the students' contributions can inspire spontaneous activities; the best ones almost always do.

A few years ago, one student brought in a particularly hot and heavy love song, "I Need Love," by the rapper LL Cool J, for her presentation in a "Love" unit. Other students in the class already knew the song but on hearing it in a new, critical arena, they collectively rejected it for being unduly saccharine and obviously insincere. This prompted a two-day reexamination of all the works we already had studied and accepted in the unit; they not only were able to transfer their newfound skepticism to other materials but felt compelled to do so.

EVALUATING THE COCREATIVE PROCESS

As stated, one crucial terminal objective for each unit of study created with students is to "reflect on and evaluate the effectiveness of the unit." I like to end semesters, courses, and units with evaluative questionnaires. When asked to comment on the student-centered approach, students have said, "For some reason, it's easier to learn from other students"; "It gave us a feeling of power"; "It made me think more about the issue"; "It showed me what the other students agree with . . . although some of them were weird."

These students have, indeed, been engaged in Freirian dialogue, whereby "education is a live and creative dialogue in which everyone knows something and does not know others, in which all seek together to know more" (Freire, 1971, p. 113). Through this process students have looked critically at a part of their reality. Their essays, stories, and discussions of the unit topic prove that another of my goals—to enable students to express their feelings about this reality—has been accomplished as well.

We have worked together to satisfy our larger objectives. These larger objectives should be determined beforehand—but teachers never should be so rigid that they cannot accommodate new concerns or subtopics that arise in the course of teaching and learning. As teachers, we must keep listening to the class—not just at the beginning of the course, when we are trying to ascertain what will "grab" them, but every day.

Curricula must reflect student experience. Larger goals and topics within courses must fit the students both academically and socially and must be determined with them. Activities and assignments must involve students at every level possible, including planning, teaching, and evaluating. Daily lesson plans need to be highly flexible in order to accommodate the unpredictable variables that are introduced when students take an active role in their own education.

PRACTICAL MATTERS: FINDING TIME TO CREATE STUDENT-CENTERED UNITS

After reading this chapter, a busy teacher might be thinking: Who's got the time to search for new materials to fit student interests? How can anyone plan ahead when daily activities depend on student participation and contributions?

There are simple answers to these legitimate concerns. First and foremost, this book is intended to be a practical, realistic resource for teachers—not another description of a plan no one really has the time to carry out.

The easiest way to incorporate student input into English curriculum is to do it piecemeal, on a small scale at first. Start slowly. Try a mini cocreative unit. Ask students for unit ideas weeks ahead of time. Look over their suggestions and pick one that you think will work, one for which you know a great article or story to use. Continue with your regular curriculum as you get a rough plan together around this idea. Determine one or two key questions and one or two terminal objectives. Decide on the one or two short materials you will use. This is the only real preplanning you need to do.

When the class finishes up the chapter, the book, or the academic marking period in which they currently are involved, spend the last week or so on their idea. Make this a short unit focusing on only one short story and one poem or article. Ask the students to write about their experiences with the unit concept in a reflective paragraph or short essay. End with a discussion about the topic. Ask students for feedback about this experiment with a student-suggested topic. Listen to what they say. If you and your students are satisfied with the miniunit, try presentations or student-written quizzes next time.

It gets easier. Students do tend to suggest some of the same topics year after year. Although class populations and concerns vary, some constants remain. Although teenagers find old news almost immediately boring (students in the 1993-1994 school year yawn at the 1992 riots and demonstrations in Los Angeles), teachers do not have to run around constantly searching for materials. When you find something that works well, save it. You can use it again. I have used an article I found in an August 1988 *Harper's* magazine, "Reflections of a Gangbanger" by Léon Bing, in four separate units: "Sacrifice and Commitment," "Denial," "Life on the Streets," and "Good and Evil."

Students respond to this short, honest interview every time. We talk about it differently, and different classes have decided to do different things with it. One class simply read and discussed it. Another class wrote a short play with the interviewed gang member featured as a character. Another class used it to set up a role-playing activity. If teachers take a second look at magazine articles they find themselves reading, if they ask their students, their children, their colleagues, and their friends for suggestions, they will find similarly effective and adaptable materials.

How can these works be recycled to address different issues? Sometimes it is a simple matter of refocusing. Teachers can serve current student interests by thinking about familiar materials in new ways. Say, for example, a teacher has collected good materials for a unit on "Success," and students have said they want to study "Money" this year. This teacher most likely can use the "Success" materials by simply modifying the unit's key questions. Specifically, this entails changing questions such as "What is success?" to "Is money always necessary for success?" In this way, the students' focus is retained, and the teacher has engaged in the most critical task of teacher's unit preparation: careful consideration of the unit topic.

I am suggesting that teachers spend some energy looking for good materials and adapting them to fit their students' interests. Depending on whether or not teachers enjoy this task, they always can be on the lookout for new materials, or they can rely on a few select materials to supplement school-supplied works. The most important thing is to reorient one's thinking about curricular materials. Check the TV guide, the video store, magazines, best-sellers, and song lyrics. These are some of the most likely places to find ideas and scenarios that will interest students.

Another way to test out the student-centered approach is to use one of the units detailed in Chapters 5 through 9. Ask students what they want to study; someone is bound to suggest one of the five unit topics offered here. This does not rob students of their prerogative. Although the teacher is working with prepared materials, students still are studying a topic they choose to study. Teachers will need to adapt these units appropriately. One class might want to study "Racism" or "Education" for different reasons than my classes did. In that case, unit rationales and key questions will have to be modified accordingly.

Students still will be the primary designers of these units. The student-supplied materials will be provided by them. The student-written quizzes will be written by them. Even though the unit will have been outlined here, it will happen, uniquely and completely, in the classroom.

MORE PRACTICAL MATTERS: PROSTUDENT DOES NOT MEAN ANTITEACHER

Busy teachers must learn not only how to solicit student input but how to utilize it to everyone's best advantage. The idea is to work with the students, not just for them. Experience and insight are assets that we teachers also bring to the classroom. Certainly, every experienced teacher has learned to establish his or her own working style, including when and how to plan classes.

This leads to another consideration in developing student-centered units: timing. Teachers must schedule student choices in a way that does not unduly complicate their own lives. If a class votes to study the topic of "Self-Destruction" and a teacher has prepared materials for a unit on "Authority," that teacher must refocus or postpone the students' choice.

If the students' suggestion is related somehow to the teachers' preparations, the situation is remedied easily. As discussed previously, the unit can be refocused so that it addresses student concerns. This requires a teacher to do a bit more thinking but does not represent a whole new enterprise. I often have been in this position and have, in fact, worked with a class to generate lists of key questions that are custom-tailored to their perspectives.

A unit on authority, however, cannot be transformed so easily into a unit on self-destruction. The class can be told that "Self-Destruction" will come next quarter, next month, or next semester. Even if more people voted for "Self-Destruction" than for "Authority," it is not always important to go with the class favorite immediately. For this reason, I never ask students to vote on choices of unit topics. It is not a contest. All student suggestions are valid.

Sometimes unit scheduling can be made to concur with outside events. For example, one of my classes voted to study war in the fall of 1990. I was not really ready to start this unit. So we waited until the winter. Coincidentally, in January, the Gulf War gave our studies real immediacy and a heightened sense of relevance. Of course, world events do not always accommodate teachers' schedules. When possible, teachers should try to synchronize unit concepts and events outside the classroom. Intensified action on the streets, scandals downtown, and conditions in the community all can bring a sense of reality to classroom studies.

Probably the biggest change teachers need to make when experimenting with student-centered curriculum is when and how they use their preparation time. English teachers always will need to spend a certain part of their week noting, correcting, and responding to student work. With conventional curriculum materials and assignments, much of teachers' prep time is spent checking written work after students have handed it in. Although it is up to individual teachers to establish the system with which they feel most comfortable, I have learned to orchestrate classroom assignments differently. I now spend more time in class working with students to determine evaluative criteria for their assignments and far less time checking student work.

This is not to say that I never find myself with a pile of essays staring up at me the day before Thanksgiving. That's the nature of the job, I believe. The difference is that each of these essays is topped with a peer evaluation sheet, with criteria specified and checked off by each essay writer's partner. For examples of peer evaluation sheets, see Chapter 8, "The Streets" (Lesson 7, HANDOUT 7),

Chapter 9, "The Hero" (Lesson 6, HANDOUT 9), and Chapter 4 (HANDOUT P: PEER EDITING/ESSAY REVISION). I am still the one who checks writing mechanics, flow, and other less objective features. Students are quite capable, however, of deciding that if a peer's paper lacks a thesis, it needs revision or that an essay with insufficient textual documentation merits only partial credit.

My postclass workload has been reduced also because of the nature of some of the assignments. Reflective writing assignments are like journal entries—I only read and make brief comments on them. They are never corrected. I usually extend another option to students, as well: If the assignment strikes them as particularly confessional or if they have written about a situation so personal that they are reluctant to share it with me, they are allowed to fold the paper over in their notebook and just show me that they have done the assignment. I don't read it. To my thinking, if students care enough to write a page or two about their own experiences, then the assignment and one of the terminal objectives (to reflect on unit concept) both have been well served. I don't need to read about every traumatic event in every student's life.

These two modifications of regular expectations—that teachers are not the only editors of students' work and that we need not read and correct every assignment—lessen my workload considerably. The time I save is time I prefer to spend designing curriculum that is responsive to my students. Yes, they need feedback on their work and help with writing and development of other academic skills. But I often think that what some students need is less red pen on their papers and more opportunities to think and write about the choices they are making every weekend.

In this way students and teachers spend more time engaged together in the true business of any classroom: learning. Students learn skills and gain insight into their own lives. Accommodating student interests has been one of the most exciting skills I have learned to develop as a teacher. Learning how to use this skill so that it does not take over my own life has been just as important.

APPLICATIONS FOR TEACHERS

1. What place, if any, have students' outside lives and concerns previously had in your classroom? Why is this the case?

2. What, in your opinion, are some of the biggest sources of conflict in your students' lives?

3. What are your concerns relating to students' expression of these conflicts?

4. Do you remember any occasions in your own education when you or classmates contributed materials and suggestions or otherwise played the "teacher's role" in the classroom? What feelings do you associate with these memories?

5. On what do you spend the bulk of your class preparation time now? Are you satisfied with this?

4

▓ Instructional Procedures and Student Guidelines

List of Handouts and Instructor's Notes

HANDOUT A: INTEREST INVENTORY

1. What was the best thing that happened to you this summer?

2. Name a few things that you are good at or like to do.

3. If you could do anything for a living, what would it be?

4. Name the last book you read.

5. Is there any kind of writing that you particularly enjoy? What is it?

6. In your opinion, what is the biggest local problem we face?

7. Name two people—famous or not—about whom you would like to know more.

8. What types of issues or subjects would you like to know more about?

9. What are your strengths in English?

10. Name the areas you know you need to improve in English.

11. What places would you like to visit?

HANDOUT B: STRENGTHS AND SUCCESSES INVENTORY

You and School

What is the best part of school?
What is the worst part of school?
What are your strong points as a student?

You and English

What have you enjoyed in English class in the past and why?
What has been the worst part of English class for you in the past and why?
What do you think you need to work on in English?

You

What will I remember about you in 20 years? What is your most outstanding characteristic?

List three things that you are really good at:

(1)
(2)
(3)

List three successes that you have experienced in your life:

(1)
(2)
(3)

Choose one of these successes and describe it on the back of this page. Make sure that you just don't say it and stop writing. Take time to think and describe:

— what obstacle you faced
— how you overcame it
— how you felt once you succeeded
— what you learned along the way and how you could apply that success to other parts of your life

HANDOUT C: CHOOSING TOPICS OF STUDY

Directions: What would you like to study? What do you feel is important to know more about? Select ideas from this list and then add more. Next to each idea, please suggest a book, film, or music that has taught you about the topic, if you can.

_____ Gender roles (male and female behavior)
_____ Racism
_____ Education
_____ Love
_____ The Streets
_____ Dreams
_____ Violence
_____ AIDS
_____ Innocence and Experience (growing up)
_____ Heroes

What else? Power? Money? Families? Working for a living? Name more ideas that matter to you:

_____

_____

_____

_____

_____

_____

_____

INSTRUCTORS' NOTES D:
STARTING OFF: OTHER IDEAS

• It is a good idea to spend some time introducing students to one another. This is especially true with smaller classes. There are many ways to do this. Here are two:

1. Pair up students who do not know each other. They are to take turns interviewing one another, using a set of questions written on the board. After these brief interviews have been conducted, each student introduces his or her partner to the class. Interview questions:

Name:
Something he or she does well:
Something she or he is proud of:
Three things he or she would like other people to say about him or her are:
By next year, she or he would like to:
One of his or her goals in life is to:
One thing she or he would like to learn is:
Someone he or she admires is:
She or he is a good friend to have because:

2. Play a "name game." This game asks students to remember and recite each other's names. Each student will say his or her name after he or she names the students who have named themselves previously, in order. For example, if Joe, Kathleen, and Renee are sitting in a row, Joe starts the game by saying simply, "Joe." Kathleen continues: "Joe. Kathleen." Renee adds her name to the list last: "Joe. Kathleen. Renee." Obviously, the game gets harder as you go around the room. It is important to establish a clear order of succession; if students are arranged in rows, make sure everyone understands the order in which the naming runs. The last person in the class, who will have to name everyone (this may or may not be the instructor), has the hardest job. I like to play this game at the end of every class for the first few days of the semester. It is how we find out the names students really want to go by and helps to give the class an initial sense of unity.

• Distribute 3 × 5 cards. Ask students to list topics or questions that they would like to see addressed in class or that they feel need resolution in their lives. This activity may workbest midyear, once a context of trust and sincerity has been established.

• Students and instructor are to list the things that they know how to do. On paper, individuals should list specific skills they have—from the trivial ("make fried chicken") to the substantial ("cheer up my mother when she's in a bad mood").

INSTRUCTORS' NOTES E: SKILL INVENTORIES

Before embarking on serious academic work with students, it is important to assess their abilities so that instruction can better use their strengths and address their deficiencies. Skill inventories—short, ungraded exercises that can measure a student's ability to read and make inferences, to write, and to use punctuation correctly—are an essential part of the cocreative classroom. These can be built into thematic units or can stand on their own as introductory exercises.

Reading inventories consist of a series of questions built around a short reading. Students answer questions about this reading. The questions are arranged from simplest to most difficult; the last few questions require sophisticated reading skills. Sample reading inventories can be found also in Chapter 5 ("Sex Roles, Power, and Identity," Lesson 6) and Chapter 8 ("The Streets," Lesson 1). I strongly urge instructors to read Hillocks's description of the reading inventory. Instructors can use the hierarchical arrangement of questions to locate students on a skill continuum, to select appropriate reading materials, and to design questions that are appropriate to the students' reading and inference levels. For a complete description of reading inventories, see George Hillocks's (1980) "Toward a Hierarchy of Skills in the Comprehension of Literature." See also Hillocks and Ludlow (1984), "A Taxonomy of Skills in Reading and Interpreting Fiction."

Writing inventories are another diagnostic tool. Instructors can use writing inventories to measure a student's ability to write complete sentences, narrative, and dialogue and to support a claim. The instructor generates specific criteria and establishes simple benchmarks. Instructors assess students' skill levels by noting which benchmarks they have reached. Writing inventories are not corrected otherwise.

Instructors may decide to use initial journal entries as writing inventories. For example, the first journal assignment in Chapter 7 ("Education," Lesson 2) is "Write about a time you took a test that was unfair." Instructors may want to use this assignment to measure a student's ability to write narrative. Entries can be assessed on a scale of 1 to 5.

"1" entries are discursive and contain no narrative elements.

"2" entries may refer to a distinct episode or event but only indirectly.

"3" entries tell a story but do not develop it.

"4" entries contain a coherent narrative but one that is told simply and without descriptive detail or sophisticated literary devices.

"5" entries are fully developed narratives complete with dialogue, descriptive detail, and a decisive narrative voice.

Here are examples of journal assignments ("Write about an educational experience—positive or negative—that was meaningful to you") that have been evaluated as narrative writing inventories. Evaluative criteria are noted in the margins.

SAMPLE 1

in medias res opening

"But Julie was cheating, too! Why doesn't Mr. Moochie send her to the principal?" I said, angrily, to Jimmy, as we walked very slowly, down the long hall to Hell—the principal's office. This was totally unfair. I was pissed.

"You know why," said Jimmy.

He was right. Julie Roseman was only thirteen years old, but she looked eighteen, and wore tighter shirts than anyone else in Amity Regional Junior High. Mr. Moochie couldn't take his eyes off her bursting buttons when she walked into class. You could just see him licking his chops. Both Jimmy and I knew that he would keep her after school himself, and probably never even call her parents.

"He is totally sickening, Mr. Moochie. Him and his shining, ping pong-ball head with the leftover hair scooped up over the top," I said. We were getting closer and closer to the glass doors that said "Principal's Office" on them. A long vinyl bench stood next to the doors. We sat down on it and waited for one of the old-bat secretaries to come swooping down and carry us off into Hell. We sat there in silence. I kept thinking about Mr. Moochie.

He was one of those pathetic teachers who felt intellectual because he knew more than you did—even though you were only twelve years old. He was one of those slimy teachers who just loved to catch kids cheating. He wouldn't stay at his desk during tests, like a normal teacher. You couldn't even see him. I didn't. He came oozing around the corner, out of nowhere, like a worm, and said . . .

SAMPLE 2

On the night of July 10, the police raided my apartment, tore my house apart trying to find certain things. A little while later they took me to the station I was arrested.

It was one of the worst experiences. Very negative. I do feel that everyone shouldn't be judged by whom you hang around. That night when they came to my apartment I felt like I was not given my proper rights.

They just bust in and wouldn't listen to me. They judged me because who I was being with. After experiencing going to jail I had stopped hanging out and having alot of company.

Now I mind my own business, come and go I don't too much hang around anymore. It seems that things are much better that way. With such a thing happening to me I has decided to go back to school and start all over. I'm trying to change my life around so positive things will happen in the future.

SAMPLE 3

I learned that if you want some thing in life you have to get it regardless of risk. I dropped out of school because it became too hard so I quit. I thought I could get along in life without school. But I was wrong.

What I did after I dropped out was I kept reading. I read military "smart" books which teach you the many way of combat, I learned how to make a variety of things . . . I learned that trust must be earned, not given. I always feel that things don't go rite. and that is the lessen I learned.

HANDOUT F: GROUP PROCESS

Working in groups provides opportunities for students to do a lot of things: talk, laugh, copy from each other, brainstorm together, ignore each other, let one person do all the work, waste time, listen to each other, learn from each other, and so forth. Some of this is okay; some is not. Have you worked in small groups before? Which of these situations have you experienced?

Working alone is easier than working in groups. Working in groups does develop other skills, though. People who work well in groups learn to cooperate, compromise, and reach consensus. They can develop better interpersonal skills than loners.

Of course, not everyone works well with other people every day. There are some classic behaviors that typically interfere with good group work.

If you want to see these behaviors in action, set up the following activity. Pick four or five people to work in a small group. Give them an activity: a class assignment or a task that requires communication and cooperation (e.g., a jigsaw puzzle). Let them interact in the middle of the room and observe the group dynamics. Note names of group members you see who are displaying the following characteristics:

"The Mother"

Watches out for everyone. Makes sure no one gets the shaft. Facilitates and encourages participation. Asks group members to put other considerations aside and focus on the matter at hand.

"The Wall"

Resists participation. Even when other group members invite the wall to participate, he or she will not. Does not interfere with others' activity but will not budge. Acts completely uninterested.

"The Saboteur"

Is more interested in derailing the group process than anything else. Distracts other group members with irrelevant information or observations. May be bitter or humorous.

"The Commander"

Takes charge of the situation entirely, doing all of the work or assigning tasks to other group members. The main objective is to get the job done, not work together cooperatively.

"The Loner"

Works as if no one else is there. Will concentrate on the matter at hand but will not communicate or share with other group members.

Based on your experiences and observations, what types of behaviors do you think help a group to work together effectively?

HANDOUT G: NOTE TAKING

Why Take Notes?

Believe it or not, the main reason for taking notes is so you won't waste your time. It is easier and quicker to take notes than it is to try and remember everything on your own. The purpose of taking notes is to record the facts, issues, and opinions that come up in class or in your reading. Once you take notes, you can go back to study and reflect on them.

Four Steps of Note Taking

1. *Record* while you are reading or during a class. Record all the facts and ideas that are meaningful. Write clearly.

2. *Read* your notes over. Try to state the facts and ideas as fully as possible, not mechanically but in your own words. Then refer to the rest of your notes and check what you have said. This helps transfer the facts and ideas to your long-term memory.

3. *Reflect* on your notes. Reread them and ask yourself, "Do I agree?" Consider your own opinions and experiences and see how they relate to what you learn. When you begin to reflect on how your life fits in (or does not fit in) with what you read and hear, you are thinking critically.

4. *Review* your notes. If you spend 10 minutes every week or so in a quick review of your notes, you will retain most of what you have learned, and you will be able to use your knowledge more and more effectively.

How to Record Notes

There is no one right way to take notes. Everyone has his or her own system. No matter what your technique, here are several hints that will make note taking easier for you:

- Use paper big enough to write more than a few words on a line. The more room you have on the paper, the more you can use the space on the paper itself to organize.

- Skip lots of lines. Write in short paragraphs or small sections. It is really hard to find one specific item in a block of writing.

- Keep it simple. Forget about complicated outlines, Roman numerals, and so forth. You can use boxes, stars, or underlining to note main ideas or new sections.

- Use abbreviations (as long as you are sure you will remember what they all mean!).

- Be as neat as you can. No one needs gorgeous notes (it's a waste of time, and you need to pay attention to fact and opinions here, not "art"), but if you can't read it easily days or weeks later, you have wasted your time.

HANDOUT H: ROLE PLAYING

You have been given the bare facts of a dramatic setup and have been given a character to play. When you meet with the other people in your setup, you will be asked to speak, react, and interact as if you are the character you have been assigned. This is improvisation. Before you start, make sure you know the answer to a couple of basic questions:

- Who are you?

- What is your relationship to the other characters in your setup?

As you begin to prepare for your setup, decide on some other basic facts about your character:

- How old are you?

- Are you basically satisfied with your life?

- How do you feel about the situation at hand?

- What do you want to happen in this situation?

- What are you willing to do to get what you want?

- How do you feel about the other characters in the setup?

When the role play begins, you should try to stay in character. Don't act like yourself; act like your character, even if it means saying and doing things you never would say or do.

Stern. *Teaching English So It Matters.* © 1995 Corwin Press, Inc.

INSTRUCTORS' NOTES I: USING MUSIC IN THE CLASSROOM

There are several reasons why I have added pop music song lyrics to the repertoire of poetry that I use in the classroom:

1. Once in a great while students will recognize the songs and feel connected to curriculum materials.
2. Music in the classroom is a variation on and a break from regular, everyday activities—a treat.
3. Songs serve as a link between unit concepts and the real, everyday world.
4. The slow pace of most singing encourages students to underline problematical lines as they read along and thus enables pointed analytical discussions.
5. When I bring in a song, it almost always compels students to choose and bring in works for their own presentations.
6. My song presentation provides a clear model for student presentations.

Instructors may be reluctant to use music in the classroom. This apprehension is legitimate but should be overcome. The important thing is to present song lyrics as poetry. Classes spent listening to and discussing songs are not a kind of throwaway musical show-and-tell; they are sessions for serious literary analysis. Students will find song lyrics to be profound, stimulating, silly, or maddening; they will come to see some lyricists as brilliant social commentators, some as poets, some as immature fools.

Instructors may not want to bring in "their" music for fear that students will hate it. They probably will. Many kids laugh when they hear music reflecting a bygone era or aesthetic. Before playing any song, instructors would be wise to stress that students are not expected to like the music. This is not music appreciation class. Students are expected to afford the lyrics the same respect that they give to any relevant piece of literature. Students may just read the lyrics without listening to the recorded song. This way, if teachers bring in a song that students deem hopelessly "uncool" or if one student plays a song that his or her peers hate, the lesson is not lost.

Instructors well may suspect that no student will want to present a song for fear that it will be subjected to the same derision as the teacher's selection. It is true that different students in the class naturally will appreciate different types of music. Instructors must stress tolerance and analysis as opposed to enjoyment.

If music is used in the classroom, it is crucial to give students a framework with which to examine each song. Handouts for typical presentations are in Chapter 6, "Racism." These handouts help students select and present songs. A presenting student knows that the selection will need to fit the questions on the handout and can use the list of questions or issues on the sheet to organize the presentation. Sometimes songs contain messages or images that require analysis beyond or in addition to the areas specified on the unit handout. In this case, employ standard questions about content and figurative language.

The most important part of the presentation is the lyric sheet. Students may transcribe lyrics or they may bring in preprinted lyric sheets. If instructors have access to copiers, they can copy the lyrics of the students' songs and distribute copies to each student in the class. Presenting students also can write lyrics on the board. Instructors will need to establish a profanity policy. They may request that students bring in songs to be previewed. Students can be forbidden to bring in works that are obscene (although I believe this may limit the effectiveness of the activity). Or teachers can tell students that they are free to bring in any work but must replace profanity with symbols (#$%&*!!) when they are writing out lyrics.

Teenagers appreciate being given the chance to share works that matter to them. Once a song has been brought in by a student, instructors have new materials with which to work. Songs can be analyzed, scanned, checked for grammar irregularities, translated into Shakespearean vernacular, or otherwise studied by students. The possibilities are endless. The only limits are the students' and instructors' imaginations.

HANDOUT J: WRITING AND USING DIALOGUE

Dialogue is conversation. There are two types of dialogue: direct and indirect. Writers use both kinds. Indirect dialogue is *talking* about talking, such as this:

Then I told her I loved her.

Direct dialogue is plain, straight-ahead talking, such as this:

"I love you," Mario said.

Direct dialogue brings a sense of excitement and immediacy to stories. Here are simple rules for writing direct dialogue:

1. Put quotation marks (" ") around the words that actually come out of people's mouths. You need to put one set of quotation marks around someone's words—at the start and at the end. That means that if you want to write a *he said* in the middle, you need to keep the words *he said* out of the quotation marks. For example:

He said, "I love you." [The three words that he spoke aloud are in quotation marks.]
"I love you," he said, "and I'll never leave you." [The speaker never said the words *he said*, so the quotation has to start, stop, and then start again.]

2. Every time a new person talks, you have to indent and start a new paragraph for them. Even if they say only one word, they still get their own paragraph. For example:

"I love you, too, Mario," Sheila screamed out. "And I want to get married and live happily ever after with you in a big house! We can have lots of children and be so happy together!"
"But—" [Mario's one word gets its own paragraph.]
"But what? Doesn't this make you happy?" she asked.

3. You can interrupt dialogue with action. This is the most natural kind of storytelling. While people talk they do all sorts of things such as sit down, look surprised, smoke cigarettes, and watch TV. For example:

"Listen, Sheila, I love you, but I don't trust you." Mario stood up and looked out the window.
"What do you mean you don't trust me?" Sheila's eyebrows shot up and her mouth dropped open. She sounded hurt.
"You know what I mean," said Mario as he started looking through the pile of cassettes lying on the table.

4. Check these short samples to see how commas and other punctuation marks fit into direct dialogue. For the most part, every quotation needs some type of punctuation mark before the final marks close the quotation.

For practice, continue the dialogue between Mario and Sheila.

Stern. *Teaching English So It Matters.* © 1995 Corwin Press, Inc.

HANDOUT K: NARRATIVE REVISION

Step 1: Reread your story.

Use a different color pen and go through your story like an editor. Decide which parts work best and which could be improved. What do you need to add? What could your story lose? Mark up your page appropriately, circling the "good stuff" and noting the parts that could be better.

Step 2: Find a new starting point.

Does your story start off with a bang, so that you want to keep reading? Put a big * (asterisk) to mark the moment when your story is most interesting. It would make a good starting point.

Step 3: Plan where you will use direct dialogue.

Underline every time your story refers to people talking, laughing, arguing. You can rewrite all these situations so that the dialogue is direct and exciting.

Step 4: Divide story into separate paragraphs.

Put a / (slash) between different sections, to note where you will start new paragraphs. You need to change paragraphs every time the speaker, emotion or mood, time, or place changes.

Step 5: Write a new rough draft.

Using all the corrections and ideas for improvement, rewrite your story. It probably will be longer and might look very different from the first story. Usually the more changes you make, the better. This is the time when you can change individual words to get more specific, more descriptive, and more colorful. Make sure your dialogue is realistic and that your characters have distinct personalities.

Step 6: Make a final check.

It is best to do this with a partner. Read over the new rough draft, making sure that it all makes sense and that you have used correct punctuation and spelling. Does the new starting point work? Are you satisfied with the ending? This is a good time to give your new revised story a title.

Step 7: Do a final rewrite.

Copy your corrected rough draft neatly into a revised final draft.

HANDOUT L: CLAIMS, EVIDENCE, AND WARRANTS

Fill in the blanks with sentences that explain why the evidence proves the claim.

CLAIM	EVIDENCE	WARRANT
1. Candy is fattening.	Sam is fat.	Sam eats a lot of candy.
2. Money can't buy happiness.	Elaine is miserable.	_____
3. Walkmen make you deaf.	Little Bobo is deaf.	_____
4. The U.S. government is in debt.	There will be new tax laws this year.	_____
5. Motorcycles are dangerous.	Bob has a broken leg.	_____
6. Alcohol is involved in most teen suicides.	15-year-old Jeannette drinks instead of talking about her problems.	_____
7. Parents can be unfair.	Susan gave Jimmy candy but didn't give any to Maria.	_____

HANDOUT M: EVALUATING SOURCES OF EVIDENCE

Directions:

1. Read the claims and supporting evidence. Decide whether you would accept or reject the evidence to support the claims.
2. Fill out column 3: Write that you would accept the evidence, or write in evidence or sources that you would trust.
3. At the bottom of the page, list four criteria for good evidence.

CLAIM	EVIDENCE	ACCEPT? OR REPLACE WITH—?
1. Bill Clinton is the best president this country has ever had.	Al Gore says so.	_____
2. Your principal is the best in the state.	The principal's mother says so.	_____
3. Lake Michigan is pure and clean.	A travel book published in 1916 says so.	_____
4. Foreign cars are better made than American cars.	A poll of mechanics says so.	_____
5. The Midwest is a boring place to live.	A lifelong resident of New York says so.	_____
6. Most cops are unnecessarily brutal on the job.	A police chief says so.	_____
7. Movies are now too stupid to watch.	A person who just saw "I Was a Teenage Bran Muffin From Hell" says so.	_____
8. All children are thieves.	The owner of a 7-Eleven convenience store says so.	_____

Good evidence must:

1.
2.
3.
4.

HANDOUT N: BASIC ESSAY ORGANIZATION

Whether it is three paragraphs, three pages, or 35 pages long, every essay follows a basic organization: introduction, body, and conclusion.

In the *introduction*, you state what you will be writing about. You let your readers know what you are going to be talking about and how you are going to break it down. There is no need to say, "I will write about blah blah blah . . ." Just go ahead and state your main point. This is the thesis of your essay. The following information must go into the introduction:

1. Thesis
2. Names of the works (literature, video, poetry, etc.) on which you are basing your study
3. Authors of the works
4. Brief outline of the major areas or claims that you will be discussing

This may take a few sentences. It may take a few paragraphs.

Next, the *body* of the paper takes each one of these areas and discusses it. There is a logical method of introducing each *claim*, supporting it with quoted *evidence*, and *warranting*, or explaining the meaning of each quotation. When using individual quotations from the book, it is important to set up each one and give some brief background information. This information assures that the reader will be able to understand the point you are making, even if she or he has not read the book. Likewise, a reference to your own experiences also needs some background information. It is important to explain why the evidence proves your point. No evidence speaks for itself. A body can be one paragraph, three paragraphs, or many pages.

Finally, the *conclusion* of your essay should tie together your several points and relate them back to the thesis. While writing your concluding paragraphs, you may discover that you have changed your focus. That's all right. In that case, you will need to go back and modify your thesis. A writer's own judgments or opinions may find their way into the conclusion—this is fine.

Also, every essay needs a *title*. Just read your essay over when it is done and name it appropriately.

Stern. *Teaching English So It Matters.* © 1995 Corwin Press, Inc.

HANDOUT O: BLANK BOXES FOR ESSAY PREWRITING

THESIS:

CLAIM 1	CLAIM 2	CLAIM 3

CLAIM 1:

EVIDENCE: (with page numbers)

WARRANT:

CLAIM 2:

EVIDENCE: (with page numbers)

WARRANT:

(Planning boxes for section 4 and 5 [the conclusion] on next page)

CLAIM 3:

EVIDENCE: (with page numbers)

WARRANT:

NOTES FOR CONCLUSION:

HANDOUT P: PEER EDITING/ESSAY REVISION

READERS: Look over your partner's essay. Check it for all the things on this sheet.

WRITERS: Read this checklist when your partner returns it with your essay. Make all necessary changes, and write your final draft accordingly.

Final draft is due on _____

Paragraph 1:

1. Is there a thesis that states the main idea of the essay? ___ YES ___ NO
2. Are the main work(s) and authors(s) named? ___ YES ___ NO
3. Are there clear, general claims stated in this paragraph? ___ YES ___ NO

Paragraph 2:

1. Is Claim 1 restated? ___ YES ___ NO
2. Is there discussion or examples that support the claim? ___ YES ___ NO
3. Is there quoted evidence that substantiates these examples ? ___ YES ___ NO
   (The more evidence, the better)
4. Is the evidence warranted? ___ YES ___ NO
5. Does the whole paragraph work to support the thesis? ___ YES ___ NO

Paragraph 3:

1. Is Claim 2 restated? ___ YES ___ NO
2. Is there discussion or examples that support the claim? ___ YES ___ NO
3. Is there quoted evidence that substantiates these examples? ___ YES ___ NO
   (The more evidence, the better)
4. Is the evidence warranted? ___ YES ___ NO
5. Does the whole paragraph work to support the thesis? ___ YES ___ NO

Paragraph 4:

1. Is Claim 3 restated? ___ YES ___ NO
2. Is there discussion or examples that support the claim? ___ YES ___ NO
3. Is there quoted evidence that substantiates these examples? ___ YES ___ NO
   (The more evidence, the better)
4. Is the evidence warranted? ___ YES ___ NO
5. Does the whole paragraph work to support the thesis? ___ YES ___ NO

Paragraph 5:

1. Is there some reference back to the thesis? ___ YES ___ NO
2. Does the essay end well? ___ YES ___ NO

(continued)

Stern. *Teaching English So It Matters.* © 1995 Corwin Press, Inc.

Check These Things as Well:

1. Is spelling correct? ___ YES ___ NO: Circle words for the writer to check.

2. Is punctuation correct? ___ YES ___ NO: Circle phrases for the writer to check.

3. Are all titles underlined or in quotation marks? ___ YES ___ NO

INSTRUCTORS' NOTES Q: STORY MAPS

All story maps outline the bare bones of a story or section of a longer work. Students who are struggling with difficult works or those who are trying to generate discussion questions benefit from constructing story maps. Students who work on story maps make generalizations, determine narrative focus and causal relationships, and synthesize information. For an example of a completed story map, see Chapter 6 ("Racism," Lesson 10 for lower level readers).

Map 1: Simple Information Type

Students find and list

Main characters:

Setting:

Main events:

Themes:

Map 2: Identifying Conflict Type

Students find and list

Main characters:

Setting:

Initial problem:

Goal:

Events:

Resolution:

Map 3: Character Type

Students find and list

Main characters:

Characters' individual goals:

Impediments to realization of goals:

Characters' successes and failures:

Students can work on either type of story map alone or in small groups. They can work with the information in any one of several ways.

- They can prepare a simple story map.

- They can prepare a simple story map and write sentence- or paragraph-long expanded accounts of the information in each category (i.e., on the setting or the resolution).

● They can construct a story map and then classify any of the instructor's statements as a main event or initial problem statement. (For example, if students were to construct a story map of "The Three Little Pigs," an instructor could say, "The big bad wolf wanted to eat the pigs"; students would then have to classify this as an initial problem statement.)

● Instructors can ask students to locate setting information or goal information in the text.

INSTRUCTORS' NOTES R: STUDENT CONTRACTS

Students who have not completed many assignments or whose attendance is irregular often benefit from individual contracts. To put a student "on contract," an instructor calls the student up to discuss the problem after school or during a class when other students are engaged in independent work. These sessions are neither lectures nor academic tutorials. They should permit discussion of the instructor's observations and give the student an opportunity to focus on the root cause of the delinquency. Students' poor performance may be caused by late nights, responsibilities at home or on the job, lack of interest in the subject matter, confusion, or poor skills. Only when the instructor knows the reasons behind a student's failure can she or he help that student. The most effective help an instructor can give a student is the chance to take control of the situation and assume responsibility for his or her actions.

A student who writes up a contract is assessing and reflecting on his or her reality, ability, and goals. Students should not make any impossible resolutions on these contracts no matter how tempting the opportunity to "turn over a whole new leaf." Contracts can specify due dates for missing written work, conditions of continued membership in the class, and consequences of violating the terms of the contract. It is most important to let the student write out the contract him- or herself and to have both instructor and student sign it. Here are a few sample student-written contracts:

SAMPLE 1

I, Ron K., agree that I cannot miss any more classes. I will not be more than ten minutes late on the days when I have to help get my brother to school. All my missing work will be made up by Friday, 10/16, or I'm out of here (dropped out of the class with no hope of graduating).

Signed: _____ Date: _____
Signed: _____ Date: _____

SAMPLE 2

I will take the quiz during lunch on Wednesday (10/10). I will hand in journal #2 plus the two missing handouts before I leave school on Wednesday (10/10). I will be absent only on my three court dates—Oct. 16, Oct. 25, and Nov. 1. I will make up all work that I miss from the court dates on the next day. Besides that, I will not be absent unless I am sick, and I will bring in a doctor's note. If I ever just blow off class I understand that I will get kicked out for good by the teacher.

INSTRUCTOR'S NOTE: I think if you blow off class, you are choosing to be out of the class. So it's up to you, not me, Barnabas.

Signed: _____ Date: _____
Signed: _____ Date: _____

HANDOUT S: STUDENT PRESENTATION GUIDELINES

There are only four things you need to do to give a successful presentation:

1. Make sure you understand the assignment.

2. Choose your work carefully.

3. Prepare what you actually will bring to class.

4. Think through your analysis *before* you come to class.

Step 1: Make sure you understand the assignment. What type of presentation are you being asked to give? Will you bring in a taped song and printed lyrics? Or will it be more of a report on a written text? When is your presentation scheduled? How much time do you have? Can you get a hold of the work you want before then? Remember, if you are bringing in a song, you also must bring in the words.

Step 2: Choose your work carefully. What is the topic you're studying? What issues should your presented work address? Start thinking about songs, movies, works of art, poems, stories, and so forth that fit the topics. Pick a work that has made you think. If you are giving a report-type presentation, make sure you know on which sections of the work you will focus.

Step 3: Prepare what you actually will bring to class. Listen to the song or read the work over several times. If you are bringing in an audio- or videotape, cue the tape to the beginning of the selection you want to play for the class. Write neatly, type, or copy the appropriate lyrics. Make sure you can get enough copies to distribute to everyone in the class.

Step 4: Think through your analysis before you come to class. Make sure you know the name of the work, the author or artist, and where we can find it. Then refer to the prepared handouts or notes on this presentation. Make sure you can answer each question on the handout for your work. You also can take general notes on your works. What are some underlying messages in your opinion? What do you think was the artist's purpose in creating the work? Do you think the artist has been successful in communicating his or her message? Why or why not? Jot all this information down and bring it with you when you give your presentation.

You can decide if you want to share your opinions, ask the class how they feel, or combine the two modes. Teach it the way you want to teach it.

Presentations must last at least _____ minutes.

INSTRUCTORS' NOTES T: STUDENT PRESENTATIONS

Presentations are tricky. They can give students a wonderful sense of power and competence—or they can make them feel like utter fools. It is the instructor's role to help each student give a good presentation. Some students will just take off: Ability, preparation, and stage presence firmly in hand, they will enjoy the task, and their peers will enjoy the presentation. Other students will not be so lucky. They will freeze, falter, or try to avoid the assignment altogether.

It is a good idea to start off by requiring students to sign up for specific presentation dates on a calendar and to leave the presentation schedule up in a public place to remind them when their due dates are coming. Students might benefit from a "predue date" on which they report which song (or other work) they will be using. This date should come a few days before presentations start.

To start presentations and decrease the intimidation factor, instructors can give a model, joint presentation with a student. The student finds the song, meets with the instructor before class to plan the presentation, and then the two of them team-teach the work to the class.

When students start presenting their works, instructors should pay close attention, making sure that the presenter goes through all formal analytical criteria. Presenting students also should write these features of their work on the board. Some students may feel cowed by this task. Even if they have prepared at home, they may feel their interpretations cannot be "right."

Be patient with these students. Instructors can take over for students who seem to be stuck and ask the class to analyze or find the specific features of the work. If a presenting student really is having trouble, an instructor should never chastise this student for poor preparation or poor analytical skills. It will be obvious that the presentation is going nowhere.

Instead, instructors will need to step in and teach the work for the presenting student. Perhaps she or he will be able to warm up and take over eventually. Many times I have had to start a presentation for a shy student, asking the class what the work says about success or love or racism, only to be relieved of my duties by the presenting student after a few minutes. It seems that I have missed some point or gotten the whole thing wrong (adults "just don't get it," for the most part). The presenting student has recovered his or her poise and is ready to lead the class through the work with the righteousness of youth and truth.

Never challenge a presenting student on his or her chosen work. Even if you suspect it was selected merely to provoke a reaction, I advise instructors to ignore the provocation and treat the work as a viable piece of literature. Apply all analytical criteria to it, and let the students challenge the presenter if the work is of questionable merit or import. Otherwise, students will start choosing works to please the instructor and compromise the purpose of the presentation.

Student presentations are the core of the cocreative classroom. I encourage instructors to adapt these procedures for their own students and find effective ways to let the students select and teach their own materials to each other. The presentation develops speaking skills, critical reading skills, and analytical abilities. It also increases self-esteem better than any other classroom activity I know.

INSTRUCTORS' NOTES U: VOCABULARY WORDS OF THE WEEK

I had difficulty finding an effective way to teach vocabulary before I happened on the "Word of the Week" technique. Although my students had tolerated vocabulary study with relatively good grace, it seemed they learned new words superficially, by rote. They learned vocabulary words like dry formulas: memorized them, took a test on them, and then forgot them. Part of the problem was that these lists of vocabulary words had no context, no purpose, or no immediate relevance to anything except a grade on a vocabulary quiz. Even if the words came from the assigned literary text, students still had trouble making the word their own.

My students need to learn new words, though. The limitations of their own vocabularies become obvious when we turn our attention to topics that matter deeply to these teenagers, such as power, success, and good and evil. Often they do not have the terms even to describe their own experiences.

One year, in frustration, I decided to do away with traditional vocabulary study. We began discussing racism in one of my classes by talking about people's assumptions and presumptions. I introduced my students to the term *stereotype*. To remind them the word existed, I wrote it with a green marker at the beginning of a long strip of adding machine tape, which I posted to run around the room up as I high as I could reach. *Stereotype* became the "word of the week," and a new word was added every subsequent week. In the coming days and weeks, every time a student used one of these words in class discussion, she or he was applauded. Whenever students used and spelled the word correctly on written work, they were awarded a point. My other classes asked about the list. They had heard that it was an easy way to get extra credit (I don't know why those two words hold such magic for my students—but they do) and wanted their own list. Another strip of tape was added.

The word of the week has turned out to be a big hit in my classes. Students ask about words from the text, or I suggest words that come up in discussion or when we read together. Usually I decide on the word of the week as I plan for the week. Any word that might enlarge my students' horizons or increase their powers of expression is a candidate.

After the chosen word is written on a long narrow strip of paper posted high on the walls around the classroom, we spend time discussing it—sometimes 10 minutes or more. In this way we can get into nuances of meaning and usage. That is why these words genuinely enter students' vocabularies: They have gotten to know each word, gotten to explore its subtleties and connotations.

The list grows longer every week, and the strips stay up on the walls all semester. In this way all the words spelled correctly are available for students to use on tests or other in-class writing. Students can be awarded one point of extra credit every time they use any form of any word of the week correctly on a test or any other writing assignment. Instructors ought to note every time a student uses one of the words in discussion in some way; I give enormous smiles to the student who uses a word from the list.

This is the most successful approach I have found to teaching vocabulary in school. It is not as intensive as most—one word a week is pretty meager—but my students end the semester with genuinely increased, enriched vocabularies.

Some words of the week from past years include: *indoctrinated, overt, motivation, exempt, naive, monotony, coerce, asset/liability, strife, rhetoric, negligent, euphemism, cynical, ambiguous, flabbergasted,* and *compassion.*

INSTRUCTORS' NOTES V: EVALUATIONS

I have been lucky enough to teach in an alternative high school in which students receive only "credit/no credit" from each instructor at the end of the marking period. Individual assignments and exams are graded, but the final evaluation is seen as a joint venture between student and teacher. I believe in this cooperative evaluation session and see it as an important part of the cocreative classroom.

We have each student sit down with the instructor for 10 minutes to talk about the academic quarter and to evaluate his or her effort and performance. It may be impossible to schedule similar sessions in more traditional schools. Still, even when regular letter grades are used to measure students' performance, I advocate some type of joint evaluative session. Instructors should try to fit a short conference into the end of each marking period. Students need an opportunity to sit and take stock of their weaknesses, their achievements, and their progress.

Here are two sample evaluations from literature classes that focused on "love" and "good and evil." Each covers one 8-week academic quarter. Students sit down with instructors and read parts I and II of the sheet, and then, together, they talk and fill out parts III and IV.

Course: *Literature I* Student: *Laura—*
Instructor: *Deborah Stern* Days Absent: *2* Tardies: *0*
Quarter: *2nd, 1991-1992* Credit Earned This Quarter: ¼
Counselor: Total Credit Earned to Date: ¼

I. Description of the Course

This course is designed to use and improve students' reading, writing, and analytical skills by examining issues close to the students' lives and concerns. This quarter we looked at different literary treatments of love: What is it? What isn't it? What forms our opinions about love?

The main focus in this class this quarter was introduction to critical thinking and analysis. We read and analyzed magazine articles, stories, and poetry and concentrated on an abridged version of Shakespeare's *Romeo and Juliet*. In addition, students were encouraged to consider these different visions of love and write a structured essay expressing their own definition of the term. Finally, students presented popular songs and poems from their own experiences, which the class then analyzed.

As always, students have been asked to reflect on the unit's varying topics as they relate to their lives and to write their responses to these topics in their journals. There was a final test on *Romeo and Juliet* that required students to learn new vocabulary words, interpret Shakespeare's language, and write essays on their opinions of Romeo and Juliet's love.

II. Course Requirements

During the second quarter, students were required to have satisfactory attendance and:

1. Write an extended definition of love.
2. Keep journal up-to-date with two assigned entries and write a complete revision that included quoted dialogue.
3. Complete the majority of the eight class assignments satisfactorily.
4. Read *Romeo and Juliet* script, in entirety.
5. Present a work of student's own choosing that presented one artist's conception of love.
6. Participate in class activities including discussions and small group work.
7. Receive a passing grade on the *Romeo and Juliet* test.

III. Student's Self-Evaluation

I really liked this class. I learned a lot especially about writing definitions and love. I wish we could learn more about it. But we need to learn other things I know.

IV. Teacher's Evaluation of the Student

This was a much better quarter for you, Laura. Your attendance and efforts in class both were excellent, and your comments in class showed a lot of maturity. Your *Romeo and Juliet* test was especially strong. Next quarter, I'd like you to check with me to make sure you understand the written assignments completely before you start writing. That way, your writing skills can catch up with your verbal skills.

Course: *Contemporary Literature*   Student: *Tina—*
Instructor: *Deborah Stern*   Days Absent: *12*   Tardies: *5*
Quarter: *2nd, 1991-1992*   Credit Earned This Quarter: *0*
Counselor: Total Credit Earned to Date: *¼*

I. Description of the Course

This course is designed to use and improve students' reading, writing, and analytical skills by examining issues close to the students' lives and concerns. This quarter we concentrated on works and issues relating to moral choice.

The works for this "Good and Evil" unit ranged widely from the historical to the philosophical to the political. We read selections from great world literature, a comic book, philosophy, short fiction, and Elie Wiesel's *Night*. Our examination of the unit topic also led us to reflect on our own beliefs through frequent discussions, current magazine articles, and analysis of popular songs and videos.

As always, students have been asked to consider the unit's key issues as they relate to their lives and to write their responses to these issues in their journals. In addition, there was a final essay exam that required students to interpret, synthesize, and express the different views of good and evil discussed in class this quarter.

II. Course Requirements

During the second quarter, students were required to have satisfactory attendance and:

1. Keep journal up-to-date with all four assigned entries.
2. Participate in class activities including discussions.
3. Complete Elie Wiesel's *Night*.
4. Complete all written and homework assignments, including reading assignments.
5. Work with other students to present one "hate article" from a popular magazine.
6. Complete the final essay exam satisfactorily.

III. Student's Self-Evaluation

I had a lot going on this quarter but all that is behind me now. I realize what I need to do and am determined to do it. I think I need literature to understand life, and I need to start applying the logic and reasoning that I did learn.

IV. Teacher's Evaluation of the Student

We missed you this quarter, Tina. I'm glad you've been able to work things out and hope that peace of mind and academic progress (especially in writing) will be yours next quarter. Your intelligence and dedication can serve again as a model for other students in the class.

INSTRUCTORS' NOTES W: ALL JOURNAL ASSIGNMENTS

I have found it useful to keep a separate account of all reflective writing pieces assigned over the year. These are the journal assignments featured in the five units of instruction described in this book:

- Chapter 5: Sex Roles, Power, and Identity
    1. Write about a time you witnessed or experienced gender stereotyping.
    2. How can a person participate in his or her own oppression in a relationship?
    3. When have you experienced a betrayal such as Celie's?
- Chapter 6: Racism
    1. Write about a time you witnessed or experienced racial stereotyping.
    2. Pick one of the sources of racism named by the class and relate a personal experience to illustrate it.
    3. Write about a time when you suffered because of people's reactions to your cultural customs.
    4. Write about a time you competed. Tell how this competition affected the way you viewed your rival(s).
- Chapter 7: Education
    1. Write about a time you took a test that was unfair.
    2. Write about a time you wanted control over your education. What happened when you tried to make decisions about your own education?
    3. Retell Journal Assignment 1 or 2 so that the experience becomes an example of optimal education.
    4. Write about a time you really were motivated to do something in or out of school. For what were you working? Why did you feel like working?
- Chapter 8: The Streets
    1. What are your responses to teens' stories of life on the streets? Write about your own experiences if you can.
    2. Tell a story that shows yourself and others facing a moral dilemma.
    3. Write about a time in your life when nothing mattered as much as other people's (or another person's) opinions of you.
- Chapter 9: The Hero
    1. Write about a hero you had as a child. What could this hero do? Why did you admire this hero? Did you want to be like this hero? How did you feel when you were in his or her presence?
    2. Write about a time you or someone you know was just acting with integrity and outsiders applauded this "heroism."
    3. How will you be a hero in your own life?

PART II

Thematic Instructional Units

Timing. I encourage instructors to vary the units to fit their students' abilities, concerns, and schedules. To shorten units, eliminate discrete lessons, such as the major work or the student presentation. As written, each unit will take about 8 weeks (give or take a few days).

Daily schedules. Each unit contains one or more sample daily schedules. Some lessons require a single day; others take a few weeks. Lessons are designed so that students work on different types of activities and in differing groupings throughout the week.

Reading the major work. Many of the units contain long lessons that detail procedures for reading and processing a major work. Separate activities are suggested for all major works; instructors should choose among them. They need not go through the activities in order. In a typical week students might spend one day reading independently, one day answering and generating questions on the work in small groups, one day working on a writing exercise, one day discussing the reading with the whole class, and one day working with a partner to edit their writing.

Activities. Although assignments vary from unit to unit, certain types of activities—working on tasks in small groups, skill inventories, story maps, and so forth—are recommended throughout. See Chapter 4 for notes and handouts on procedures for these activities.

Student writing samples. Units contain examples of student writing, which have been reprinted as they were turned in, with all errors intact.

Reading levels. Some units are appropriate for students reading at any level. Some specify materials and assignments that require a higher reading level. A few suggest a range of readings and activities to accommodate different skill levels. See Contents.

Materials. Wherever possible, I obtained permission to reprint the works suggested in the units. Many are here. Many are not. I encourage instructors to find the materials listed in individual lessons and/or search for alternate works. *Instructors who wish to copy and distribute these works must obtain permission from the authors, their publishers, or their agents.* See the reference section for complete bibliographical information on all works suggested in the units.

5

▓ Sex Roles,
Power,
and Identity

In the jail he lies on his cot
Staring at the ceiling,
Cigarette hanging from his mouth,
in his blue uniform.
Ain't he a man? everyone said.

—Mike

And another woman has the baby,
lives there, inside the diapers and days of babysitting
so that her boyfriend can go out into the world
toward a future, which she had to forget.

—Anonymous

RATIONALE

What Is the Topic of Study?

This unit will focus on the different roles that men and women play in society and in personal life. We will examine what it means to be male or female in different social contexts. Students will bring up the issues of both power and identity as we analyze our own observations and discuss real and fictional characters.

We address these basic questions: How are gender and power related? What powers are girls supposed to have? What powers do they have? What powers are boys supposed to have? What powers do they have? We will look at the relationships between the sexes in our society and examine the ways power affects those relationships as well.

Why Will Students Be Interested in Studying This?

This is a hot topic that most definitely will engage students. They will be allowed and encouraged to talk about their collective social lives and to register complaints about some of the different injustices they have seen and felt. There will be enough references to student observation (regarding gender stereotypes, division of labor, and male and female images in the media) to sustain even uninterested students. We will talk about what they know and about the power and abuse of power they have felt. We will talk about male and female identity as they struggle to create their own.

Why Do Students Need to Study This?

Both male and female students will take a good look at the stereotypes and roles they accept. They may be physically mature but probably have not had the opportunity to question the gender stereotypes dictated by society in general and by their own individual cultures in particular. The peer pressure to play into these sex roles is overwhelming. Students live in a world in which girls need to be sexually attractive and available without being too promiscuous. They know that physical abuse is a possibility in a relationship. The girls will say that they don't want to accept the boys' disrespect, but most often they do accept it—giggling—and do not think the situation is remediable. That is the status quo. For their part, most of the boys do not know how to relate to women as anything but caretakers and/or sexual-romantic objects. They buy into machismo wholeheartedly and do not consider themselves limited by it. They are romantic and do not understand the contradictions of their fantasies. Both boys and girls need the chance to examine the various personal, social, and cultural ramifications of being men and women.

The Color Purple, the major work for this unit, offers the opportunity to focus on power and abuse of power in male/female relationships. In addition, *The Color Purple* ought to raise some interesting questions about homosexuality, expose feelings of homophobia, and provide a chance to look at this issue calmly and responsibly, without fear.

Why Teach This Unit Now?

This is a good unit of study for the start of a new semester. The combination of themes in the unit will allow us to move between the abstract and the concrete. This is essential at the start of a new class, given the reality of new students with unknown abilities. Because this is a long book, we will limit our supplementary reading materials and make reading assignments short enough to accommodate any slower readers in the class. Several of the better readers may finish *The Color Purple* ahead of schedule. Slower readers can take time to read in class, while those students who are done can get started on the nuts and bolts of essay writing. The last week or so of class will be spent writing the essay and will be tutorial.

The personal nature of the issues in this unit suggests that a longer essay, rather than a test, would be appropriate. Students will write essays on topics of their choice around the issues of sex roles, power, and identity. They will learn how to generate theses and to substantiate a thesis with evidence from both text and personal experience. In this way students will come to recognize that their own experience and understanding are as valid and valuable as Alice Walker's or as any author's. The reflective work necessary for this type of insight will bolster student confidence. Although they are at vastly different levels in terms of their writing, they all can master the required forms. These forms include making a claim, substantiating it with evidence, and explaining how the evidence proves their point.

KEY QUESTIONS

1. What are sex roles? What are male and female sex roles in our society?

2. What determines the different roles men and women play in society?

3. What gives a person power in a relationship?

4. How does gender affect identity?

TERMINAL OBJECTIVES

- To consider unit concepts carefully

- To reflect on these concepts as they impact students' lives

- To read a longer novel (even if students already have seen the movie)

- To write a longer, analytical, coherent essay, with prewriting

MATERIALS

General References (for instructors)

- Foucault, Michel (1980), *Power/Knowledge: Selected Interviews and Other Writings, 1971-1977*

Major Works (Novel)

- Walker, Alice (1982), *The Color Purple*

Chapters and Excerpts From Longer Works

- Fausto-Sterling, Anne (1985), "The Biological Connection: An Introduction" from *Myths of Gender: Biological Theories of Men and Women* (reprinted here with permission)

- Sabo, Don (1987), Excerpt from "Pigskin, Patriarchy, and Pain" from *New Men, New Minds: Breaking Male Tradition* (reprinted here with permission)

Articles

- Jarrett, Vernon (1985), "The Beast in 'Purple' "

- LeBlanc, Adrian Nicole (1991), "Girlfriends: Three Lives in the Drug Trade" (reprinted here with permission)

Short Stories

- Merimee, Prosper (1961), "The Pearl of Toledo"

Poems

- Dugan, Alan (1983), "Prayer" (reprinted here with permission)

- Piercy, Marge (1971, 1973, 1982), "A work of artifice" and "Barbie doll" (reprinted here with permission)

- Rilke, Rainer Maria (1981), "Sometimes a man stands up during supper . . ." (reprinted here with permission)

Songs

- Ice T (1988), "Power"

- Sweet Honey in the Rock (1980), "Oughta Be a Woman"

- Was/Not Was (1983), "Out Come the Freaks"

SAMPLE DAILY SCHEDULE

Day 1: Lesson 1: Distribute HANDOUT 1: MALE/FEMALE ATTRIBUTES. Discuss gender stereotyping.

Day 2: Lesson 2: Write Journal Assignment 1 in class.

Day 3: Lesson 3: Watch TV in class. Complete HANDOUT 2: GENDER ROLES ON TV. Discuss.

Day 4: Lesson 4: Review Journal Assignment 1 entries; assign revision.

Day 5: Lesson 5: Begin taking notes on two theories. Read unit materials on sources of gender roles.

Day 6: Continue taking notes and discussing theories.

Day 7: Lesson 6: Read "Pearl of Toledo." HANDOUT 3: "THE PEARL OF TOLEDO" QUESTIONS. Have students answer questions in class. Homework: Read unit materials: "Girlfriends" article.

Day 8: Finish reading article. Generate discussion questions in small groups. Use HANDOUT 4: "GIRLFRIENDS: THREE LIVES IN THE DRUG TRADE" QUESTIONS.

Day 9: Discuss story and article. Assign Journal 2.

Day 10: Lesson 7: Read poetry. Students work in small groups using HANDOUT 5: POETRY GROUP WORK TASKS. Write new version of one of the four poems.

Day 11: Continue writing poetry.

Day 12: Lesson 8: Introduce Foucault's categories of power. Small groups work on HANDOUT 6: POWER SCENARIOS.

Day 13: Discuss handout, applying categories to characters in works already read.

Day 14: Lesson 9: Begin reading *The Color Purple*. Homework: HANDOUT 7: CASEWORKER ASSIGNMENT.

Day 15: General discussion. Continue to read for homework.

Day 16: Independent reading day.

Day 17: Simple reading quiz.

Day 18:   Group activity: Students formulate quiz and discussion questions.

Day 19:   General discussion using groups' questions.

Day 20:   Assign Journal 3.

Day 21:   Short reading quiz.

Day 22:   Introduce essay writing skills.
               Distribute HANDOUT 8: PROVING A POINT IN AN ESSAY; discuss.

Day 23:   Continue introducing claims, evidence, warrants.
               Use HANDOUT L: CLAIMS, EVIDENCE, AND WARRANTS.

Day 24:   Independent reading day.

Day 25:   General discussion. Begin prewriting with HANDOUT 9:
               CELIE'S IDENTITY.

Day 26:   Short reading quiz. Go over HANDOUT 9. Remind students
               to save this!

Day 27:   Work with partners to start HANDOUT 10: CELIE AND MEN AND WOMEN.
               Homework: Complete sheets.

Day 28:   Independent reading day.

Day 29:   General discussion. Review HANDOUT 10.
               Remind students to save this and all prewriting handouts.

Day 30:   Class works together on part I of HANDOUT 11: GENDER STEREOTYPES
               IN *THE COLOR PURPLE*; small groups work on part II.
               Homework: Complete handout.

Day 31:   Assign HANDOUT 12: POWER IN *THE COLOR PURPLE*. Students work
               on this in class.

Day 32:   Solicit students' questions. General discussion on final scenes
               in novel, novel in entirety.

Day 33:   Catch-up day: Independent reading/work on written assignments.

Day 34:   Go over all handouts and essay prewriting work.

Day 35:   Lesson 10: Introduce basic format of the essay. Distribute HANDOUT
               13: BOXES PLANNING SHEET FOR ESSAY WITH SAMPLE NOTES.
               Work out essay-writing schedule; assign due dates.

Day 36:   Concentrate on generating provocative theses. Start selecting
            and modifying supporting claims, evidence, and warrants
            from the four prewriting handouts.

Day 37:   Continue formulating argument and planning structure of essay.

Day 38:   Write essay.

Day 39:   Write essay.

Day 40:   Write essay.

Day 41:   Hand in completed essay and prewriting.

LESSON 1: WHAT IS GENDER STEREOTYPING?

Objectives

- To open issues and terms pertaining to key questions

- To examine personal conceptions of gender roles and gender stereotyping

Materials

- HANDOUT 1: MALE/FEMALE ATTRIBUTES

Procedures

- Begin with general discussion of the terms *gender* and *sex roles*. Do not assume that the class recognizes the difference between a person's sex role and having sex. Discuss the different roles women and men need to fill in society, in their families, in the classroom, on TV.

- Distribute HANDOUT 1: MALE/FEMALE ATTRIBUTES. Ask students to fill these out on their own according to their first reactions. Explain any unfamiliar terms. It may be interesting (but could be merely gratuitous) to read the list aloud and ask for students' individual responses. Discuss the three questions at the end together as a class.

- Stress the concept of *gender stereotyping*. Ask students to relate a time they were expected to act in a certain way because of their gender.

- Read the following sample gender stereotype journal entry if desired, written by Baba, age 17:

One summer afternoon at about 2:00 some of my friends got together to play baseball at the park. I didn't really know how to play but I wanted to play anyway. My friend Tony said I could if I went and got some more people. So I went and got my two oldest sisters and my best friend who lived on the next block from me. We talked for awhile and went up to the park to play baseball. When my friends saw us they said we couldn't play cause baseball is not for girls it's a man's game. All the other boys laughed and said yeah, go play jump rope or something. I said why did you tell me to go get some more people if you knew you wasn't going to let us play. James (another boy) said go play rope. That's a girls' game. So me and my sisters and my friend left and came back with a lot of rocks. We threw the rocks at the boys and took all their bases and messed up their game. My sister said, "If we can't play, you can't, either."

HANDOUT 1: MALE/FEMALE ATTRIBUTES

Do not write your name.
What is your gender? _____

Directions:

1. Read through this list of words quickly, rating them "F" for "female" or "M" for "male." Mark your first reaction.

adventurous	giggling	sensitive
aggressive	gossip	sexy
artistic	good cook	strong
assertive	graceful	sweet
big	hairy	tall
boss	hard	talkative
bold	hard-working	takes risks
brave	heavy	teaches
cute	helpless	tender
communicative	hero	tough
dutiful	independent	unmechanical
domineering	innocent	ugly
dumb	loud	vicious
emotional	loving	wholesome
funny	nagging	wicked
gentle	quiet	responsible

2. Answer the following questions:

   a. What features characterize those qualities you have labeled "male"? In other words, sum up a male, according to this sheet.

   b. What features characterize those qualities you have labeled "female"? In other words, sum up a female, according to this sheet.

   c. In your opinion, what does this activity demonstrate?

LESSON 2: PERSONAL EXPERIENCE WITH GENDER STEREOTYPING

Objectives

- To review concept of gender stereotyping

- To tie the abstract concept to students' own experiences

Materials

- None

Procedures

- (Re)read sample aloud.

- Assign in-class writing: Journal Assignment 1: Write about a time you witnessed or experienced gender stereotyping. Tell the class that this is an inventory assignment to enable the teacher to get an idea of where students stand as writers. Explain to the students that they will not be graded on this assignment and that the important thing is to tell the story as completely as possible.

- If class looks lost, a good technique is to relate a personal experience or observation of your own showing gender stereotyping. It is best to keep these truthful but not too personal. I have had success recounting memories of receiving many unwanted, dress-up girly dolls for presents, and of teachers' expectations that girls would be better behaved in school than boys.

LESSON 3: GENDER STEREOTYPES IN THE MEDIA

Objectives

- To observe men's and women's roles as presented in popular media

- To reflect on the messages promulgated by these images

Materials

- HANDOUT 2: GENDER ROLES ON TV

Procedures

This exercise can be assigned as homework, or you can bring a TV into the classroom and complete the worksheet together as a class.

- Distribute HANDOUT 2: GENDER ROLES ON TV. Explain how it is to be filled out, what types of attributes to note, and so forth.

- If this is to be done for homework, explain that anything students see on TV or in the movies (including commercials and music videos) is appropriate to observe and analyze.

- After viewing various images on TV (it is not necessary to watch whole shows to do this exercise) or after students return to class after doing their homework, it is important to discuss the reflective question at the bottom of the worksheet ("What did you learn from this activity?"). Have students write responses to this question. Ask for volunteers to read their responses out loud.

HANDOUT 2: GENDER ROLES ON TV

Every time you watch TV you are getting messages about the ways men and women relate to the world and to each other. Fill out the following sheet based on what you see on TV.

SHOW AND CHARACTER	GENDER	OCCUPATION	MAIN PERSONALITY TRAITS	IS SHE OR HE POWERFUL? WHERE? HOW?

What did you learn from this activity?

LESSON 4: REVIEW OF JOURNAL ENTRIES

Objectives

- To share personal experiences and observations

- To recognize possible conflicts between self-concept and socially pre-scribed gender roles

- To note and correct errors in mechanics and style (for classes focusing on writing skills)

Materials

- Students' Journal Assignment 1 entries. Instructors should read and write supportive and constructive comments on these before returning them.

Procedures

- Return journals. After taking private note of outstanding entries, ask selected students if their entry may be shared with the class. Give many options for this reading: Piece can be read by teacher, anonymously by teacher, by a friend, or by the writer him- or herself. Discuss assets of entries read aloud (humor, honest language, good use of detail and dialogue, an example of particularly unjust gender stereotyping, etc.).

- If desired, class can focus on writing by passing out sample (or copy a student's piece with permission); class either can correct mechanics (spelling, dialogue punctuation, and other punctuation) or can revise writing (insert dialogue, add description, etc.). Of course, they can do this with their own journals after or instead of working on a sample piece.

LESSON 5: SOURCES OF GENDER STEREOTYPES

Objective

- To name, explain, and examine two theories of gender roles and stereotypes

Materials

- UNIT MATERIALS: Sources of Gender Roles, including excerpts from Fausto-Sterling's "The Biological Connection: An Introduction" and Sabo's "Pigskin, Patriarchy, and Pain"

Procedures

- Pose the following questions to the class, moving to the issue of the origins of gender roles. (This issue already has come up, no doubt.) Discuss:

  1. What is the problem with gender stereotyping?
  2. Aren't there some general truths about guys and girls that we just can't ignore?
  3. If you are a girl who wants to play baseball or a boy who loves to cook, aren't you just an exception to the general rule?
  4. Where did gender roles come from?
  5. Does gender stereotyping have any legitimate basis?

- Write these terms on the board and ask the class to take notes:

  1. *Biological determinism:* the theory that biology is destiny. We act as we do because nature gave us the appropriate anatomies to do so. (Example: Women are responsible for taking care of babies because they can provide nourishment [breast-feeding].)
  2. *Sociocultural pressure:* the theory that upbringing is everything. We are compelled to act as we do because of the myriad role models, social pressures, and messages conveyed to us throughout our lives. (Example: Women are responsible for taking care of babies because they are expected to—little girls are given baby dolls, not toy soldiers.)

- Ask the class to provide and note other examples that support either side of the "nature versus nurture" controversy. Discuss:

  1. What choices in life are ruled by our bodies?
  2. What cultural institutions have we created that determine our lives as men and women?

- Distribute UNIT MATERIALS: Sources of Gender Roles. These are readings that explain how biological determinism ("The Biological Connection: An Introduction") and sociocultural pressure ("Pigskin, Patriarchy, and Pain") account for gender roles. Because this is pure theory, you should take students through the material slowly—reading aloud, stopping to ask and answer questions, and writing notes on the board to be copied by students.

UNIT MATERIALS: SOURCES OF GENDER ROLES

The Biological Connection: An Introduction

by Anne Fausto-Sterling

These are difficult times. The middle-class family of the 1950's, headed by a husband, managed by a wife, and enlivened by two children and a collie, is no more. In its stead we have single-parent families, contract marriages, palimony suits, and serial monogamy. Women demand equal pay for work of equal value, take assertiveness training, and feminists organize to change long-standing political and social structures. Men are unsure about whether to expect a thank you or a snarl when they hold a door open for a woman, and clothing designers offer us the world of unisex dress. Hair length doesn't matter, the gender gap in finishing marathon races gets smaller every year, and "affirmative action" has become embedded in our language. The variety and rapidity of the changes symbolized by these random examples have generated an expressly political backlash by the "New Right," doubts about individual identity, and fears of sexual obliteration-through-equality. In response to such personal and social upheaval, professionals throughout the country—scientists, journalists, economists, and politicians—have begun to search out the real truths about sexual differences. And therein lies a tale.

Over the years physicians, biologists, and anthropologists have had a lot to say about women's place in the world. In the nineteenth century, some scientists wrote that women who work to obtain economic independence set themselves up for "a struggle against nature,"[1] while author after author used Darwin's theory of evolution to argue that giving the vote to women was, evolutionarily speaking, retrogressive.[2] Physicians and educators alike warned that young women who engage in long, hard hours of study will badly damage their reproductive systems, perhaps going insane to boot. With these warnings came grim predictions about the end of the [white, middle-class] human race.[3] Ironically, feminists of the period often used the same biological arguments to support their own points of view.[4] Antoinette Brown Blackwell, for example, garnered evidence from the natural world to prove the fundamental equality of men and women,[5] and Eliza Gamble argued outright for the natural superiority of the female sex.[6]

Today, too, many scientists respond to the issues of sexual equality and the social and political upheaval that has accompanied it by offering us their insights, suggesting in all sincerity that, however well intentioned, the women's liberation movement and its fellow travelers want biologically unnatural changes that would bring grief to the human race. Sociobiologists, for example, suggest that our evolutionary history deeply affects our most intimate personal relationships. Man's natural sexuality sends him in search of many sex partners, making him an unstable mate at best, while women's biological origins destine her to keep the home fires burning, impelling her to employ trickery and deceit to keep hubby from straying. The battle between the sexes is ancient; its origin lies hidden deep in our genes.[7] One sociobiologist even argues that male and female sexuality are so different, so at odds, that it makes sense to think of the two sexes as separate species.[8] In general these scientists emphasize difference, the biological logic of male-female conflict, and the dim prospects for change.

Even physical violence fits into the picture. Dr. Katharina Dalton, a British physician who has made a name for herself by publicizing and then inventing treatments for something she calls the Premenstrual Syndrome, suggests that monthly hormone fluctuations may cause afflicted women to unknowingly injure themselves, claiming afterward that their husbands had beaten them: "All too often the patient herself is not fully aware of the distress caused by her periodic tantrums . . . When a woman demonstrates bruises as signs of her husband's cruelty it is well to remember the possibility that these may be spontaneous bruises of the premenstruum."[9]

Biologically based argumentation has even invaded the criminal court system. In the trial of a woman who had used an automobile to run over and kill her boyfriend, Dalton testified that the woman had suffered from premenstrual derangement and should not be held legally responsible for her acts. As a result the woman received a conditional discharge from jail.[10] A similar defense is now valid in French courts,[11] while in the United States a judge recently acquitted a dentist accused of rape and sodomy, after the defendant claimed that his girlfriend had filed the charges during a period of premenstrual irrationality.[12] Whether the idea that we are mere agents of our own bodies will make inroads into the criminal justice system remains to be seen. If this idea does take hold, the erosion of personal responsibility for one's actions—be it a woman who commits murder or a man who batters or rapes—would be an inevitable consequence.

Lost also would be our society's ability to recognize large-scale violence as a social problem to be dealt with in a public arena. One recent study, for instance, suggests that a woman in a large city stands a 26 percent chance of being raped during her lifetime. This statistic increases to 50 percent when the possibility of rape attempts is taken into account.[13] Are we to believe that these statistics result from the male's ungovernable mating urge combined with the false reporting of distraught premenstrual women? Or must we face up to the conclusion that sexual violence is somehow embedded in the social fabric? If we believe the former, then there's not much to be done about it; if we believe the latter, we must collectively endeavor to change the assumptions and attitude of our culture—a complex and difficult task. Clearly, what we think about the biological basis of criminal violence matters a great deal.

NOTES

1. W. Bagehot, "Biology and 'Women's' Rights," *Popular Science Monthly* 14 (1879): 201-13.

2. M. K. Sedgewick, "Some Scientific Aspects of the Woman Suffrage Question," *Gunton's Magazine* 20 (1901): 333-44; G. Ferrero, "The Problem of Woman, From a Bio-Sociological Point of View," *The Monist* 4 (1894): 261-74; E. D. Cope, "The Relationship of the Sexes to Government," *Popular Science Monthly* 33 (1888): 261-74; J. Weir, Jr., "The Effect of Female Suffrage on Posterity," *American Naturalist* 29 (1895): 815-25.

3. H. Maudsley, "Sex in Mind and in Education," *Popular Science Monthly* 5 (1894): 198-215; A. L. Smith, "Higher Education of Women and Race Suicide," *Popular Science Monthly* 66 (1906): 466-73; G. DeLawney, "Equality and Inequality in Sex," *Popular Science Monthly* 20 (1881): 184-92; M. A. Hardaker, "Science and the Woman Question," *Popular Science Monthly* 20 (1882): 577-84; N. Morais, "A Reply to Miss Hardaker on: The Woman Question," *Popular Science Monthly* 21 (1882): 70-78; Stephen J. Gould, "The Mismeasure of Man" (New York: Norton, 1981); W. L. Distant, "On the Mental Differences Between the Sexes," *Journal of the Anthropological Institute* 4 (1875): 78-85.

4. Janet Sayers, *Biological Politics: Feminist and Anti-feminist Perspectives* (London: Tavistock, 1982).

5. Antoinette B. Blackwell, *The Sexes Throughout Nature* (New York: Putnam, 1875; Westport, Conn.: Hyperion, 1976).

6. E. B. Gamble, *Evolution of Woman: An Inquiry into the Dogma of Her Inferiority to Man* (New York: Putnam, 1893; Westport, Conn.: Hyperion, 1976).

7. D. Barash, The Whisperings Within (New York: Penguin, 1979); D. Symons, *The Evolution of Human Sexuality* (New York: Oxford University Press, 1979); and J. Durden-Smith and D. DeSimone, "The Main Event," *Playboy*, June 1982, 165.

8. Symons, *Evolution of Human Sexuality*.

9. Katharina Dalton, *The Premenstrual Syndrome* (London: William Heinemann Medical Books, 1964), 94.

10. M. B. Rosenthal, "Insights into the Premenstrual Syndrome," *Physician and Patient* (April 1983): 46-53.

11. T. O. Marsh, *Roots of Crime* (Newton, N.J.: Nellen, 1981).

12. W. Herbert, "Premenstrual Changes," *Science News* 122 (1982): 380-81.

13. D.E.H. Russell and N. Howell, "The Prevalence of Rape in the United States Revisited," *Signs* 8 (1983): 688-95.

Pigskin, Patriarchy, and Pain

by Don Sabo

Sport is just one of the many areas in our culture where pain is more important than pleasure. Boys are taught that to endure pain is courageous, to survive pain is manly. The principle that pain is "good" and pleasure is "bad" is crudely evident in the "no pain, no gain" philosophy of so many coaches and athletes. "The pain principle" weaves its way into the lives and psyches of male athletes in two fundamental ways. It stifles men's awareness of their bodies and limits our emotional expression. We learn to ignore personal hurts and injuries because they interfere with the "efficiency" and "goals" of the "team." We become adept at taking the feelings that boil up inside us—feelings of insecurity and stress from striving so hard for success—and channeling them in a bundle of rage which is directed at opponents and enemies. This posture toward oneself and the world is not limited to "jocks." It is evident in the lives of many nonathletic men who, as tough guys, deny their authentic physical or emotional needs and develop health problems as a result.

Today, I no longer perceive myself as an *individual* ripped off by athletic injury. Rather, I see myself as just *one more man among many men* who got swallowed up by a social system predicated on male domination. Patriarchy has two structural aspects. First, it is a hierarchical system in which men dominate women in crude and debased, slick and subtle ways. Feminists have made great progress exposing and analyzing this dimension of the edifice of sexism. But it is also a system of *intermale dominance,* in which a minority of men dominates the masses of men. This intermale dominance hierarchy exploits the majority of those it beckons to join its heights. Patriarchy's mythos of heroism and its morality of power-worship implant visions of ecstasy and masculine excellence in the minds of the boys who ultimately will defend its inequities and ridicule its victims. It is inside this institutional framework that I have begun to explore the essence and scope of "the pain principle."

SOURCE: Excerpt from "Pigskin, Patriarchy, and Pain" by Don Sabo, in Franklin Abbott (Ed.), *New Men, New Minds: Breaking Male Tradition,* 1987, Freedom, CA: Crossing Press. This piece also can be found in *Sex, Violence, and Power in Sports: Rethinking Masculinity* by Michael Messner and Don Sabo, 1994, Freedom, CA: Crossing Press. Used with permission of the author.

LESSON 6: POWER IN RELATIONSHIPS

Objectives

- To examine and reflect on the ways in which power is used and abused in some relationships between men and women

- To demonstrate ability to make inferences from readings

- To discuss individual perspective and affective response to readings

Materials

Short works showing men and women in traditional and nontraditional gender roles. I have used:

- Merimee's short story "Pearl of Toledo"

- HANDOUT 3: "PEARL OF TOLEDO" QUESTIONS

- UNIT MATERIALS: "Girlfriends: Three Lives in the Drug Trade"

- HANDOUT 4: "GIRLFRIENDS: THREE LIVES IN THE DRUG TRADE" QUESTIONS

Procedures

- Distribute Merimee's "Pearl of Toledo." Do not engage students in a discussion of this work so that you may use HANDOUT 3: "PEARL OF TOLEDO" QUESTIONS to take inventory of students' abilities to make inferences, read for implied relationships between characters, and so on. These questions begin with simple queries about basic stated information and advance through questions that require progressively more sophisticated powers of inference and interpretation. Explain any unknown words (e.g., *swarthy*) out loud to entire class as they are reading. See INSTRUCTORS' NOTES E: SKILL INVENTO-RIES (Chapter 4) for an explanation of the reading inventory.

- After students have finished writing (or after you have read their responses, if you prefer), discuss questions. Make sure class considers the last three questions critically.

- Discuss with students whether strict sex roles and conventional expectations still play a part in relationships today or if everything has changed. Distribute UNIT MATERIALS: "Girlfriends: Three Lives in the Drug Trade" to read in class or for homework. Instructors should note and take appropriate measures to deal with the graphic language used in this article.

- Divide students who complete the reading early into small groups to create their own discussion questions. Examples of student-generated questions are given with a list of provided questions. When entire class has finished reading, distribute HANDOUT 4: "GIRLFRIENDS: THREE LIVES IN THE DRUG TRADE" QUESTIONS or use a combination of provided questions and student-generated questions.

- Ask class to respond to "Pearl of Toledo" and "Girlfriends: Three Lives in the Drug Trade" by relating a story in which someone stayed in a relationship that was oppressive. Ask them if they can understand any of the factors that allowed the relationship to continue.

- Write Journal Assignment 2 on the board: How can a person participate in his or her own oppression in a relationship? (Because of the nature of this assignment, make it clear to students that they do not have to hand in their journal to be read by the instructor.)

After giving the class time to write, I obtained permission to read the following student-written sample aloud:

One reason could be they're scared. For example, I know a girl who met a guy and they fell deeply in love. When he met some new friends that sell drugs, all he see is fast money.

After a while he start cheating on her. And she knows it. Then, he start to beat on her and when he finish he apologize and says he hit her because he loves her.

A lot of girls have heard this line and if they believe it they are fooling themselves. This girl believed her man like a stupid ass. He kept beating her. After a while she got fed up with it. She wanted to leave him but she was scared if she did he would find her and beat her even worse.

My written comment to this student offered support for her and listed a few phone numbers (a crisis hot line, women's shelters) for her friend. In class, we had a moving discussion about passivity, fear, responsibility, and so forth. We did not treat this discussion as an academic one, or try to analyze anything. Classes dealing with such real-life issues must be prepared to diverge from preplanned daily objectives to focus on the personal dilemmas and conditions that present themselves.

HANDOUT 3: "THE PEARL OF TOLEDO" QUESTIONS

1. Who is the Pearl of Toledo and what is special about her?

2. Who is Don Guttiera de Saldana?

3. Why does swarthy (dark) Suzani want to fight Don Guttiera de Saldana?

4. Who is killed at the fountain of Almami?

5. Why does the Pearl of Toledo approach the wounded man?

6. What significance does his "last effort" have for him? For the Pearl of Toledo?

7. How does this story address the issue of racism? Sexism?

8. What is the greatest abuse of power in this story?

UNIT MATERIALS

Girlfriends: Three Lives in the Drug Trade

by Adrian Nicole LeBlanc

At Grande Billiards on 184th Street and the Grand Concourse in the Bronx, Lucy hooks her beeper into the V of her cleavage. Her friend Isabella smiles, a little embarrassed, and tucks her own on the waistband of the leggings she wears under her thigh-high black leather boots. Isabella and Lucy met because their boyfriends dealt heroin together, and the girls have license to come out on this cold Saturday night only because their boyfriends are in jail.

Tonight's excursion is a rare show of female defiance. More familiar are their project apartments and their routines of babies and soap operas. The girls are more comfortable visiting their incarcerated boyfriends dutifully, riding the No. 6 train for 45 minutes to the MCC, the Metropolitan Correctional Center at the intersection of Park Row and Pearl Street in lower Manhattan, or the two-hour bus ride to Otisville; tending to the boys' requests for cassettes and Playboy; gathering enough money for their commissary purchases; writing letters; staying home to receive the boys' collect calls; reassuring them with coos of faithfulness and love. Although they will be interrogated when the boys call in from jail tomorrow morning—what did they wear, who was at the pool hall, what time did they leave their homes and arrive, how did they get there, who spoke with them, how and what time did they get home—the girls have decided to go out.

Everyone in the pool hall has a beeper—strung on a belt, hanging in a pocket, tucked in a jacket. Isabella proudly says that many of the people here are involved in drug dealing. She is a stunning Puerto Rican girl with long, shining, straight black hair, bangs sprouting from a barrette at the top of her head, all bold and charm. The heavy gold necklaces she wears tonight, some with medallions, belong to someone she calls "just a friend." The chains are significant status symbols; it is rare that a girl would buy them on her own. Her wearing them suggests that Isabella is an important girl. That is, a girl an important boy wants.

Like all people who operate from the assumption that they exist for other people, the girls are unsure of their own experiences of fun. At their table, between checks out the window to see who in what Maxima or Mercedes is pulling up, Lucy, 23, and her 14-year-old cousin Marisa attempt to organize their game. They laugh self-consciously (they don't know how to play pool) and young men saunter to their rescue. The flirtations begin—here is how one breaks, leans over, holds the cue.

At 11:30 more guys stream in. After they pass the first check at the downstairs entrance, where they are frisked, the group's movements are radioed up to the second entrance at the top of the stairs. Girls to whom the boys pass their guns can flirt their way by the entry booth, hiding the boys' guns beneath their shirts. "Three bad bitches coming" the doorman calls up, and the girls know they are in. They pass the bouncers, the guys follow suit, then the girls pass the guns back to the boys. In return, the boys will pay for their hours of pool.

More and more guys—all under 20—arrive, in leather hats with maps of Africa, hats with thin diamond bands. The coats the boys step out of are nothing less than leather—thick sheepskin, black Northbeach with dark brown fur, all-yellow bombers with white fox-trimmed hoods. They walk around in red leather sweatsuits, wearing weight in chains—diamond chokers, wide gold link-ropes with pendants, sapphires, onyx, rubies, jade. There are many Rolexes, 18-karat bracelets, diamond-studded namebar rings. The gold medallions they wear—the size of large cookies—are of Spanish patron saints.

A Cuban boy steps over to help Lucy break. She tends to her teacher courteously, but seems distracted, as if being out with the girls ought to be more fun. Isabella, 20, spreads out the skirt of her chiffon baby-doll dress and begins to weave through the pool hall's 42 tables. It is the girlish stroll of the movies—pivoting, eyes down, the lag of the toes—by group after group of boys. Lucy's and Isabella's boyfriends were some of the most popular boys, feared and rich. Isabella's boyfriend David managed a location and supposedly murdered a person. "He could have become anything he wanted to," says Isabella. "He looked Italian." He is Puerto Rican, very handsome. Isabella was his.

So when David's friends come into the hall and Isabella spots them with the speed of instinct, she is tearing off her borrowed gold necklaces and shoving them into Lucy's hands, over Lucy's cousin Marisa's neck, begging, low-voiced, to her girlfriends to, please, take them and put them on. Isabella then rushes to David's friends. Her attentiveness is expected and it does her nerves some good. She escorts them back to the table—eyes finding home on the ground—and as they approach, Lucy's pool teacher says, "I am getting out of here. Now."

David's friends are drug dealers, significant ones, and in the pool hall, as on the street, they accord respect, the silent caterings of fear. If David's friends saw Isabella in jewelry, they would think she was playing David dirty. At the very least, his friends would report her indiscretion to him. At the worst, they would destroy the jewelry's owner.

One of David's friends gives Isabella money to buy him cherry brandy, and she puts on her leather coat and hurries down to the street. She scurries past two men under a car they are dismantling, and grabs each pay phone on every other freezing, locked-up block. "Shit!" she says, as she slams a receiver down, onto the next, then, "Shit!" another. Isabella needs to beep her new friend and warn him not to show up— David's friends would never understand. When she finds a dial tone, she punches in 9-5-8, a code that will recite the pay phone's number back. If it doesn't, Isabella says, the phone is tapped. She moves past the chicken palaces and video stores, past the cashiers behind their thick plastic shells. After 10 blocks she finds a phone where the 958 code registers, so she tests the number from another nearby phone, but the incoming call won't ring in. She's running the blocks and each phone faster now—she stops, she checks, it doesn't work. As she hustles, the fear ebbs into excitement. She darts into a bar.

Inside, two chubby Spanish girls sit in dark blue satin, like bridesmaids under the red tinsel strung above their heads. Isabella plugs her free ear, punches in her friend's beeper code, and sighs, hanging up the phone. "You can play guys dirty as long as you don't do it in front of their friends," she says, as she waits for him to call back. "That's disrespect."

When you are beeped, the number of the person calling flashes on your beeper's mini-screen. If you are the girl you're supposed to be, you return the call in seconds, exactly the amount of time your boyfriend would have the patience to stand by the phone waiting, wherever he is. (More than one girlfriend had three or four beepers lined up by her phone.) Some codes mean simply, "I'm on my way home" (there is no code for "I'm staying out") or, whatever-we-discussed-is-taken-care-of, which could be anything from a covert meaning to "Yes, I got the baby's diapers." You can beep your boyfriend whenever you like, but whether or not he'll call back will depend. If it's urgent you add 911; his friends use 411 when they have information. There may be private digits for other kinds of specification: if Lucy used 888 after her usual code to her boyfriend Jack, only he would know what it meant. Close associates sometimes punch in the street corners where they may be found, or the street number and a building number.

Everybody has a code so that each caller can be identified immediately. Lucy is 89, and Isabella is 128 and their friend Dolores, who went out with another of Jack's dealers, is 165 because of the cross streets where they live. Some people use their building or apartment numbers, and others are known by their age or the digits from their prison IDs. David was always 117, the number of a street where he managed a spot. Often dealers prefer girls to use only codes instead of entire phone numbers (it is rare they would beep from anywhere but home), just in case other girlfriends are near the beeper when the numbers flash. A few years ago, having a beeper was an indication of being on the inside, but now almost anyone can have one, so they've lost the bulk of their status. Still, for these girls, the beeper is an object rife with conflicted assumptions about ownership and honor, a little flash into what being a drug dealer's girlfriend can mean.

How close the girlfriends actually are to the drugs depends upon the parameters of their relationships with the men who sell them, which in turn depends upon circumstance and convenience as much as the variables of personality and a dealer's work ethics. Some girlfriends are encouraged to act as dispatchers of a sort. They steer business phone calls and deliver instructions from their apartments, where their children play at their feet. Others run deliveries or supervise mill tables. Some—and this seems the most common girlfriend duty—are entrusted to count money. Some girlfriends want no part of it, some draw the line at hiding guns. Some girls regularly work the tables (bagging and stamping may be how they became girlfriends), while others will only fill in when large shipments demand their labor.

Of course there are girlfriends, like there are always girlfriends, who do whatever their boyfriends want done, from washing underwear in the kitchen sink, to awakening early in the morning for unwanted anal sex, to making reservations for dates with other girls, to acting as a decoy to lure in associates and enemies targeted to be killed. And plenty of girlfriends cheat.

A boyfriend's positioning of his girlfriend can depend on his reading of love, but as often as not it depends on his need for a person he can trust. This need varies in relation to his negotiations on the street, but a girlfriend is likely to be the one constant in his life. All the girlfriends, from those who knew their boyfriends before they became drug dealers, to those who gladly affect the false stupidity of mafioso mothers and wives, are afforded the vicarious power that comes with their connection to "successful" men. Beyond this, the lives of these girlfriends are as complex and varied as the lives of just regular compromised girls.

The women that drug dealers come home to are actually girlfriends, but they are known, at least in a fair portion of the South Bronx, as wives. The title is as unoriginal and oppressive as its ancient meaning, and has nothing to do with adolescent absorption of modern urban culture or the values specific to the selling of drugs. It is, finally, about being a girl perceived as useful to a guy, for the kinds of reasons that guys find girls they like useful. "When you meet a guy, in the Bronx, and you go out with them for about a month, you are permanently his wife," Dolores explains. She is a tiny girl, with a raspy, vacant voice. "Even if you say, 'Excuse me, I have no ring on my finger, no paper in my wallet,' they go, 'You still his wife.' It's like everybody give you the respect. Sometimes you feel good about it like, 'Oh, I'm his wife.'"

"We stay home and we cook and we clean," says Isabella. "We the wives." The girls do benefit: they get deference and protection on the streets; their rent and food are paid for; they have money for their kids' clothes and toys. Your husband's friends will talk to you, but they usually won't try to pick you up. The downside is your husband's constant absence, his growing ego,

and the times of trouble. A year after he began dealing, Joey had a bad encounter and the dissatisfied client threatened to kill Dolores and her son, Jose. Joey ushered Dolores into the midtown Marriott for a few weeks and he didn't let her outside. He told her their apartment building was leaking gas and kept the truth to himself until the danger passed.

The other girls, the ones most heard about—the ones that get taken to Atlantic City, or discovered on the guys-only vacations in Puerto Rico, or flown into New York from Belize or Hawaii to go to clubs—they are only mistresses, or just girls. Girls who the dealers would pick up and—just as a joke—leave in a restaurant on the highway. Girls who might give them head for drugs, or for nothing more than being "shown a good time out." Girls unknowingly videotaped during sex for the amusement of the neighborhood (in one Harlem video game a guy earns points for the speed in which he can steer a girl through his hidden schedule of sexual service). Like most peripheral sexual players to the institution of marriage, the nonwife girls have better odds of acquiring the most romanticized material expressions of male-female association—hotel rooms, plane tickets to exotic places, perfume, jewelry, candy, lingerie. The only jewelry Isabella ever got from David was a bracelet; he passed it along to her when he bought an identical one with thicker links. To the wives who know about their husbands' wanderings at all, these girls are just the other girls, the drinking partners, the slimy wannabes, girls their husbands fucked. Little skeezers, sluts, money-hungry leeches, bitches. Dogs.

Lucy met Jack on a blind date. Before he was arrested with his crew in 1989, when he was 20, he led a South Bronx heroin operation that employed 30 people and made him a millionaire by the age of 18. Except for the countable bursts of celebration—a trip to Puerto Rico when she was his mistress, a few coats, birthday shopping sprees, and a nice, nice ring—in their two years together, Lucy saw little of Jack's money. She often had to beep him to buy her lunch or to pick up diapers for her little girls. But she was always around the money and the activity that was around Jack. Members of Jack's organization claim that Lucy was a mill worker at his table, but Lucy denies this. She claims she knew nothing about any involvement Jack is supposed to have had with heroin at all.

The phone taps that were part of Jack's federal trial present Lucy as a girl who spent most of her long days talking, discussing soap operas with friends, taking messages for Jack, seeking out advice about caring for her little girls when they were sick or acting up. Much of her days Lucy spent worrying and wondering about Jack's other girlfriends, whom she regularly attempted to locate by phone. Most of the time, Lucy sounds tremendously lonely and bored.

Jack had plenty of other girls and children of his own—another "wife" with the first-born son whom he adores, girls he'd pick up and girls he'd take out for three or four months at a time—but Lucy hung in there because she was at least second. "You know how they say drug addicts can't live without their drug?" she says. "Jack's like my drug."

Lucy's father died of hepatitis when she was three, and her mother was always afraid of the streets. Growing up, Lucy left the apartment only when her mother went to buy food or would take her and her little brother to the park. When she was 16, Lucy became pregnant and had a little girl. She found out about her second pregnancy—twins—as she was getting her stomach pumped after a suicide attempt when she was 17. "I never got the attention I deserved when I was little," Lucy says. "I would do anything for attention."

Jack's attention included beatings, at least one of which required the services of a doctor. That night, Lucy ventured out to a club to dance, and Jack unexpectedly returned from a vacation—he never liked to discuss the details of his plans. More infuriating to him than her actual absence was the fact that he didn't have keys to the apartment. So he hunted her down and escorted her to his waiting car. While one of his lieutenants drove, Jack beat Lucy in the back seat of the Lincoln Town Car until she passed out. He dumped her bloodied body at his mother's feet. "Whenever I woke up to his mother, I knew he beat me," Lucy says. She feels she deserved that beating, that she deserves his wrath in general, but she is hurt by the fact that Jack seemed distracted. "It wasn't like it was about me," she says, ashamed. "It didn't seem like it had nothing to do with me."

And Lucy is proud that she is finally Jack's main girl, even if it took jail to make him realize it. "Ask him yourself," she dares you. "He says he wouldn't have made it without me." They are now engaged. On her 23rd birthday they were supposed to marry in the visiting room of the MCC. Lucy is still waiting.

She'll show you the ring to prove his love and her half dozen tattoos in his honor—his name is inscribed on her back, on her thigh and ankle, and on her butt, along with hearts and roses and a love poem to him and, in one spot, the stamp "Property of Jack"—as well as the pictures of him on Hawaiian vacations with the other girls cut out of the frame. Since his conviction on drug charges, Lucy has returned to her mother's two-bedroom apartment in the South Bronx. She lives with her girls, her mother and stepfather, and sometimes her brother's baby daughter. She couldn't maintain the apartment she had downtown because Jack doesn't want her to work. Her phone bills alone, from all the collect calls from jail—Jack, their friends serving time out-of-state, her brother, upstate in a juvenile facility for attempted murder—had reached more than a thousand dollars before they turned her phone off. "My brother knows the guys that are in the Central Park rape," Lucy says, in her drained way of talking, all words breathing out like a sleepy joke.

When Lucy had a telephone, her answering machine message had the same sexy voice: "Hello. Yes. I accept a collect call . . ."

It seems the perfect response to the contours of her difficult life and the appropriate tone to match her full-lipped, voluptuous body. It might even seem possible that her troubles could all be under control were it not for the exhaustion that seeps through the words, and for her eyes. Lucy has the fearful eyes of every damaged kid.

Isabella's boyfriend David was not a major dealer. He worked for Jack managing a location at 117th Street and Brook Avenue. He oversaw the location's lookouts, street runners, and pitch men, and made at least $1000 a week. Now, at 21, he is awaiting his sentence for conspiracy; he's also been charged with a murder, allegedly committed the first few weeks he was out on bail.

In retrospect, although she still loves him, Isabella is not sure why she liked David. Every night he used to come home drunk, leave in the morning, and come back drunk. She used to cry a lot and he hated her crying. "I'd be there sleeping," Isabella says, "he'd try to butter me up. I'd take his shoes off and have to make him comfortable, but when he'd wake up, he'd be in a bad mood. There would be a phone call and he'd be gone. I'd be like, 'David?' "

They lived with David's mother in the projects where they both grew up. Isabella stayed in David's bedroom watching TV and crying.

David's mother would encourage Isabella to stand up for her rights and Isabella knows that she should have been stronger, but she just wasn't. It was two years before she felt comfortable enough to go into the refrigerator and get food for herself.

David would always call when he got arrested, and Isabella would wait at the courthouse—usually, for 72 hours—until he came before the judge. In the two years they were together, this happened more than half a dozen times. Whenever he was incarcerated, she tried to open his spot for business, but only after David threatened his dealers would they listen to her instructions. The only other thing David ever let her do was to count some of the money, usually $50,000. "He never let me do anything big," Isabella says. But he would always tell her all the details if something exciting happened.

When David eventually moved Isabella into a house of her own, she liked it—a real neighborhood with Italian people and trees—even though it was lonely. He would beep her when he was done working, and she would cook him dinner, but he never made it home to eat. At four or five in the morning, he would come in and tell her to heat it up. "He called me the Microwave Queen, " Isabella says, still embarrassed.

Three months after they moved, David got arrested for the final time. Isabella had no money for rent and food and David had nothing saved, so she immediately moved back in with her parents. "I never had no shopping sprees," says Isabella. "That was all bull. He would spend it on his friends; he would pay for everybody. Sometimes we'd go out to eat, or we'd go to Playland, but we would always end up running because they got drunk and started fights." The one time he promised to take her on a trip, after she had her bags packed and ready, he called and told her to forget it. " 'It's gonna just be the guys,' he says. And they went to the Poconos, and I found out it wasn't just the guys. But that was okay, I didn't need none of those trips," she says.

Neither Lucy nor Isabella was—or is—bothered by the nature of their boyfriends' business; they approached it as the unquestioned commerce of their neighborhood streets. Although the American Dream metaphor for drug dealers—the entrepreneurs of denied opportunity—is a tired and sloppy one, there remains in it a strong seed of pure American truth: If Joey or David or Jack didn't do it, somebody else would, and not everybody can. At least, the girls felt,

their boyfriends commanded respect. Better yet, their boyfriends were employed.

David's friend Joey was also one of Jack's dealers, and his "wife" Dolores became Isabella's friend. Dolores' explanation of her life has an eerie quality of inevitability. She describes a father, an alcoholic and a gambler, who regularly beat up and threatened to kill her mother when she wouldn't hand over the family money. Still, Dolores says he took care of them all. When he was shot in an abandoned building—Dolores was six—life became frightening. "We couldn't get what we wanted," she says. "We was scared. My mother panicked." As her mother's depression grew, she became superstitious nearly to the point of paralysis, and Dolores grew up indoors. Her mother was afraid of the streets, and Dolores spent afternoons practicing cheers and the baton inside their apartment. She was never allowed out alone.

Still, at 15, Dolores got pregnant. Her boyfriend was an alcoholic, so she broke up with him when she was six months pregnant and got a job filing at a doctor's office. One day she bought everything her son would need—shoes, Baby Wipes, blankets, a stroller, playpen, toys, a crib—and wrapped the gifts and put music on. "I gave myself a baby shower," she says. "I started dancing, and I sat on the chairs, and opened all the gifts. And I put on all these clothes, I came out of the closet, and go doo, doo, doo, and I would pose. I would do stuff like that, all by myself. And I made it fun, you know. If I didn't do it, nobody was going to do it for me." She was eight months and two weeks pregnant by then. She walked herself to the hospital when she went into labor; her mother met her there.

She saw Joey in his Hawaiian shorts in the schoolyard, and he asked her if she was calling him Baby when she was actually calling to a friend. He was her sister's husband's best friend, and it only took a little while until he moved in. He worked in a gift shop on 125th then, he hadn't yet started dealing. "Little things he would take home," Dolores says, like a cupcake. "It was real, real nice."

Then Joey began coming home late, and there was lots of running around. He tries to deny it for three months, but Dolores knew. " I said, 'It's obvious Joey. All these people are looking for you. You got beepers.' "

Dolores didn't like Joey's dealing because it took him away from home. She had no moral dilemmas about the business and possessed no clear fear of the inherent dangers, but she wouldn't give him her blessing. He didn't have to deal drugs; she never loved him for money. She resented his absence and the lying, even though it took her a year to tell him so.

Jack's operation fell, and almost everyone involved was arrested. "It was exciting at first," says Isabella. "We finally found out what they were doing all that time they was away from us."

"We love them but we hate them," Dolores says. "You know when you love somebody but you hate them?" Dolores and Isabella went to the courthouse each day of the months-long trial. They would dress up beautiful in their best outfits, bought for them by their parents—hair pulled back, makeup, miniskirts, leather coats—and lean over the deep mahogany benches to get as close to the guys as the court marshals would permit. But on the days the guys' friends showed up—which were rare—the guys seemed almost to forget that their wives even existed. The guys' friends always come first.

Lucy went to court whenever she could get a babysitter. Sometimes she bought Kaitlin, her oldest girl, and Kaitlin would sit quietly on those same deep mahogany benches drawing pictures of her mother.

According to the boys' lawyers, Jack will likely receive at least 30 years, Joey was recently sentenced to 20 years, and David will receive at least 20. Parole is unlikely.

Joey has been in MCC for more than six months. Jose has been told the MCC is a hospital, and that Daddy is very sick, so that Jose believes that hospitals are bad because they never let their patients go home. Dolores doesn't like the untruth, but Jose is too young to understand.

With their boyfriends in jail, the girls have begun, for the first time in their young lives, to think of themselves as people with goals beyond the tasks of daily survival for themselves and their relationships and their kids. There are the lawyers' offices, the courtrooms, the jails to visit. The girls have been forced to consider the uncertain terms of futures they've never before questioned, not because they were so satisfied with their lives, but because the concept of futures never came to play in their experiences at all. Isabella is the only one who is concerned about launching herself beyond her predicament rather than re-establishing the same form of half-security again.

Significantly, she is also the only one to come from an intact home and the only one whose father worked (he was a porter). Nobody in her immediate or extended family has ever been in jail, and she has no illusions of marrying David while he's doing time. She is not proud of these details—they are offered only as explanation. To her, the significant consequence of her upbringing was that she was "whack": a bore.

She is willing to accept the fact—as much as she hates to have to—that her life is in her own hands now, and that, except for the rent and food for which David paid, it always was. She is getting her GED and for a while enrolled in Continuing Ed. Business courses at night. While the other girls push their understanding of their immediate situation no further than pained confusion, Isabella has it analyzed. "David made me think everybody's a liar. He made me cold-hearted. So if somebody was like, 'Oh, I love you,' I would be like, 'Oh yeah, it doesn't mean nothing to me,' " she says. "I think like a guy now. I think the same way they use girls, I use them. I don't think because a guy offers to pay that it's because I am special anymore. I can talk and get over on guys now. I can say things without meaning them. My cousins are pretty and guys come to pick them up in cars and they are flattered. I tell them, 'Cars are nothing. Take a cab.' "

She became involved with David before he began to deal drugs, but—if she were to stay with guys from her neighborhood—she would go out with only drug dealers again. She doesn't think dealing is admirable, but she finds "the life" exciting: Isabella loves danger and the dark of nights. It is the way to make money. "You know what's the weird thing," Isabella says, "everybody I ever knew is involved and the ones that aren't are bums and they stay home and you have to support them. I don't want to support those guys. For me, it's about independence. I was crazy with David because I got dependent on him. But now I'm independent. Nobody's there but me. I just want the money to come in steady, and to get the money, I have to work. I wasn't happy [with David], but I was secure. He paid the rent and the food."

Lucy's mother is pregnant. Lucy wishes that she were pregnant, too. When Jack first went to jail, he wrote to her about it in letters. "P.S." one said, in slanted writing at the bottom underlined by squiggles, "I hope you are PREG-

NANT!" lots of flying exclamation points. It is believed to be a sign of deeper love when a guy wants you to have one of his babies.

Lucy believes in Jack. The first night Lucy stayed with him, he didn't make her have sex, and he'd taken her to a hotel. "You know how guys nowadays are. 'Wow. she gots kids, she can't tell me no.' He was saying, 'I hope you feel free, you know, to lay down.' And I was. I can still picture to this day how we slept in each other's arms and we just spoke and the next morning when I got up he had pancakes there with strawberries and he fed me in bed. I was like, I guess this was the first time I fell in love with him. I never been treated that way, and I've always wanted to be treated like, you know, a princess, like." When a beeper goes off on a coat in the hallway, Kaitlin's the only one to hear it—over her twin sisters' screaming, over the TV and Latin music and her grandmother's clanging in the kitchen—and she messengers the information straight to Lucy, who is kneeling, sewing a blouse on the bedroom floor.

"Mommy! Mommy! Your beeper went off!" screams Kaitlin, a hostile dare to her mother's face. Kaitlin, five, has already learned that sly way of covering up her need with a tentative curtness. She's a clinging child; when she was two years old, she had gonorrhea in her rectum, and she hates to go to sleep without her mother in the room.

Then Kaitlin long-legs it to the other bedroom, where her four-year-old sisters and the 12-year-old boys from downstairs are piled wrestling on the bed. Kaitlin is hyper tonight at her grandmother's apartment, running in her torn underwear shirt. She is so beautiful, little princess, round bright baby round brown eyes.

"Your beeper, Lucy!" yells Lucy's mother from the kitchen where she's stirring arroz con pollo. It wasn't hers that went off—she checked the stretch waistband where her own beeper hangs just below her large belly. But this time it's not Lucy's either, like it always used to be; this time it's for Marisa, Lucy's cousin.

Marisa is 14 and tall with no hips and nervous, wide-open eyes. Her light-brown skin is pure and soft and she is proud of her new boyfriend. She cannot claim that he's a well-known dealer, and he's not in jail, but he is married. He gave the beeper to her recently—it is her first—after they had a bad fight. He wants to know where Marisa is all the time when she's not with him, and Marisa is anxious to go downstairs and return the call; the apartment does not have a phone.

Marisa hurriedly puts on her coat in the hallway, as Kaitlin darts from the kitchen and loops around Marisa's long legs. But Marisa ignores her, she's got to get down to a pay phone; she's got to call him back.

SOURCE: LeBlanc, Adrian Nicole, "Girlfriends: Three Lives in the Drug Trade." Photographs by Kristine Larsen [not shown here]. *Village Voice*, April 23, 1991, pp. 30-35. Copyright © 1991. Reprinted with permission of the author.

HANDOUT 4: "GIRLFRIENDS: THREE LIVES IN THE DRUG TRADE" QUESTIONS

1. What do the girls get from their relationships with their boyfriends?

2. What do the guys get from their relationships with their girlfriends?

3. Are these girls oppressed in their relationships? Explain.

4. Why do these girls seem to be unsure of their own experiences?

5. What role do beepers play in these girls' lives? How are they like wedding rings? How do they differ from wedding rings?

6. Why did Lucy feel she deserved a beating from Jack? What was worse than the beating, for her? Are her tattoos like a wedding ring? How so? How not?

7. What, if anything, bothers Isabella and Dolores about their boyfriends' dealing?

8. "We love them but we hate them." Is this feeling common in relationships? How are these relationships different from ones you have seen? How are they the same?

9. How have the boys' jail sentences affected the girls? What impact did this have on Isabella's life?

10. We end with Lucy's 14-year-old cousin Marisa. What is the final message of the article?

Students' Questions

1. Is it better to be a "wife" or a "mistress," in your opinion?

2. Is Lucy crazy for staying with Jack? Why does she stay with him?

3. Isabella talks about trading excitement for independence. Which would you choose and why?

LESSON 7: GENDER AND IDENTITY

Objectives

- To continue observation of sociocultural expectations based on gender

- To begin examining the ways in which gender roles impact an individual's identity

- To characterize features of written poetry

- To write poetry demonstrating students' ideas about pressures and expectations for men and women in their own cultures

Materials

Poetry that challenges or exposes the limitations of traditional gender roles in some way. I use:

- UNIT MATERIALS: "Barbie doll" by Marge Piercy

- UNIT MATERIALS: "Sometimes a man stands up during supper . . ." by Rainer Maria Rilke

- UNIT MATERIALS: "A work of artifice" by Marge Piercy

- UNIT MATERIALS: "Prayer" by Alan Dugan

- HANDOUT 5: POETRY GROUP WORK TASKS

- SAMPLE STUDENT-WRITTEN POETRY (included for teachers' reference)

Procedures

- Divide poems into pairs. I pair "Barbie doll" with "Sometimes a man stands up during supper . . ." and "Prayer" with "A work of artifice."

- Give each student a copy of HANDOUT 5: POETRY GROUP WORK TASKS. Go over directions with students altogether. Divide class into small groups of four or five. Distribute one pair of poems to each group.

- In groups, students are to read each of their two poems and answer short questions on them. This will generate discussions of familial and societal expectations based on gender.

- After group work, each of the four poems should be read aloud by a student. Take this time to go over any puzzling sections or phrases in poetry. Discuss poems as a class, using the questions on the handouts as a starting point.

- After poetry readings, explications, and discussions, each student must write a new version of one of the poems (e.g., a "Ken Doll" version of "Barbie doll" poem, "Sometimes a Woman" for Rilke's "Sometimes a man stands up during supper . . ."). See SAMPLE STUDENT-WRITTEN POETRY. Read and discuss these examples aloud to illustrate the assignment, if desired.

HANDOUT 5: POETRY GROUP WORK TASKS

Names of people in group: _____

Your group has been given copies of two poems. You will work with both poems.

Someone in your group needs to read each of the poems aloud.

Answer the following questions on each of the poems:

Poem 1 Title: _____

1. Which gender is in focus?

2. According to the poem, what are the expectations for people of this gender?

3. According to the poem, what are the consequences of meeting those expectations?

4. According to the poem, what are the consequences of not meeting those expectations?

5. Characterize the style in which the poem is written (conversational, mysterious, sarcastic, detailed, excited, calm, etc.).

Poem 2 Title: _____

1. Which gender is in focus?

2. According to the poem, what are the expectations for people of this gender?

3. According to the poem, what are the consequences of meeting those expectations?

4. According to the poem, what are the consequences of not meeting those expectations?

5. Characterize the style in which the poem is written (conversational, mysterious, sarcastic, detailed, excited, calm, etc.).

Independent Work

After answering these questions and hearing the other two poems, start thinking about with which of the four poems you want to work.

UNIT MATERIALS

Barbie doll

by Marge Piercy

This girl child was born as usual
and presented dolls that did pee-pee
and wee lipsticks the color of cherry candy.
Then in the magic of puberty, a classmate said:
You have a great big nose and fat legs.

She was healthy, tested intelligent,
possessed strong arms and back,
abundant sexual drive and manual dexterity.
She went to and fro apologizing.
Everyone saw a fat nose and on thick legs.

She was advised to play coy,
exhorted to come on hearty,
exercise, diet, smile and wheedle.
Her good nature wore out
like a fan belt.
So she cut off her nose and her legs
and offered them up.

In the casket displayed on satin she lay
with the undertaker's cosmetics painted on,
a turned up putty nose,
dressed in a pink and white nightie.
Doesn't she look pretty? everyone said.
Consummation at last.
To every woman a happy ending.

SOURCE: "Barbie doll" by Marge Piercy. From CIRCLES ON THE WATER. Alfred
A. Knopf, Inc. Copyright © 1971, 1973, 1982 by Marge Piercy. Used by permission
of the Wallace Literary Agency, Inc., and Random House, Inc.

Sometimes a man stands up during supper . . .

by Rainer Maria Rilke

Sometimes a man stands up during supper
and walks outside, and keeps walking
because of a church that stands somewhere
in the East.

And his children say blessings on him as if
he were dead.

And another man remains in his own house,
stays there, inside the dishes and in the glasses,
so that his children have to go far out into the world
toward that same church, which he forgot.

SOURCE: "Sometimes a man stands up during supper . . ." by Rainer Maria Rilke. From *Selected Poems of Rainer Maria Rilke.* Copyright © 1981. HarperCollins Publishers. Used with permission.

UNIT MATERIALS

A work of artifice

by Marge Piercy

The bonsai tree
in the attractive pot
could have grown eighty feet tall
on the side of a mountain
til split by lightning.
But a gardener
carefully pruned it.
It is nine inches high.
Every day as he
whittles back the branches
the gardener croons,
It is your nature
to be small and cozy,
domestic and weak;
how lucky, little tree,
to have a pot to grow in.
With living creatures
one must begin very early
to dwarf their growth:
the bound feet,
the crippled brain,
the hair in curlers,
the hands you
love to touch.

SOURCE: "A work of artifice" by Marge Piercy. From CIRCLES ON THE WATER. Alfred A. Knopf, Inc. Copyright © 1971, 1973, 1982 by Marge Piercy. Used by permission of the Wallace Literary Agency, Inc., and Random House, Inc.

Prayer

by Alan Dugan

God, I need a job because I need money.
Here the world is, enjoyable with whiskey,
women, ultimate weapons, and class!
But if I have no money, then my wife
gets mad at me, I can't drink well,
the armed oppress me, and no boss,
pays me money. But when I work,
Oh I get paid!, the police are courteous,
and I can have a drink and breathe air.
I feel classy. I am where the arms are.
The wife is wife in deed. The world
is interesting! except I have to be
indoors all day and take shit, and make
weapons to kill outsiders with. I miss
the air and smell that paid work stinks
when done for somebody else's profit, so I quit,
enjoy a few flush days in air, drunk, then
I need a job again. I'm caught in a steel cycle.

SOURCE: "Prayer" by Alan Dugan, copyright © 1961,1962,1968,1972,1973,1974, 1983 by Alan Dugan. From NEW AND COLLECTED POEMS 1961-1983, first published by Ecco Press (Hopewell, NJ) in 1983. Reprinted by permission. (Poem also found in A. Poulin, Jr. [Ed.], *Contemporary American poetry*, pp. 117-118, New York: Houghton Mifflin.)

SAMPLE STUDENT-WRITTEN POETRY

Ken Doll
(after Piercy's "Barbie doll")

by Mike (1992)

This boy child was born as usual
and presented racecars that spit fire
and miniature GI Joes and Ninja Turtles
and tiny guns and robots that fit together like weapons.
Then in the magic of puberty, a classmate said:
You have big hips and you walk like a girl.

He was healthy, tested intelligent,
possessed strong arms and back,
abundant sexual drive and manual dexterity.
He went to and fro keeping to himself.
Everyone saw big hips and a swish when he walked.

He was told to play tough,
Had to come on strong,
Lift weights, fight everyone, be bold, and talk loud.
His good nature wore out
Like a fan belt.
So he went out one night and killed someone he didn't even know
And offered him up.

In the jail he lies on his cot
Staring at the ceiling,
Cigarette hanging from his mouth,
in his blue uniform.
Ain't he a man? everyone said.
Consummation at last.
To every man a happy ending.

Woman's Prayer
(after Dugan's "Prayer")

by Candace (1990)

God, I need a man because I need reputation.
Here the world is, enjoyable with clothes,
flirting, nights on the town, and class!
But if I don't have a man, then my friends
pity me, I never feel like going out,
my teachers oppress me, and what my boss
pays me isn't enough. But when I have a man,
Oh I get paid! My friends envy me,
and I can have a drink and breathe air.
I feel classy. I am where the action is.
I am a woman in deed. The world
Is interesting! Except I have to be
indoors all the time and take his shit, and
Lie to everyone and say how great he is.
I miss my freedom and feel tied down to
someone else's happiness, so we break up,
enjoy a few days of freedom, drunk, then
I need a man again. I'm caught in a steel cycle.

Sometimes a Woman
(after Rilke's "Sometimes a man stands up
during supper . . .")

by Anonymous (1990)

Sometimes a woman stands up during her pregnancy
and goes to the clinic, and walks out a few hours later,
because of a future that stands somewhere
in her own mind.

And her parents and her boyfriend curse her as if
she was dead.

And another woman has the baby,
lives there, inside the diapers and days of babysitting
so that her boyfriend can go out into the world
toward a future, which she had to forget.

LESSON 8: EXAMINING A FORMAL THEORY OF POWER

Objectives

- To introduce students to a formal scheme for analyzing use and abuse of power

- To give students practice applying this framework to fictional and real-life characters

Materials

- HANDOUT 6: POWER SCENARIOS

Procedures

- Introduce students to terminology associated with Michel Foucault's analysis of power dynamics. Foucault (1980) names four types of power: custodial, indoctrinary, visionary, and oppressive. Students usually grasp this easily. They should take notes for future reference. Ideas to discuss are as follows:

Almost every powerful action can be classified as one of the following four types: custodial power, indoctrinary power, visionary power, and oppressive power. It is possible for a person to have more than one type of power or for an act to be classified in more than one category.

1. Custodial: This is the type of power that includes caretaking, record keeping, and monitoring. It, like all types of power, can be abused when it is used to repress rather than to sustain and nurture. Some people who have custodial powers are teachers, parents, police, the IRS, and pet owners.
2. Indoctrinary: This is the type of power that includes consciously persuading, educating, or otherwise informing another person. People who use indoctrinary power usually have an agenda they wish to further. Politicians, teachers, lawyers, and advertisers use indoctrinary power.
3. Visionary: This is the type of power exercised by charismatic leaders, entertainers, and preachers. Visionary power appeals to the soul, taking the listener out of his or her world and creating a new vision altogether. Dr. Martin Luther King, many evangelists, and some musicians have this power.
4. Oppressive: Although all types of power can be used abusively, oppressive power is the force in play during acts of cruelty, hatred, and violence. Oppressive power exists only to hurt—there is no other motive (such as nurturing, educating, or inspiring).

- Encourage students to think of, discuss, and debate examples of each type of power.

- Distribute HANDOUT 6: POWER SCENARIOS. Students may work on this alone or in groups.

- Apply these terms and concepts to characters and relationships in "The Pearl of Toledo," "Girlfriends," and to sex roles poetry. If class is willing, students can use these categories to review their Journal 1 and 2 entries in discussion or in writing.

HANDOUT 6: POWER SCENARIOS

Directions: Read the following scenarios and determine what type of power each represents. Many illustrate more than one type of power. You need to decide which type is most prevalent.

1. David Churlish: Churlish has been leading a group of people who believe that he is the messenger of God. Recently a group of investigative reporters searched and found Churlish in the deepest, most isolated part of a Louisiana bayou. They described Churlish as an obese man with no hair who most resembled a wild pig. His hut was guarded by 50 believers armed with sharpened spears. The hut was surrounded by a fence on which were hung shrunken heads. From afar the reporters watched the group perform bizarre rituals of sacrifice over which Churlish presided. At another time, they witnessed a meeting of some sort, at which Churlish sat on a throne. Another man jumped up and down on a raised platform and danced wildly. This seemed to hypnotize the crowd, who immediately filed past Churlish, kissed his feet, offered up jewelry and stereo equipment, and sacrificed their youngest daughters. The reporters thought it best to leave Churlish alone.

2. Colon Powerful: Powerful is a top military officer. He is well regarded as a competent and rational man who smokes expensive cigars. Although he is extremely short, standing only 4 ft. 9 in., he has overcome his size to gain friends and influence important people. Powerful began as a drill sergeant. He was famous for his obsession with details and for his systematic way of promoting people. Not a single soldier in his troop could get away with a small wrinkle or smudge on his uniform or his record. He never yells—he has lieutenants for that. He runs a very tight ship. His officers keep precise records on everything from ammunitions ordered to Kleenexes used. There is no room for error.

3. Sigmund Skinner: Sigmund is a famous professor of psychology. A rather ugly man with embarrassing nostril hair, Sigmund always has felt uneasy about his appearance. Consequently, he spent his entire life defining what is normal. He is most famous for creating a system of rewards and punishments that trained deviant chickens to become normal laboratory rats. He later applied his methods to schoolchildren and established a school named after his mother, Beatrice. Through a meticulous keeping of records, files, and progress reports, Sigmund managed to produce a class of 12-year-olds who looked and behaved exactly like him. Fortunately, Sigmund quickly was locked away. His system, however, is alive and well in some American public school systems.

4. Mother Jones: Mother Jones, or Mother as her friends call her, is well known in some political circles, although she never participates in negotiations or treaties. Mother leads small groups of people who help to find and build housing for the homeless and food kitchens for the hungry. She rarely speaks in public but seems to deeply affect everyone she comes into contact

Stern. *Teaching English So It Matters.* © 1995 Corwin Press, Inc.

with. She uses simple words effectively and sincerely. She leads many people to religion with her kindness and the example of her selfless life.

5. Jackie Lord: Lord controls a large business empire that includes companies in world capitals as well as her hometown, Podunk, Arkansas. Lord is a master analyst who keeps firm, if not always legal, control of her holdings (which include as many people as dollars). She has several connections with the underworld, using those thugs to keep investors investing. In order to assure the mob's loyalty, she also runs a secret service that has all the dirt on the mob. She is well respected and is, in fact, thinking of running for senator. She keeps her name clean by effectively controlling all would-be informers: She has them chopped into tiny bits and sells them to frozen food companies as sausage.

LESSON 9: SEX ROLES, POWER, AND IDENTITY IN *THE COLOR PURPLE*

Objectives

- To read and understand the novel in entirety

- To discuss gender roles, power, and identity as they impact characters in the novel

- To work effectively in groups, especially on textual analysis

- To write creative, reflective pieces based on themes in the novel and these works

- To become conversant with the concepts of claims, evidence, and warrants

- To develop abilities to make claims about literary works and themes, search text for evidence to support claims, and generate warrants for claims and evidence

- To complete prewriting exercises and understand formal writing structures

Materials

- Walker, Alice, *The Color Purple*

- HANDOUT 7: CASEWORKER ASSIGNMENT

- HANDOUT 8: PROVING A POINT IN AN ESSAY

- HANDOUT 9: CELIE'S IDENTITY

- HANDOUT 10: CELIE AND MEN AND WOMEN

- HANDOUT 11: GENDER STEREOTYPES IN *THE COLOR PURPLE*

- HANDOUT 12: POWER IN *THE COLOR PURPLE*

- HANDOUT L: CLAIMS, EVIDENCE, AND WARRANTS (see Chapter 4)

- HANDOUT M: EVALUATING SOURCES OF EVIDENCE (see Chapter 4)

Procedures

- *Activity A: Initial Ideas About **The Color Purple**.* Begin reading *The Color Purple*. Students will want to discuss narrator's childish and uneducated narrative voice. Distribute HANDOUT 7: CASEWORKER ASSIGNMENT. Ask students to imagine the following scenario: They are social workers assigned to 14-year-old Celie. They must prepare a factual report on the events covered in the first 12 pages of the novel.

• *Activity B: Discussing **The Color Purple**.* The following questions can be used to start general class discussions.

Pages 1-22. Why is this book written in nonstandard, incorrect English? What information does this give us about Celie? What are Celie's feelings toward her father? Toward Nettie? Why does Celie marry Mr. _? Why does Mr. _ marry Celie? When Kate and Celie discuss power on page 22, Celie considers her own situation. Do you think she has any power?

Pages 23-55. What type of power does Shug have over Celie? Over Mr. _? What type of power does Sofia have over Harpo? Does he have any type of power over her? Why does Celie tell Harpo to beat Sofia? What does Shug Avery represent to make Celie obsess over her? How does Shug show her power over Mr. _? Are Shug and Celie friends?

Pages 56-83. Explain Celie's happiness with Shug in the house. What do you think about Harpo's ideas about power and marriage? Why does Sofia leave Harpo? How does Celie feel about Shug when she sings? Why does she finally decide to tell Shug about Mr. _ beating her, that is, how does Celie gain power over Shug? What type of power is it?

Pages 84-118. What happens to Sofia? How does this decrease her power? How does it increase her power? Why does the family decide to send Squeak to speak to the prison warden? What changes does this visit bring about in Squeak? How does Sofia feel about her White employers? How does Celie telling Shug about her father raping her at 13 change the women's relationship? Do you think this change came as a surprise to Celie? To Shug?

Pages 119-151. Why had Celie not received any letters from Nettie? What has happened to Nettie? What is Nettie's mission in life? Why are Nettie's impressions of New York significant? What conflicts exist in Nettie's mind (see p. 145)? How does Shug talk Celie out of killing Mr. _?

Pages 152-198. What are sex roles for Olinka boys and girls? How does Olivia link sexism and racism? Are Tashi's parents superstitious (see pp. 166-167)? What changes does the new road bring to the village? Why did Samuel and Corrine adopt Olivia and Adam? What does Celie gain from visiting the man she thought was her Pa? How does Nettie finally put Corinne's mind at rest?

Pages 199-228. Why does Celie stop writing to God? What brings Nettie and Samuel together? Who in this book is deeply spiritual? Would Nettie agree with Shug's thoughts on religion (pp. 202-204)? What is Celie's response to Mr. _'s refusal to let her leave? Does Mr. _ seem affected by the curse Celie lays on him as she goes (p. 213)? Why does Celie succeed in her business venture?

Pages 229-249. How has Mr. _ changed his ways? Why? What happened to the Olinka village? How did the African chief show respect for Doris Baines, and why is this important? Explain Tashi's feelings about her initiation and Adam's feelings about Tashi's initiation.

Pages 250-283. How do Shug and Celie share power in their breakup? How has Nettie's concept of God changed (p. 264)? Why does Celie talk to Mr. _ on page 267? How does he help her? What does their conversation about Shug, Sofia, and "typical women" tell you about each of them? About their culture? What finally brings Mr. _ and Celie together?

Pages 284-end. How do Harpo and Sofia learn to be happy with each other? What is the lesson Celie figures she is here to learn? What is Celie's attitude toward Shug when she returns? Why is her last letter written to God and to "dear everything"? What is the significance of the book's title?

• *Activity C: Quizzes on* **The Color Purple.** Encourage consistent reading by holding frequent short quizzes. When giving quizzes, it is important to ask two kinds of questions: ones that ask students to recall simple events and ones that ask them to explain their own interpretation of events in the novel. In this way, slower and more advanced readers are both challenged. Here is a sample quiz on pages 1-115 of the novel:

1. Name Harpo's wife and his girlfriend.
2. Name the woman loved by both Celie and Mr. _.
3. Why did Harpo's wife have to go to jail?
4. Who begins to make Celie aware of her own sexuality?
5. Why didn't Mr. _ marry the woman he loved?
6. Which woman in the novel so far most defies gender stereotype? Explain.
7. Celie appears to be almost powerless in her life at this point, and yet she is gradually "coming into her own." Identify and explain the sources of her newfound sense of self and/or power.

• *Activity D: Group Formulation of Quiz and Discussion Questions.* One effective technique to use with students of varying abilities is to gather those students who are at the same approximate place in the book together in groups of two, three, or four. In these small groups, students can generate discussion questions for later use by the whole class or for use as a quiz. The students who need to catch up on their reading can read on their own and not join a group that day.

Groups of students who create quiz questions also can write "ideal" answers to these questions and specify criteria for evaluating responses to their questions. Students are then exempt from answering their own questions on such a quiz. Student-written questions usually take a different tack than questions written by adults. Here are a few questions from a quiz on *The Color Purple* written by students:

1. Since he lives with two different women (one who is beautiful and sexy, and one who is ugly and just there like a servant), what do you think Mr. _'s attitudes are about women?

2. There are strict sex roles for men and women to follow in both the southern American and Olinka cultures. In your opinion, which society is more repressive? Give at least four reasons for your answer.

• *Activity E: Applying Formal Theories of Power.* Discussions of *The Color Purple* will gain depth and relevance if instructors teach Lesson 8: Examining a Formal Theory of Power before or while students read the novel. Once students become comfortable with Foucault's categories, assign short group writing or discussion assignments analyzing the power dynamics of relationships in *The Color Purple*. For example:

> What type of power do Pa and Mr. __ have over Celie? Explain using textual citations.
>
> What type of power does Shug first have over Celie? Explain using textual citations.
>
> What type of power does Sofia first have over Harpo? Explain using textual citations.

• *Activity F: Betrayal.* When students have read of Mr. __'s concealment of Nettie's letters, assign Journal 3: When have you experienced a betrayal such as Celie's? Issues of (women's, children's, or people of color's) powerlessness may arise. Teachers should beware of returning journal writing marked with lots of mechanics or other corrections: These are private pieces. Students have told me that they resent it when I "correct their lives" and generally appreciate more personal responses. Correct and edit other, less confessional writing assignments.

• *Activity G: Introducing Essay Writing Skills.* Introduce the concept of substantiated claims by distributing HANDOUT 8: PROVING A POINT IN AN ESSAY. This sheet and the following procedures should be completed by students in class together.

After students understand the basic criteria for proving a point in an essay, begin with basics: Explain what a *claim* is. Give examples: Girls in this class are smarter than boys. The sky is blue. Michael Jordan is the best basketball player ever. Make it clear that the most interesting claims are the ones that state a bold, controversial point. ("The sky is blue" is not much of a claim because it isn't all that bold a statement.)

Next, go on to *evidence*: What proof do we have that girls are smarter than boys? (Girls' average test scores are 75; boys' are 71.) That the sky is blue? (We can look outside and see for ourselves.) That Michael Jordan is the best? (He led the NBA in scoring for 6 consecutive years.) The students may tell you that your evidence does not prove anything. (If they don't, ask if this proof would suffice: Girls are smarter because they wear nicer clothes. Michael Jordan was the best because his head is the shiniest.)

Also useful at this point is HANDOUT M: EVALUATING SOURCES OF EVIDENCE (see Chapter 4). Good sources of evidence are impartial, up-to-date, and knowledgeable.

Not all proof "works." That is because it is not warranted. Explain to students that a *warrant* is the part of an argument that explains why the evidence proves the point. Ask the class to explain what the word *warrant* means to them: They might say that a warrant gives an individual the right to do something, such as arrest someone. It is a guarantee, authorizing and justifying an action. In an argument, a warrant justifies and puts an official stamp of authorization on evidence. It is the part that is missing most often in student writing. Warrants for the above claims would be like this:

CLAIM	EVIDENCE	WARRANT
1. Girls in this class are smarter than boys.	Girls' average test score is 75; boys' is 71.	Test scores give some measure of intelligence.
2. The sky is blue.	I look up and see blue.	I am outside looking up and seeing blue sky.
3. Michael Jordan is the best basketball player ever.	He led the league in scoring six consecutive seasons.	Scoring points is one measure of skill. No other player has ever done this.

Have students generate warrants for unrelated, supplied claims and evidence. Use HANDOUT L: CLAIMS, EVIDENCE, AND WARRANTS (see Chapter 4). It is best to do this together in class.

Continue prewriting for essays by having students complete progressively more difficult claim-evidence-warrant worksheets. Assign any of the following provided worksheets. Some need to be done in class; some can be done independently. Make sure students save all claim-evidence-warrant worksheets for use in their essays.

Activities H through K help students write their final essays.

• *Activity H: Prewriting/Finding Good Evidence.* When students are up to about page 80 in *The Color Purple*, distribute HANDOUT 9: CELIE'S IDENTITY. Students will work independently to find quoted evidence and deduce claims based on the evidence they have found. When students have finished this sheet, go over sample student responses until all students seem to grasp the basic idea.

• *Activity I: Prewriting/Warranting Evidence.* Next, distribute HANDOUT 10: CELIE AND MEN AND WOMEN. With partners, students can find two pieces of relevant evidence. Students then work alone—or continue with partners—to generate warrants for supplied claims. Review and discuss particularly strong warrants with the class as a whole.

• *Activity J: Prewriting/Claims, Evidence, and Warrants and Gender Stereotypes.* Distribute HANDOUT 11: GENDER STEREOTYPES IN *THE COLOR PURPLE*. The class generates claims together. Instructors can introduce this task by saying: "You are elders belonging to one of these cultural groups. You must instruct the local children on their roles in the families and in society. What will you say?"

Together the class writes four claims (two for southern, early 20th-century African American culture and two for traditional Olinka culture). Then divide students into small groups to find evidence. Finally, let individual students work on their own to supply warrants.

- *Activity K: Prewriting/Claims, Evidence, and Warrants and Power.* Distribute HANDOUT 12: POWER IN *THE COLOR PURPLE.* Students work on their own to supply claims, evidence, and warrants. This worksheet relies on the analytical framework introduced in Lesson 8.

HANDOUT 7: CASEWORKER ASSIGNMENT

The Color Purple (pp. 1-12)

You are a Department of Children and Family Services (DCFS) caseworker who comes across these letters written by Celie. Write a report about the facts—or at least as much as reasonably can be sorted out from Celie's letters. Describe Mr. _'s actions and decisions in relation to Celie. What has he done to her? What has he told her?

Remember, you are not a teenager writing this—you are completing a report for your boss. Use appropriate phrases and language.

HANDOUT 8: PROVING A POINT IN AN ESSAY

Which paragraph is most successful in proving its point?

1. ___ Celie, the main character in Alice Walker's *The Color Purple*, is totally disrespected by the men in her life. They do not treat her as a fully empowered, independent person. Celie is emotionally and physically abused by both her father and her husband, Mr. _. All she can do is work, be sexually available to them, and care for their children.

2. ___ Celie, the main character in Alice Walker's *The Color Purple*, is totally disrespected by the men in her life. They do not treat her as a fully empowered, independent person. When Mr. _ talks about Celie, he doesn't even refer to her as a person. She is just someone who will work for him, be sexually available to him, and take care of his kids.

3. ___ Celie, the main character in Alice Walker's *The Color Purple*, is totally disrespected by the men in her life. They do not treat her as a fully empowered, independent person. When Celie's prospective husband, Mr. _, is considering marrying Celie instead of her sister, Nettie, he says, " 'I ain't never really looked at that one' " (p. 9).

4. ___ Celie, the main character in Alice Walker's *The Color Purple*, is totally disrespected by the men in her life. They do not treat her as a fully empowered, independent person. When Celie's prospective husband, Mr. _, is considering marrying Celie instead of her sister, Nettie, he says, " 'I ain't never really looked at that one' " (p. 9). This callous statement shows that Mr. _ does not value Celie as an individual. Referring to a woman, a prospective wife, as "that one" is clear indication of strong disregard and disrespect.

Key:

1. Clear claim, no evidence
2. Clear claim, reference to specific situation without textual citation
3. Clear claim, quoted evidence
4. Clear claim, quoted evidence, definite warrant

HANDOUT 9: CELIE'S IDENTITY

SAVE THIS SHEET   *PREWRITING FOR ESSAY*

Directions: Find a section of the text that shows how each one of these characters has affected Celie's character, self-perception, or feelings about her life. Copy the quotation and make sure you note the page number. Then interpret the quotation: Tell what you think it shows.

CHARACTER & QUOTATION   INTERPRETATION
(from the novel)   (in your own words)
This will be your evidence.   *This will be your claim.*

Her Father
pp. —————

Mr. __
pp. —————

Nettie
pp. —————

Shug Avery
pp. —————

Sofia
pp. —————

HANDOUT 10: CELIE AND MEN AND WOMEN

SAVE THIS SHEET   *PREWRITING FOR ESSAY*

Directions: Read the following claims. Find one or two pieces of evidence from the book that support the claim. Copy the evidence down word for word from the book. Make sure to write down the page number. Then try to explain how your evidence proves the claim: Warrant it.

Claim 1: Celie's confidence has been destroyed by the men in her life.

Evidence 1a:

Evidence 1b:

Warrant(s):

Claim 2: Celie receives positive reinforcement from the women in her life.

Evidence 2a:

Evidence 2b:

Warrant(s):

Claim 3: Celie is confused by the different signals she receives from the men and women in her life.

Evidence 3a:

Evidence 3b:

Warrant(s):

HANDOUT 11: GENDER STEREOTYPES IN *THE COLOR PURPLE*

SAVE THIS SHEET   *PREWRITING FOR ESSAY*

Directions:

1. List the basic sexual stereotypes and expectations based on gender for these two groups of people. It is all right to make bold statements. These statements are claims. Example of a claim: The Olinka consider women to be inferior to men.

2. In groups, find evidence from the book that supports these claims. Example of evidence: "The Olinka do not believe girls should be educated" (p. 144).

3. On your own, explain why your evidence proves your point; in other words, warrant your evidence. Example of a warrant: As we know, a society will work to educate only the people it values. Olinka society does educate its boys but does not consider girls worthy of education. Girls thus are considered inferior to boys.

Two sets of claim/evidence/warrants about early 20th-century, southern, African American men and women:

   1. Claim:
       Evidence:

       Warrant:

   2. Claim:
       Evidence:

       Warrant:

Two sets of claim/evidence/warrants about traditional Olinka men and women:

   1. Claim:
       Evidence:

       Warrant:

   2. Claim:
       Evidence:

       Warrant:

HANDOUT 12: POWER IN *THE COLOR PURPLE*

SAVE THIS SHEET   *PREWRITING FOR ESSAY*

Directions: Fill out boxes using this example as a model.

Character: *Mr. __*
Type of power (claim): *Mr. __* has oppressive power over Celie when they first get married.
Quoted evidence: *"Mr. __ say ['I beat Celie'] cause she my wife"* (p. 23).
Warrant: *To beat anyone casually, for no reason, is cruel and oppressive. To beat someone for no reason except that she is married to you is twisted and oppressive.*

Character: Type of power (claim):

Quoted evidence:

Warrant:

Character: Type of power (claim):

Quoted evidence:

Warrant:

Character: Type of power (claim):

Quoted evidence:

Warrant:

LESSON 10: WRITING THE ESSAY

Objectives

- To focus and organize prewriting

- To conceive a thesis and outline a supporting argument

- To work independently toward self-imposed deadlines

- To write an organized, coherent, honest essay on sex roles, power, and/or identity in *The Color Purple*

Materials

- HANDOUT 13: BOXES PLANNING SHEET FOR ESSAY WITH SAMPLE NOTES

- SAMPLE STUDENT-WRITTEN ESSAY (included for instructors' reference)

Procedures

- Explain that students now can begin to put their essays (on sex roles, power, and/or identity in *The Color Purple*) together. Distribute and explain HANDOUT O: BLANK BOXES FOR ESSAY PREWRITING (see Chapter 4). This sheet helps students map out the structure of the essay. To avert panic (the handout is a little daunting the first time students see it), show students HANDOUT 13: BOXES PLANNING SHEET FOR ESSAY WITH SAMPLE NOTES almost immediately. This will help them get an idea of how to use the boxes worksheet: It can act as a rough draft, or students can use it only to get the sequence of their points straight and then continue planning and writing according to their own process. The sample notes are unfinished; if necessary, teachers can work with individual students to complete notes to ensure that students understand the process.

Students may say that they have "already done this" work on the last four handouts. They are correct. Explain that the new handouts show them how to select and organize the information and analysis that they already have completed. In other words, they may be halfway done with writing their final essays already.

- Circulate around the classroom, working with students to help them with the boxes worksheet. Students should start by writing theses. Explain to students that a *thesis* is the main point that an essay makes and defends. How can a student develop a thesis? One simple and effective way is to have the student think about the book personally—about what affected him or her most as a reader. Each student should try to articulate what she or he feels is the most obvious, most gripping, most disturbing, or most important aspect of the book. Instructors can help students generate theses by posing general reflective questions:

1. What do you think *The Color Purple* teaches us about power?
2. How do men's and women's roles differ in *The Color Purple?*
3. What happens when men and women don't follow the rules in *The Color Purple?*
4. How would you react to Mr. __ if you were Celie?

Students can jot down notes addressing the questions that they find most appealing and work with their responses to create bold, declarative theses. It is best for them to work through these experimentations and phrasing efforts on the back of the handout first. After developing working theses, students will generate claims, find evidence, and write warrants. Students can adapt notes from their claims, evidence, and warrants worksheets to fit their chosen theses.

- After most students seem confident with the boxes worksheet, clarify all formal expectations for the essay. Help students meet those expectations by developing realistic due dates for each step of the essay-writing process. With students, assign due dates for:

completion of the thesis
outline of the argument (i.e., completing the rest of the boxes worksheet)
the rough draft (unless the completed boxes worksheet suffices as a rough draft)
final draft

- Give students time in class to receive help with writing. They also can work on essay at home. Students need not bring texts home: Most of the quotations they will be using will have been written out on their claims, evidence, and warrants worksheets.

- When essay is completed, teachers should collect packet consisting of:

1. The claims, evidence, and warrants worksheets that students used to write their essays;
2. Boxes worksheet;
3. Rough draft (Judge if this step is necessary; some students will have used their boxes worksheet as a veritable rough draft);
4. Final draft. (See SAMPLE STUDENT-WRITTEN ESSAY. This paper was written by Candace, a student who admitted she never had finished reading any book assigned in high school before *The Color Purple* and "hated writing" because she "didn't know how to do it." She used the boxes worksheet carefully. Although her essay is a bit stiff, she was grateful for the organizational guidance and was proud of this essay.)

HANDOUT 13: BOXES PLANNING SHEET FOR ESSAY WITH SAMPLE NOTES

Directions: Notes that you take on this sheet are the outline of your essay. When you copy this into paragraphs as your essay, you will need to add phrases, whole sentences, and missing information to make it flow smoothly and make sense.

THESIS: *Although they suffer consistent oppression by men throughout the novel, the women in* The Color Purple *by Alice Walker actually have more power than the men.*

CLAIM 1	CLAIM 2	CLAIM 3
When the men resort to physical force and intimidation, it is because of their own powerlessness.	*Celie handles sorrow and heartbreak more constructively than Mr. __.*	*Shug has visionary power over both men and women in the novel.*

CLAIM 1: *When the men resort to physical force and intimidation, it is because of their own powerlessness.*

EVIDENCE: (with page numbers) *Harpo and Sofia, p. 37: "How you 'spect to make her mind . . . good sound beating."*

Mr. __ and Celie, p. 79: ". . . he beat me for . . . bein' me and not you."

Pa and Celie, p. 1: "You better not never tell."

WARRANT: *Harpo is taught by his father that the way to assert male superiority, to "be a man," is to use the only advantage he has over a woman: physical force. Mr. __ himself feels like a loser without Shug, so he beats Celie out of frustration, because he can't make her Shug. Pa tells Celie not to tell anyone about his attack on her, threatening her with more.*

CLAIM 2: Celie handles sorrow and heartbreak more constructively than Mr. __.

EVIDENCE: (with page numbers)

WARRANT:

CLAIM 3: Shug has visionary power over both men and women in the novel.

EVIDENCE: (with page numbers)

WARRANT:

SAMPLE STUDENT-WRITTEN ESSAY

Body and Self

by Candy

In the book, *The Color Purple* by Alice Walker, Shug Avery taught Celie how to feel, love, and live for herself. In the beginning, Celie felt she didn't have any power over her body. Then, Shug taught Celie how to look at herself. After that, Celie began to feel something for Shug. And finally, Celie began to gain control over her feelings.

In the beginning, Celie didn't have any power over her body. Celie asks Shug: "You like to sleep with him? I ast . . . what is it like? He git up on you, heist your nightgown round your waist, plunge in. Most times I pretend I ain't there. He never know the difference. Never ast me how I feel, nothing. Just do his business, get off, go to sleep" (81). Celie could not say, "Mr. _, get up offa me!" cause she would of gotten beat by him. So, Celie felt she had no choice about what she wanted to do with her own body. Celie had no power or feelings when Mr. _ had sex with her.

Then, Shug Avery taught Celie how to look at herself. "She say, Here, take this mirror and go look at yourself down there. I bet you never seen it, have you?" (81). Celie goes and looks at herself and finds it fascinating. She never experienced looking at herself before. It gives her a feeling of power and independence. It teaches Celie to feel that she can have fun with sex and her own body.

After that, Celie started feeling something for Shug. "One night Shug was singing in Harpo's jukebox. All the men got their eyes glued to Shug's bosom. I got my eyes glued there too. I feel my nipples harden under my dress. My little button sort of perk up too. Shug, I say to her in my mind, Girl, you look like a real good time, the Good Lord knows you do" (85). Celie is starting to feel something for Shug and started feeling changes about her body. She is attracted to Shug now, and before, she did not feel she had the right or the power to be attracted to anyone.

Finally, Celie started to gain control over her feelings. At the end of the book, she says, "And then, just when I know I can live content without Shug . . . Shug write me, she coming home. Now. Is this life or not? I be so calm. If she come, I be happy. If she don't, I be content" (290). Celie says she can live a normal life with or without Shug. That's the biggest lesson of all. Celie finally has the power to realize that she is the one who is charge of herself. In spite of Mr. _'s abuse, her own ignorance, and her love for Shug, Celie has learned that she is in control.

In conclusion, Celie learns a lot from Shug Avery. Shug was an independent woman in the book. She had the strength to support a lot of people, she loved Celie and Celie loved Shug. By Shug's example, Celie learned how to become independent and live for herself.

ADDITIONAL LESSONS

Objective

- To continue application of unit concepts to popular works and other media

Materials

Any provocative works that question or reinforce popular depictions of gender and male/female sexuality are appropriate. Suggestions:

- Ice T, "Power" (lyrics and recording of song)

- Lyrics and recordings of other songs, supplied by teacher and/or students

- Film, *The Color Purple*

- Jarrett, Vernon, "The Beast in 'Purple' "

Procedures

- Make and distribute copies of the lyrics to a song of your choice. I have used Ice T's "Power," Sweet Honey in the Rock's "Oughta Be a Woman," and Was/Not Was's "Out Come the Freaks." Tell the class that this song must be treated as literature today and that, whether they like the song or not, it deserves their attention and respect, like any other piece of literature. Play the song and ask:

1. Is it sexist?
2. What types of power are in use?

Apply key questions and/or the four questions used to analyze the poetry in Lesson 7. See also INSTRUCTORS' NOTES I: USING MUSIC IN THE CLASSROOM (Chapter 4).

- Ask individuals or a group of students to bring in other song(s) to analyze. All students in the class must be given clear copies of lyrics; otherwise, critical analysis becomes impossible, and the class turns into music appreciation. Apply rigorous questioning and the four types of power detailed in Lesson 8 to characters in pop songs. Make sure students understand that the song must be relevant to the unit topic.

In past years, students have brought in "She's Always a Woman" by Billy Joel (1977), "Boys Don't Cry" by The Cure (1979), "I Ain't tha One" by NWA (1988), and "I Wonder if I Take You Home" by Lisa Lisa and Cult Jam/Full Force (1985) to illustrate the different ways power and identity are affected by gender and how all three issues impact relationships. Although not all songs were enjoyed by every student in every class, each one was listened to and analyzed. Students always have responded positively to this activity.

• See the film. Compare and contrast film with book. Do this orally, ask individual students to prepare a presentation for class, or assign it as a written exercise.

• Ask students if they think *The Color Purple* is racist or sexist. Distribute or read aloud Vernon Jarrett's commentary, "The Beast in 'Purple.' " Discuss and/or have students write opinions on his views.

6

⚎ Racism

Why do the white police officers think all Puerto Ricans are thieves?

—Migdalia

If someone who doesn't even know me gives me a hard time, I'm going to give it to them right back. But I don't want to be like that. I'm so tired of racism.

—Lettan

I know everyone here cares about me and they say they understand where I'm coming from. And everyone sees how fucked up the world is. But what if these things have a different impact on our lives than they do on yours?

—Ilia

RATIONALE

What Is the Topic of Study?

This unit tries to encourage honest communication between and about different peoples. We concentrate on ethnic groups represented in the class and in the surrounding area. We will begin with basic questions about racism: Why does it exist? What are the reasons for the conflicts between different groups of people? Will there always be tension between different peoples?

It is important to focus on *racism* rather than *race*. Although students might welcome the opportunities to celebrate their different heritages, this unit investigates issues of fear and bigotry more successfully than it teaches racial or ethnic pride. Besides, our time is too limited to do justice to any one group, and we want to be inclusive, not exclusive in our focus. Of course, classes who decide to study African American history or literature or who want to develop units on Latino culture should be encouraged to do so. The mix of students in many U.S. classrooms in the 1990s provides the imperative, opportunity, and resources we need to learn about each other.

Why Will Students Be Interested in Studying This?

Urban students are interested in the phenomenon of racism because they encounter it firsthand virtually every day. Students of all ages, at all levels, can recognize preferential treatment, name-calling, and the many other manifestations of racism that permeate life in the city. Just ask the students if they ever encounter racism. They will tell you.

Students will want to share stories about the racial stereotyping they have encountered themselves and also about the different customs and traits they have observed among various ethnic groups. Some will appreciate the opportunity to express frustration with the intolerance they have experienced or witnessed in school, in society at large, or at home. In this way the unit will investigate the different ways teens' lives are impacted by racism.

Why Do Students Need to Study This?

Beyond their personal experiences with racism, students invariably are drawn to examinations of injustice and imbalances of power. Currently, trendy T-shirts and radio songs promote messages of both separatism ("It's a Black Thing—You Wouldn't Understand") and interracial harmony ("Love Knows No Colors"). Students must go beyond the rhetoric of racism. This unit requires students to delve more deeply into the factors that make racism so universal and, at the same time, so personal. We will examine the fear, jealousy, and ignorance that leave none of us immune to racism. The long-range goal is to teach students to search for the real causes—competition for resources, education, and economic position—of racial bias and racism. These factors define their lives and limit their opportunities. Ultimately, students might reconsider redirecting their anger at the institutions and habits that pit them against, instead of in solidarity with, each other.

Why Teach This Unit Now?

This unit is designed for classes of varying reading levels. Everyone— even the uninterested and/or low-skilled students who do not read or watch the news—is aware of racism, hate groups, and racist and antiracist activism. There are good materials dealing with racism available for students reading at lower levels. These materials may be simplistic, but they engage the students, thereby improving reading skills, and afford us time to work on grammar basics.

On the other hand, more advanced students will be able to engage in critical debates on this difficult issue and read thought-provoking literature. These more sophisticated works engender discussions about our culture's simultaneous rejection and promotion of racism.

Racism is not always a good unit with which to begin a course. Although this is a universal and commonplace occurrence, racism's manifestations and impact are acutely personal. Students have been more comfortable sharing their perspectives after they know each other and the teacher. It is best to schedule this unit once the course has gotten off to a solid start. This unit does, however, serve as a good introduction to the student presentation. Lower level readers usually are able to find songs dealing with racism quite easily. Presentations give more advanced students a chance to read, formulate, and express critical responses to other's perspectives.

KEY QUESTIONS

1. What is racism? How has racism been apparent in our lives?

2. Why are individuals racist?

3. In what ways is our whole society racist? Why is it racist?

4. What can an individual do about racism?

TERMINAL OBJECTIVES

- To read stimulating works that are both challenging and engaging

- To present artistic works or sociohistorical perspectives of students' own choosing

- To consider and reflect on unit's key questions honestly and express views in writing

- To practice selected grammar basics

MATERIALS

Major Works

- Bennet, Jay (1991), *Skinhead*

- Terkel, Studs (1992), *Race: How Blacks and Whites Think and Feel About the American Obsession*

Articles

- Dreyfuss, Joel (1992), "White Men on Black Power"

- Malone, Bonz: Any of the "Radio Graffiti" columns in *Spin* magazine

- Marriott, Michel (1993), "Rap's Embrace of 'Nigger' Fires Bitter Debate"

- Nichols, Len M. (1990/1991), "Reducing Economic Inequality Can Stop Racism" in *Racism in America: Opposing Viewpoints*

- Smith, Danyel (1994), "Dreaming America: Hip Hop Culture"

- "The Roots of Economic Violence: Dim Economic Prospects for Young Men" (1987/1989) (excerpt reprinted here with permission)

Poems

- Chou, Noy (1990), "You Have to Live in Somebody Else's Country to Understand" (reprinted here with permission)

- Mora, Pat (1984), "Elena" (reprinted here with permission)

- Parker, Pat (1978), "For the white person who wants to be my friend" (reprinted here with permission)

Songs

- Paris (1989/1990), "The Hate That Hate Made"

Other Materials

- I found the Southern Poverty Law Center's magazine *Teaching Tolerance* to be a useful tool in putting together this unit. It lists useful books and other media and describes programs and policies in use around the world that promote cooperation and understanding among different peoples. Along with other resources (videos, texts, and teaching kits), it is available free to educators by writing to Teaching Tolerance, 400 Washington Avenue, Montgomery, AL 36014.

SAMPLE DAILY SCHEDULE
FOR LOWER LEVEL READERS

Day 1:   Lesson 1: Discuss stereotypes; stage role play.
          Characterize ethnicities according to popular stereotypes.

Day 2:   Lesson 2: Journal Assignment 1.

Day 3:   Lesson 3: Students work independently on HANDOUT 1:
             RACISM OPINIONNAIRE.
          Begin discussion of controversial statements on opinionnaire.

Day 4:   Continue discussing HANDOUT 1.
          Revise Journal Assignment 1 entries.

Day 5:   Lesson 4: Read and discuss poems by Mora and Chou;
             select vocabulary words.
          Homework: Define vocabulary words.

Day 6:   Refine vocabulary definitions; discuss usage and connotations.

Day 7:   Lesson 5: Class creates school racism survey.

Day 8:   Lesson 6: Students read and highlight articles on sources of racism.
          Homework: Complete reading.

Day 9:   Go over choices of highlighted sections.
          Discuss article. Begin questions on article (HANDOUT 3:
             "WHITE MEN ON BLACK POWER" QUESTIONS).

Day 10:   Complete handout; begin to discuss responses to questions
             handout.

Day 11:   Continue review of responses on handout; edit and revise responses.

Day 12:   Lesson 7: Review surveys from Lesson 5; tally results on
             poster paper.
          Try to characterize generic sources of racism.

Day 13:   Journal Assignment 2.

Day 14:   Lesson 8: Discuss and define nonstandard English; read sample.
          Consider and compare standard versus nonstandard English.

Day 15:   Work on selected standard English grammar exercises as needed.

Day 16:   Continued work with standard English exercises; students work
             in teams to correct each other's work.

Day 17:   Lesson 9: Journal Assignment 3.

Day 18:   Lesson 10: Introduce *Skinhead*; read opening chapter aloud.

Day 19:   In-class reading day.

Day 20:   Short reading quiz; discussion.

Day 21:   Complete HANDOUT 5: STORY MAP in groups.

Day 22:   Create discussion questions in groups.

Day 23:   Discussion using class-generated questions.
                 In-class reading.

Day 24:   Short reading quiz.
                 Homework: Students respond in writing to an "essay question"
                   of their choice.

Day 25:   Discuss homework essays.
                 Prepare for test.

Day 26:   Test on *Skinhead.*

Day 27:   Lesson 11: Discuss competition, economics, racism; read article.

Day 28:   Discuss article;
                 Journal Assignment 4.

Day 29:   Lesson 12: Model presentation using pop song; analyze song,
                   explain presentation criteria.
                 Schedule student presentations.

Day 30:   Work on journal revisions (Journal 4, other entries).

Days 31-38:   Student presentations.

Day 39:   Students evaluate presentations.

SAMPLE DAILY SCHEDULE
FOR HIGHER LEVEL READERS

Day 1: Lesson 1: Discuss stereotypes; stage role play.
Characterize ethnicities according to popular stereotypes

Day 2: Lesson 2: Journal Assignment 1.

Day 3: Lesson 3: Students work independently on HANDOUT 1:
RACISM OPINIONNAIRE.
Begin discussion of controversial statements on opinionnaire.

Day 4: Continue discussing HANDOUT 1.
Revise Journal Assignment 1 entries.

Day 5: Lesson 4: Read and discuss poetry by Mora and Chou.
Small groups define vocabulary associated with race and racism.

Day 6: Discuss vocabulary terms: usage, relevance in literary
and personal contexts.
Read Parker poem, discuss separatism.

Day 7: Lesson 5: Students discuss in small groups using HANDOUT 2:
DISCUSSION GUIDE ON SOURCES OF RACISM.
Assess discussions as a class.

Day 8: Lesson 6: Students read and highlight articles on sources of racism.
Homework: Complete reading.

Day 9: Go over choices of highlighted sections.
Discuss article.
Begin questions on article (HANDOUT 4: "REDUCING ECONOMIC
INEQUALITY CAN STOP RACISM" STUDY GUIDE).

Day 10: Complete handout; begin to discuss responses to questions
on handout.

Day 11: Continue review of responses on handout.
Edit and revise responses.

Day 12: Lesson 7: Review HANDOUT 2: DISCUSSION GUIDE ON SOURCES OF
RACISM and the poster prepared in Lesson 5.
Try to characterize generic sources of racism.

Day 13: Journal Assignment 2.

Day 14: Lesson 8: Discuss and define nonstandard English, read sample.
Consider and compare standard versus nonstandard English.

Day 15:   Work on selected standard English grammar exercises as needed.

Day 16:   Continued work with standard English exercises; students work
            in teams to correct each other's work.

Day 17:   Lesson 9: Journal Assignment 3.

Day 18:   Lesson 10: Introduce Terkel's *Race* and independent reading format.
            Distribute sample chapter, finish for homework.

Day 19:   Model presentation on sample chapter (presentation given
            by instructor).
            Distribute notes on chapter's necessary information.
            Assign reading sections to students.

Days 20-23: Read individual assigned sections in class and at home.
            Begin to prepare for presentations.

Day 24:   Discuss and process characters in assigned sections with a partner.
            Choose one character to present to the class; prepare notes on
            necessary information.

Days 25-28: Student presentations.

Day 29:   Student presentations.
            Students who already have presented can share effective strategies
            for preparation and presentation.

Day 30:   Lesson 11: Discuss competition: Relate competition for economic
            resources to racism.
            Read article.

Day 31:   Journal Assignment 4.
            Continue with student presentations as needed (through day 35).

Day 36:   Evaluate presentations; discuss larger picture of racism that has
            become apparent.

Day 37:   Lesson 12: Introduce scenario to be discussed on panel talk show;
            create and assign roles.
            Write short position papers "in character" to prepare for videotaping.

Day 38:   Stage and videotape panel talk show.

Day 39:   Watch and discuss yesterday's taped exercise.

Day 40:   Evaluate unit.

LESSON 1: WHAT ARE RACIAL STEREOTYPES?

Objectives

- To begin discussions of race and racism

- To define and demonstrate the predominance of racial stereotypes

- To discredit the notion of racial stereotypes

Materials

- "Hello my name is" tags or other name tags students can wear

Procedures

- Begin with an explanation of the word *stereotype*. Ask class to describe a stereotypical character in a TV show or movie: the "dumb blonde," the "nerd with glasses," the "black gangsta," and so forth. Discuss with students whether these characterizations are true and why or why not.

- Extend this concept to the idea of race using a carefully staged role play. Explain the purpose of the activity beforehand. If desired, distribute HAND-OUT H: ROLE PLAYING (in Chapter 4).

We need to be careful with the role play. It can become a type of sanctioned opportunity for students to display real bigotry and insensitivity. Teachers must be careful to stress the conclusion just reached by the class in discussions of blondes on TV: Generalizations are unfair and pointless.

Before we start this exercise I post a note on the board:

WARNING!

You probably will be offended by some statements made during this next activity. Please—do not show your responses to the ignorant, improvised comments you hear about different ethnic groups. Our purpose is to expose these racist stereotypes. We will examine all statements after the activity.

- Choose a small group of students to role play for the next step of this activity. Assign ethnic identities: Give students name tags that list their "new" ethnic groups: African American, Asian, Latino, White, and Jewish. (It is interesting to assign a few of these roles so that they are consistent with students' ethnicities and to assign others so that they differ from students' actual ethnicity.) Vary the categories as appropriate for the community, naming each group as specifically as possible. Tell the rest of the class to pay attention and note the generalizations that characters make about themselves and each other.

- Set up a role play: Participating students all are competing for the one remaining 3-bedroom apartment in a safe, newly rehabbed building. They have been waiting outside the landlord's office for almost an hour and are starting to get frustrated. Remind students to play roles—try to keep the dialogue realistic and stay in character. Let the dialogue play out so that students not only spoof their own "identities" but start to call names and comment on each other's supposed characteristics. Depending on the actors, role plays can last from 2 to 10 minutes.

- Call a halt to the role play when it starts getting ugly or once it goes on long enough to have established the characters' tendencies to resort to racial stereotypes. Ask students to identify the stereotypes and assumptions made by characters in the role play.

- Across the top of the board, write *African American, Asian, Latino, White,* and *Jewish* (adding or substituting other appropriate categories depending on your community) and ask students to supply the stereotypical characteristics of these groups. You can add groups that were not used in the role play. The purpose is to expose racial stereotypes espoused—consciously and not—in our society. Everyone will be uncomfortable with this at first. Keep emphasizing that this exposure seeks not to concede but to destroy stereotypes.

This acknowledgment of racist aspersions is a highly provocative and potentially dangerous activity! Teachers who are unsure about their ability to maintain a respectful and academic discussion around these issues should cut out this step. Students of various ethnicities will feel singled out and maligned if the goal of the lesson—to note and then discredit the idea of ethnic stereotyping—is not effectively presented and stressed.

- Define and discuss the concept of *stereotype.* If students have been engaged in this activity, it is best to try to retain and use that momentum by segueing immediately into Lesson 2. If time permits, assign Journal 1 (see next lesson) in class or for homework.

LESSON 2: PERSONAL EXPERIENCE WITH RACIAL STEREOTYPING

Objectives

- To recount personal experiences with racial stereotypes

- To consider peers' accounts of racial stereotyping and to begin to examine some of the ways in which teens' lives are affected by racism

Materials

- None

Procedures

- Write Journal Assignment 1 on board: Write about a time you witnessed or experienced racial stereotyping.

- Take a few minutes to review yesterday's activity. Discuss situations in which students may have been treated particularly because of other people's racist assumptions. Suggest sites where this can happen: on the streets, in stores, in schools, and visiting friends' houses.

- Tell students that it is important that they try to tell the whole story, not just what was said to them. If they can relate facial expressions, tones of voice, body language, and their own feelings, their stories will do a much better job describing the idiocy and injustice of racial stereotypes.

- Read the following samples aloud, if desired. If Journal 1 entries are to be revised, both versions can be used to illustrate the importance of revision:

Chris's first entry:

My mother and I decided to go to the Brickyard to by some pants for me. We were walking around looking for the pants that I wanted to buy. She was in back of me.

There was a police officer there and when he seen me he started walking in front of my mother. He thought that I was by myself. He was following me all over the store. My mother told me in Spanish that he was following me. She yelled at him for following me.

Revision:

"I don't have all day, Ma. I got to go to work."

"Don't worry, hijo. We'll just run in the store and get those pants you want," she said. So we went to the Brickyard Mall to buy some pants, and instead we found racial stereotyping.

We started walking around together. My mom was in back of me. A cop saw me, and was on my tail in a minute. He started following me, walking in front of my mother. He thought that I was by myself. He was following me all over the store.

My mom came up to me. "I think this police officer is following you," she said in Spanish.

"I know. Since we came in the store he's been following me."

My mom got so mad she turned and yelled at the police officer, "What is your fucking problem, following my son around?"

"Sorry," said the cop.

"Let's go home," interrupted my mom. "Just because we're Spanish, this officer thinks we're thieves. We will come buy your pants another day."

White police officers are going to see you first, and ask questions later. The cop wasn't really sorry at all. So what, we left. All the while I was asking myself, did her telling him off really do anything?

• This is a good exercise for revision. Depending on formal objectives, instructors can ask for revisions that include dialogue, description, language mechanics, and so on. I like to (ask permission and then) read two students' journals out loud to the class, both of which tell a good story—one of which is detailed and descriptive, the other of which is not. We spend time generating criteria for a good story, and then students work in pairs to revise their journals. Sample criteria for "What makes a story good?":

Dialogue—with correct punctuation

Descriptions of characters' looks and voices

Descriptions of setting

Main character describes how she or he feels

• Once students are done writing or once their journals have been returned, it is a good idea to have as many of these revisions read aloud as possible. Have each student who reads his or hers aloud prepare one discussion question about it (I had students pose this question as the final line of their journal revisions).

LESSON 3: STUDENT OPINION ON RACE AND RACISM

Objectives

- To identify and reflect on student opinions about racism

- To identify and reflect on student opinions about other races

- To begin to examine sources of beliefs concerning race and racism

Materials

- HANDOUT 1: RACISM OPINIONNAIRE

Procedures

- Distribute HANDOUT 1 and ask students to work on this independently. Explain that there are no right or wrong answers and that no one is being graded on his or her opinions. Students should understand the purpose of the opinionnaire: to allow each of them to get in touch with his or her own beliefs and prejudices, and to try to identify the sources of these feelings.

- Gauging class reaction, engage students in discussions of selected opinionnaire questions. Ask students to explain their responses by giving examples and relating anecdotes. Discussion formats should accommodate class's interest and skill levels.

Lower skilled classes (sixth- to seventh-grade reading level) who have responded positively to this exercise have enjoyed short discussions focusing on only three or four questions. We chose three questions to focus on the first day and then came back to two more questions the next day. With classes who have expressed disdain or who otherwise reject the exercise, I have had success asking students to pick one question and explain their feelings on the back of the paper in writing.

Of course, students who enjoy discussions easily can devote the rest of the class period to an open discussion of the issues presented in the opinionnaire. I also sometimes ask students to move into small groups of four or five as they finish the opinionnaire and to discuss their responses there.

- After class has discussed the racism opinionnaire, ask students what they learned from the exercise.

- Because this activity sometimes can take only 15 minutes or so in classes in which students do not engage readily in discussions, it can be combined with a lesson on writing mechanics (for use in revising Journal 1 entries).

HANDOUT 1: RACISM OPINIONNAIRE

Directions: Read each of the statements below and tell whether you strongly agree (circle 1), strongly disagree (circle 5), or fall somewhere in the middle (circle 2, 3, or 4). Think of your own experiences and feelings and be as honest as you can.

1. Small children start out with no prejudices.
   1   2   3   4   5

2. No ethnic group or race is better than any other.
   1   2   3   4   5

3. Because of their experiences or natural abilities, some groups do deserve special benefits.
   1   2   3   4   5

4. Everyone is racist.
   1   2   3   4   5

5. It is important to learn as much as possible about all cultures and ethnic groups.
   1   2   3   4   5

6. My ethnicity is a very important part of my identity.
   1   2   3   4   5

7. I share many of my parents' opinions about other races and ethnic groups.
   1   2   3   4   5

8. I share many of my friends' opinions about other races and ethnic groups.
   1   2   3   4   5

9. The media represent my ethnicity accurately.
   1   2   3   4   5

10. I feel that racism is a huge problem in our society.
    1   2   3   4   5

11. I feel that racism is a huge problem in my life.
    1   2   3   4   5

LESSON 4: RESPONDING TO HATRED

Objectives

- To read direct and emotional accounts of prejudice in interpersonal relations

- To define terms related to race and racism

Materials

- UNIT MATERIALS: "You Have to Live in Somebody Else's Country to Understand" by Noy Chou

- UNIT MATERIALS: "Elena" by Pat Mora

- UNIT MATERIALS: "For the white person who wants to be my friend" by Pat Parker

Procedures

- Distribute UNIT MATERIALS: "You Have to Live in Somebody Else's Country to Understand" by Noy Chou and "Elena" by Pat Mora. Students should read poems aloud. Discuss the emotional weight carried by the speakers in the poems. Ask students to delineate the hardships both Elena and Noy undergo. Ask them to compare the two and judge which character "has it rougher." Tally votes on the board and ask students to defend their judgments. This exercise can be done in writing.

- Discuss with students:

  1. Are Elena's children prejudiced?
  2. Are Noy's classmates racist? Bigoted? Discriminatory?
  3. What is the difference between these terms?

Write a list of words on the board that will help students articulate their observations about race and racism. Select words as appropriate for students' reading levels. Here is a sample list of words:

Prejudice. Racism. Bigotry. Discrimination. Intolerance. Xenophobia.
Race. Ethnicity. Creed.
Militance. Integration. Segregation. Separatism. Depersonalization.

Have students define the words in groups, looking up those that are new to them and differentiating between related terms such as *discrimination* and *bigotry.* Students can use these words to identify characters and situations in the poems and relate them to personal experiences.

• Distribute copies of the Pat Parker poem, reprinted here as UNIT MATERIALS: "For the white person who wants to be my friend." Students reading at lower levels have trouble with the satire in this poem. Have students read the poem and ask for their reactions. Here are some ideas to start with:

1. What are the contradictions in this poem?
2. Are such contradictions inherent in any relationship between people of different races?
3. What implications does this have for peaceful coexistence and co-operation between the races?

Responses to these and similar questions may be assigned as written exercises.

You Have to Live in Somebody Else's Country to Understand

by Noy Chou

What is it like to be an outsider?
What is it like to sit in the class where everyone has blond hair and you have black hair?
What is it like when the teacher says, "Whoever wasn't born here raise your hand."
And you are the only one.
Then, when you raise your hand, everybody looks at you and makes fun of you.
You have to live in somebody else's country to understand.

What is it like when the teacher treats you like you've been here all your life?
What is it like when the teacher speaks too fast and you are the only one who can't understand what he or she is saying, and you try to tell him or her to slow down.
Then when you do, everybody says, "If you don't understand, go to a lower class or get lost."
You have to live in somebody else's country to understand.

What is it like when you are an opposite? When you wear the clothes of your country and they think you are crazy to wear those clothes and you think they are pretty.
You have to live in somebody else's country to understand.

What is it like when you are always a loser?
What is it like when somebody bothers you when you do nothing to them?
You tell them to stop but they tell you that they didn't do anything to you.
Then, when they keep doing it until you can't stand it any longer, you go up to the teacher and tell him or her to tell them to stop bothering you.
They say that they didn't do anything to bother you.
Then the teacher asks the person sitting next to you.
He says, "Yes, she didn't do anything to her" and you have no witness to turn to.
So the teacher thinks you are a liar.
You have to live in somebody else's country to understand.

What is it like when you try to talk and you don't pronounce the words right? They don't understand you.

They laugh at you but you don't know that they are laughing at you,
and you start to laugh with them. They say, "Are you crazy, laughing
at yourself?
Go get lost, girl."
You have to live in somebody else's country to understand.

What is it like when you walk in the street and everybody turns
around to look at you and you don't know that they are looking at you.
Then, when you find out, you want to hide your face but you don't
know where to hide because they are everywhere.
You have to live in somebody else's country to feel it.

SOURCE: "You Have to Live in Somebody Else's Country to Understand" by Noy
Chou, ninth grade, first appeared in *Locked In/Locked Out: Tracking and Placement
Practices in Boston Public Schools.* 1990. Boston: Massachusetts Advocacy Center.
Reprinted with permission.

Elena

by Pat Mora

My Spanish isn't enough.
I remember how I'd smile listening to my little ones,
understanding every word they'd say,
their jokes, their songs, their plots.
    Vamos a pedirle dulces a mama, Vamos.
But that was in Mexico.
Now my children go to American high schools.
They speak English. At night they sit around
the kitchen table, laugh with one another.
I stand by the stove and feel dumb, alone.
I bought a book to learn English.
My husband frowned, drank more beer.
My oldest said, "Mama, he doesn't want you
to be smarter than he is." I'm forty,
embarrassed at mispronouncing words,
embarrassed at the laughter of my children,
the grocer, the mailman. Sometimes I take
my English book and lock myself in the bathroom,
say the words softly,
for if I stop trying, I will be deaf
when my children need my help.

SOURCE: "Elena" by Pat Mora is reprinted with permission from the publisher of *Chants* (Houston: Arte Publico Press—University of Houston, 1984).

For the white person who wants to be my friend

by Pat Parker

The first thing you must do is forget i'm Black.
Second, you must never forget that i'm Black.

You should be able to dig Aretha,
but don't play her every time i come over.
And if you decide to play Beethoven—don't tell me
his life story. They made us take music appreciation too.

Eat soul food if you like it, but don't expect me
to locate your restaurants
or cook it for you.

And if some Black person insults you,
mugs you, rapes your sister, rapes you,
rips your house or is just being an ass—
please, do not apologize to me
for wanting to do them bodily harm.
It makes me wonder if you're foolish.

And even if you really believe Blacks are better lovers than
whites—don't tell me. I start thinking of charging stud fees.

In other words—if you really want to be my friend—*don't*
make a labor of it. I'm lazy. Remember.

SOURCE: "For the white person who wants to be my friend" by Pat Parker. From MOVEMENT IN BLACK by Pat Parker. Firebrand Books, Ithaca, NY. Copyright © 1978 by Pat Parker. Reprinted with permission.

Two sets of procedures are specified for the next lesson, one for students reading at a lower (6th- to 7th-grade) level and one for those reading at a higher (11th- to 12th-grade) level. Instructors of students whose skills fall between these levels should gauge which lesson would be most effective for their students.

Skip to page 164 for Lesson 5 (for Higher Level Readers).

LESSON 5: STUDENT INVESTIGATIONS INTO SOURCES OF RACISM
(for lower level readers)

Objectives

- To encourage student dialogue about sources of racism

- To expand the scope of student investigation into race and racism

- To lead the investigation into student-directed routes and areas of interest

Materials

- SAMPLE: MODEL SCHOOL RACISM SURVEY (included for instructors' reference; each class should create their own survey)

- Large piece of poster paper or newsprint

Procedures

- Select questions from the MODEL SCHOOL RACISM SURVEY, writing them on the board (or distribute copies of the provided MODEL SCHOOL RACISM SURVEY and ask students to fill them out as a first step to creating their own survey). Ask students to report their responses. Run a tally of these responses on the board. Examine the statistics, breaking them down by respondents' racial categories, noting general agreements and wide disparities. Ask students if they think their friends and families would give the same responses they did.

- Suggest that the class create a better survey, one that asks the questions that really get at the roots of racism. Work with the class to refine and personalize the questions to accommodate their concerns. If you have access to a copier, ask one or more students to draft a copy-ready version of the survey. Duplicate copies for students to distribute. I prefer this format to oral polling: It provides more accessible and precise results.

- Tell students to use this racism survey to poll their friends and family members.

- Give students most of a week to collect responses to the survey questions. Specify the date by which all responses are to be collected and tallied. Students should be able to choose how many people they survey or if they want to participate in the survey at all. Set up a collection box for all completed surveys.

- On the specified date, create a large grid to report and tally survey results. List each question along the left side of one large piece of poster paper. Across the top, write all racial/ethnic categories of survey respondents. Students should organize completed surveys and call out responses to be tallied and recorded.

- Tally responses. Work with the class to note general trends. The class should take notes (title these notes "School Racism Survey") to help them process the information. They should save these notes for use later on in the unit.

- Post survey results in the room. It will serve to remind students of their investigation into race and racism and will provide a reference point for future discussions.

SAMPLE: MODEL SCHOOL RACISM SURVEY

No names necessary; what is your race? _____

1. Did you have friends of other races when you were growing up?
   ___ no   ___ some   ___ a lot

2. When you were growing up, were you taught that people of other races were
   ___ better   ___ the same   ___ worse than you?

3. Now that you're older, do you feel ___ the same or ___different (about other races) as you did when you were a child?

4. What race or ethnic group do you remember hearing something negative about when you were young?
   ___ African American   ___ White
   ___ Latino   ___ Jewish
   ___ Asian   ___ Arabic
   ___ Native American   ___ Other(s) _____

5. Did you ___ agree, ___ disagree, or ___ feel confused about these negative remarks?

6. Can you remember receiving any positive messages about your own race or ethnic group?
   ___ yes   ___ no   ___ can't remember

7. Where did these positive messages come from? (Check all that apply)
   ___ family   ___ friends   ___ school
   ___ the media (TV, movies, newspapers, etc.)

8. Have you been a victim of racial stereotyping or other prejudice?
   ___ constantly   ___ sometimes   ___ never

9. When you were younger and you saw people of other races getting special treatment, did this make you feel
   ___ confused   ___ inferior (not as good as)
   ___ upset or angry   ___ all of the above

10. Are any of your relatives ___ more racist or ___ less racist than you? Or are you ___ all the same?

11. Do you feel that things are getting ___ better or ___ worse as far as racism is concerned? Do you think anyone can do anything about it?
    ___ yes   ___ no

Survey created and evaluated by Lettan, Tennille, Keith, Janice, Charles, Dalia, Mike L., Chris N., Roman, Mario, Danny, Sarina, Dahnetta, Rob, Thomas, Sandra, Daisy, Justin, Liza, Demont, Kitty, James G., Irene, Evernell, Jennifer, Tito, Darvin, Angela, and Vikkiey. THANK YOU.

LESSON 5: STUDENT INVESTIGATIONS INTO SOURCES OF RACISM
(for higher level readers)

Objectives

- To encourage student dialogue about sources of racism

- To expand the scope of student investigation into race and racism

- To lead the investigation into student-directed routes and areas of interest

Materials

- HANDOUT 2: DISCUSSION GUIDE ON SOURCES OF RACISM

- Large piece of poster paper or newsprint

Procedures

- Distribute HANDOUT 2: DISCUSSION GUIDE ON SOURCES OF RACISM. Have directions read aloud. This handout works well with older/higher skilled students; it does not engage the less mature or lower skilled students who often are uncomfortable with sustained class discussions.

- Ask students to divide themselves into small groups that will engender the most candid discussions: They can choose to mix ethnicities in groups or keep these groups homogeneous. For the purposes of this activity, it is essential that students feel comfortable.

- After students have discussed the issues suggested on the guide or when there are about 10 minutes left in class, reconvene class to assess discussions. Ask class to consider the question at the bottom of the guide ("Based on your group's stories and experiences, can you identify any sources of racism?"). Ask them to articulate what they learned from this exercise.

- Note possible sources of racism or other striking conclusions and commentary reported by students in the course of their discussions. Write or ask a student to write these notes on a large piece of poster paper. Post this in the room. It will serve to remind students of their investigation into race and racism among teenagers and will provide a reference point for future discussions.

HANDOUT 2: DISCUSSION GUIDE ON SOURCES OF RACISM

Directions:

1. Assign someone in the group to read the questions aloud. This person will act as group leader today.

2. After each question is read, each group member can talk about his or her experiences, or she or he can "pass," if necessary.

3. Go with new issues or subtopics as they come up—but your group leader should try to rein things in after a few minutes so that the group can discuss all issues on this sheet.

Your group should try to work together, giving each person as much time as they need to remember and contribute to the conversation.

1. As a child, did you have friends of other races? Did you go to their houses? Did your parents support or try to prevent these friendships?

2. What can you remember thinking about other races when you were a small child? Did you grow up thinking that some people were better than others? Explain.

3. What was the first thing—negative or positive—you can remember hearing or learning about people of another race? What were the circumstances surrounding this "lesson"?

4. What TV shows or movies did you watch that were about other races? What stereotypes did they reinforce? Did you believe them? Do you still?

5. As a child, were you ever jealous of people of another race or culture? What was the situation?

6. Are there some people in your family who are more or less racist than you, yourself? How do you know this? What effect do you think this has had on you?

7. Do you have friends who you know are more or less racist than you are? How do you know this? What effect do you think this has had on you?

8. What do you think is the future of racism? Will the problem of the 21st century also be "the color line"?

9. Based on your group's stories and experiences, can you identify any sources of racism?

This lesson can be used both for students reading at a lower (6th to 7th grade) level and for those reading at a higher (11th to 12th grade) level. Instructors of students whose skills fall between these levels should gauge which materials would be most effective for their students. The procedures are the same for both. Materials and handouts are specified as to lower or higher level readers.

LESSON 6: FURTHER INVESTIGATION INTO THE SOURCES OF RACISM
(for lower and higher level readers)

Objectives

- To develop critical reading skills (for lower level readers)

- To stress and practice critical reading skills (for higher level readers)

- To understand and process concepts presented in challenging reading materials

- To practice underlining and other good note-taking habits

- To identify some of the sources of racism

Materials

Short articles dealing with individual perceptions about the sources of racism. I use:

- Dreyfuss, Joel, "White Men on Black Power" (For lower level readers, I copied and abridged this article from *Essence* magazine in four concise pages. I knew these students would have trouble with the vocabulary and sophisticated tone so I made sure that they would not be put off by its length. For higher level readers, the article can be used in its entirety.)

- Nichols, Len M., "Reducing Economic Inequality Can Stop Racism," in *Racism in America: Opposing Viewpoints* (for higher level readers)

- HANDOUT 3: "WHITE MEN ON BLACK POWER" QUESTIONS (for lower level readers)

- HANDOUT 4: "REDUCING ECONOMIC INEQUALITY CAN STOP RACISM" STUDY GUIDE (for higher level readers)

Procedures

- Distribute readings. Explain to class that this reading is different from most other assignments: In order to complete the assignment, they must read and then *write* on the handouts.

- After each student has received a copy of the reading, demonstrate critical reading of one passage. Start by reading the first paragraph aloud. Ask the students what was important in that paragraph. Have students note these selected passages. Check that each student does underline the noted section(s). Next, ask the class for their reactions to the underlined section or any other part of the paragraph. Have them jot down their ideas in the margins. Explain that critical readers never just blindly accept what they read, that student response to the information is at least as important as what they read. Give a few examples of subjective commentary that a critical reader might note in margins (e.g., for lower level readers: "No poor white men were interviewed by *Essence!*" For higher level readers, "Nichols is talking about white urban dwellers only!").

- Explain to students that this is intended to make less, not more work for them. When the time comes for them to skim the article (to answer questions on the reading), all the salient points will be highlighted and easier to find. When the time comes to discuss the reading, their own objections and agreements already will be noted (right next to the textual support that teachers require). Not every paragraph will contain something to underline, question, or agree with. Students need mark only the parts that matter.

- As students read (if they are completing the assignment for homework, this next step will need to be adapted the next day, in class), monitor their highlighting. Stop periodically to bring attention to particularly critical commentary or to issues that have escaped students' attention. It is not important that all students underline and/or comment on the same passages. This exercise is designed to recognize and appreciate students' individual viewpoints and perspectives.

- Assign questions or study guides designed to show students the efficacy of underlining significant passages in their readings. Use HANDOUT 3: "WHITE MEN ON BLACK POWER" QUESTIONS for lower level readers. Use HANDOUT 4: "REDUCING ECONOMIC INEQUALITY CAN STOP RACISM" STUDY GUIDE for higher level readers. Tell students that they are to try to answer all questions. Allow students to work at their own pace.

- When the majority of students are done working, go over the questions. Read each aloud, discuss, and have students self-correct their responses. Tell them to listen to peers' opinions and commentary, to add to and adapt these ideas, and to make their own answers complete. These answers are their notes, which they will use to complete the final assignment in the study of racism's sources. Discuss each question, asking students if they highlighted any information pertinent to it when they were reading, and if this highlighting helped them answer the questions efficiently.

HANDOUT 3: "WHITE MEN ON BLACK POWER" QUESTIONS

1. What does Sey Chessler think drives White men to push Black men "to some edge"?

2. What does Bill Adler say makes White men fear Black men?

3. On page 3 of the article, Jonathan Van Meter (who is 29 years old) argues with Andrew Hackler (age 62) and Anthony DeCurtis (age 41). What do they disagree about? Which side do you agree with and why?

4. What are two ways that White society has tried to "de-male" Black men?

5. In what important way are famous Black rappers successful?

6. Read the paragraph spoken by DeCurtis on page 4. Look up the word *immaterial*. What do you think DeCurtis is saying here?

7. Why is Jesse Jackson a threat to White America?

8. What role does the media play in presenting Black men in a negative way? Explain your answer to this question by giving an example. On the back of this paper, write about something you actually saw or read.

HANDOUT 4: "REDUCING ECONOMIC INEQUALITY CAN STOP RACISM" STUDY GUIDE

What does Len M. Nichols do for a living?

1. What, according to Nichols, defined the racism of his youth? What does he believe is the foundation of racism today?

2. What differences between Blacks (which had been submerged before) did the successes of the civil rights movement make obvious? Why is this important?

3. In the past, various ethnic groups—Italian, Russian Jews, and Irish—emigrated to the United States and "made it." What, according to Nichols, is the primary difference between those groups and the current Black underclass? What could be some reasons for this difference?

4. In what sense does Nichols say it is more "costly" for a young, inner-city Black boy to take school seriously than it is for a suburban, middle-class boy of any race? Explain his reasoning. Do you think he is sympathetic to young, inner-city Black boys? Or is he blaming them? Give evidence for your answer.

5. What does Nichols mean when he says, "The decision to take the lawful, hard-working path within the inner city is a hard choice for attempting to emigrate slowly from an oppressive and dangerous land"?

6. How are crime and economic inequality related, according to Nichols? Do you agree?

7. What is the critical "impossibility" for White suburbanites (which is responsible for what Nichols calls the "new racism")?

8. Sum up Nichols's viewpoint on the sources of racism in one or two sentences. Feel free to comment.

LESSON 7: SUMMING UP AND COMMENTING ON SOURCES OF RACISM

Objectives

- To identify all sources of racism raised by recent class activities and in readings

- To evaluate those sources of racism

- To reflect on and express feelings about at least one of these sources

Materials (students should have completed handouts)

- Completed HANDOUT 1: RACISM OPINIONNAIRE

- Completed school racism surveys and poster of tallied results (lower level readers) or

- Completed HANDOUT 2: DISCUSSION GUIDE ON SOURCES OF RACISM and "Sources of Racism" poster (higher level readers)

- Completed questions/study guides that accompanied Lesson 6 readings:

HANDOUT 3: "WHITE MEN ON BLACK POWER" QUESTIONS or
HANDOUT 4: "REDUCING ECONOMIC INEQUALITY CAN STOP RACISM"
    STUDY GUIDE

Procedures

- Ask students to produce all specified materials. As a final summary exercise, ask them to call out the various sources of racism each activity or reading brought out. Try to group similar emotional sources (intimidation and suspicion) into broader categories (fear). These sources need not have been expressed explicitly; ask students to "read between the lines" if necessary and name the more implicit sources of racism present in their studies. List the sources on the board.

When my students did this exercise, we came up with the following sources of racism: fear of different peoples, jealousy of different peoples, ignorance about other cultures, and desire for retaliation. It is a good idea for teachers to reflect on the results of the various exercises and the readings first and then facilitate the students' discussion. In this way, teachers can help students with the difficult task of making inferences and generalizations.

- Write Journal Assignment 2 on the board: Pick one of the sources of racism named by the class and relate a personal experience to illustrate it.

Begin by asking students if they think the resulting list is accurate. Ask them if they have had any experiences witnessing racism that came out of jealousy, fear, ignorance, or retaliation. Suggest the following opening lines for Journal 2: (substituting your class's conclusions for fear, jealousy, ignorance, and so forth): "Fear, jealousy, ignorance, and a desire for retaliation are all sources of racism. I, myself, have seen racism born of _____." Have each student end his or her piece with a reflective question. Here is an example of one student's journal entry that could have focused on a specific incident but did not. Instead, the writer, 18-year-old Lettan, speaks in generalities, only hinting at real-life experience, pain, and knowledge. The piece would benefit from revision:

Fear, retaliation and jealousy are all sources of racism. I've seen racism born of jealousy. There are some people out there who are in love with other races. I think that we should all stop and learn about each other. But the way some people think, they are too good for their own kind, or maybe they hate they self. It can't be a good feeling, even though I know some black boys who like to run after only white girls or real light skinned girls.

To me, I like all people. I may be jealous of a person because I'm only human, but this is not going to make me a bigot. When someone say things I don't like I do sink to their level, and I even say worse things back. When it's all over I feel bad because people don't need to fight especially when we are the same race. But honestly, I'm getting tired of all that. I'm not sure how it can stop, when people are so petty. Sometimes I wonder why there's so many small minds in the world?

LESSON 8: IS "DIFFERENT" WRONG? EVALUATING NONSTANDARD ENGLISH

Objectives

- To discuss the advantages and the limitations of nonstandard English

- To consider the consequences of adopting and of rejecting this norm

- To determine and improve individual weaknesses in writing standard English

Materials

- Any one of Bonz Malone's "Radio Graffiti" columns from *Spin* magazine

Procedures

- Ask students to read the column, which is written in the nonstandard English used by rappers and street kids. Note students' reactions and questions on one side of the board. (My students said: "This is crazy!" "I can't read this!" "What?" "This man can't spell!")

- Focus on style rather than on the piece's content. Inform students: Malone is a "real" writer, whose work has appeared in several publications. What is the point of writing like this? Is it more difficult or easier to read than standard English? What might Malone be trying to accomplish? Is he successful?

- Using Malone's column as a reference point, work with the class to define standard and nonstandard English. List a few common nonstandard expressions (i.e., "I be fittin' to . . ." "What up?" "He don't never . . .") on the board. (Instructors may have to provide these if students are unsure about what is and is not standard.) Discuss where each style is most commonly found. Ask students to discuss the limitations of nonstandard phrases:

  1. When is it okay to use them?
  2. When might using them hurt you in some way?

- Let the class analyze any one of these issues:

  1. What is the relationship between this language issue and racism?
  2. Is *standard* just a politically correct term for *White?*
  3. Do people of color always need to change they way they communicate in order to succeed? Does this signify advancement? Assimilation? "Selling out"?
  4. What are the consequences of being unable to speak or write standard English when applying for a job? In school? On the streets?

5. Are there any negative consequences of being able to speak only standard English?

Here is a sample from one of my classes:

If people of color "talk White," they can:

Pros	Cons
make good impression in school	lose credibility on streets
make good impression on job	be considered conceited
"get away with shit," sometimes be perceived as smarter	alienate friends and family
get in a position to help their people have more power in society	betray their nation diminish cultural diversity

- Evaluate the benefits of studying standard (White) English in class:

  1. What do you think about cultural variations in expression?
  2. Is "different" wrong?
  3. Is slang unacceptable? Where? In what situations?

My students agreed with the following sentiment: "I believe that a student who says 'he don't' and 'I ain't' for 14 years probably will not change his language patterns in high school. Therefore, we should not spend time and money attempting to correct such errors in high school English classes" (Hayden, 1967).

They did, however, feel compelled to learn and practice certain grammar basics (notably, parts of speech for grammar tests and subject-verb agreement for other writing assignments). Ideally, they said, people should be able to speak however they want and should have the skills to "sound White" on paper, because that is what is still considered correct by most readers.

- Based on student need, assign short grammar exercises from standard textbooks. I use *English Grammar and Composition* (Warriner & Graham, 1977) and GED preparation materials (Mulcrone, 1990; Romanek, 1987), assigning exercises that students agree they need to work on—mostly subject-verb agreement, pluralization, and using compound verbs. Depending on student skill level, this grammar work can take one day to one week. I have found it best to keep the focus on racism and limit straight grammar exercises to three days at the most. Always, we stress the reasons why we are choosing to develop these writing skills. In general, the White students I teach come from backgrounds in which few family members received formal education: They, too, speak the nonstandard language they learn on the streets. If there are students in your class who speak and write standard English correctly, pair them up with peers as grammar tutors.

LESSON 9: IS "DIFFERENT" WRONG?
SOCIETY AND RACE IN STUDENTS' EXPERIENCES

Objectives

- To reflect on the claim that society gives preference to certain White standards

- To consider personal experiences supporting or refuting this claim

Materials

- None

Procedures

- Ask class to consider the work with grammar that they have been doing for the past few days:

    1. Do you think it will make a big difference, some difference, or no difference at all in the way you are perceived socially?
    2. Why do you feel the way you do?
    3. Why do some people of color feel that society always will judge them as inferior?

- Discuss what is unjust about society's preference for standard English. Explain that one injustice is that nonstandard English speakers' accomplishments or intelligence go undervalued. Ask students:

    1. Is this true only as far as language is concerned?
    2. What other cultural traditions or habits are devalued in mainstream American culture?
    3. Have you ever been in a situation when some feature of your ethnicity was found wanting? When something special (or merely different) was treated as something wrong?

- Go around the room and listen to students' stories. Teachers should be prepared with a few of their own reminiscences: I've told stories about being embarrassed in front of friends when talking about religious practices and about hiding part of my identity in order to win a friend.

- Assign Journal 3: Write about a time when you suffered because of people's reactions to your cultural customs.

- Because this topic is so broad, students need to focus their stories of injustice on differences among customs of different peoples. Ask them to consider the following questions:

1. When other people recognized your differences, were you asked to change? Were you rejected outright?
2. Did you make any compromises in order to be accepted or to succeed?

Variations/Extensions of This Lesson

1. Students can write their journal entries in nonstandard English/dialect if they feel it would be appropriate or might add resonance to their story. Refer to the "Radio Graffiti" column written in an African American/hip-hop style.

2. When one of my classes worked on this assignment, some kids "couldn't think" of a relevant experience. They were paired with students who chose to write in dialect. The assignment was to rewrite the partner's journal entry in standard English. This turned out to be a beneficial pairing because the students who had trouble thinking of an experience to recount for Journal 3 were, for the most part, the same students who needed to work on "writing White." They worked in tandem with the students who had written in dialect and who generally had stronger writing skills.

Two sets of procedures are specified for the next lesson, one for students reading at a lower (6th- to 7th-grade) level and one for those reading at a higher (11th- to 12th-grade) level. Instructors of students whose skills fall between these levels should gauge which lesson would be most effective for their students.

Skip to page 183 for Lesson 10 (for higher level readers).

LESSON 10: RACISM IN JAY BENNET'S *SKINHEAD* (for lower level readers)

Objectives

• To develop reading skills including basic comprehension, analysis of character development, and affective response

• To gain exposure to characters who espouse various levels of tolerance and racism

• To engage in independent, self-paced reading

• To create lessons and evaluative exercises based on students' reading

Materials

• Bennet, Jay, *Skinhead*

• HANDOUT 5: STORY MAP

• HANDOUT 6: CREATING DISCUSSION QUESTIONS

Procedures

Depending on students' reading pace, these activities can require from 5 to 10 class periods.

• Notes for instructors on *Skinhead:*

This is a young adult book, written simply and in a style with which students will feel comfortable. There is a lot of dialogue and short, declarative sentences. Most chapters end suspensefully. Because the reading is easy and not too demanding, I found that even the most low-skilled, recalcitrant students were eager to take the book home and read on their own. If you have enough copies to give each student a book, I strongly encourage assigning reading homework. I sometimes let students sign books out if they want to take them home. I do lose quite a few copies this way. Students will read the book quickly enough to finish it in a few days, even if they read only in class.

We may, as teachers, scoff at such a low-effort read: Don't these poorer readers, especially, need to be challenged by books they read in school? Not always, I say vehemently. These students will continue to devalue and disregard reading if it is always a difficult chore. What we must remember, I think, is that we all enjoy easy reading: Even English teachers (maybe especially English teachers) like to curl up occasionally with mystery/romance/adventure novels. They're easy reading. They're fun. Poorer readers will enjoy reading *Skinhead* for the same reasons: Here is a book, finally, that they can call a page-turner. If teachers are unable to find this novel, I recommend works that are similar in style and are as easy to read.

- *Activity A: Introducing **Skinhead.*** Begin by asking students to tell what they know about skinheads.

   1. What are skinheads? Who are skinheads?
   2. Are there local skinhead groups? For what do they stand?
   3. What generalizations do people typically make about skinheads?

Distribute copies of *Skinhead*. Read the opening chapter aloud with students.

- *Activity B: Establishing Basic Facts.* Students will read at their own pace. Devote the first day or two to this independent reading, pausing only to ask basic questions near the end of the class period, such as:

   1. Who is Jonathan?
   2. Is he rich or poor?

- *Activity C: Discussing **Skinhead.*** The following questions can be used to start general class discussions:

Chapters 1-4. Describe Jonathan's attitude about the phone call from Seattle. Why do you think he doesn't tell his grandfather what is going on? How would you describe the man on the plane? Why do Jonathan and his mother have different last names? What type of relationship does Jonathan have with his parents? With his grandfather?

Chapters 5-7. Are you surprised that Jonathan arrives too late at the hospital? Detective Ward calls Jonathan a "spoiled, rich brat." Do you agree with him? What makes Detective Ward finally show Jonathan some sympathy? What do we learn about the detective? How did the man in the hospital die?

Chapters 8-11. What would you do if you got a phone call like Jonathan got in the hotel room? What makes Jonathan stay in Seattle? Who do you think controls the situation at the airport, Jonathan or Jenny? Who are Mitch and Carl? What role have they played in Alfred Kaplan's life? In Jonathan's?

Chapters 12-14. What does Jonathan learn about Alfred Kaplan when visiting his house? What strange feeling comes over him? Why was Alfred Kaplan a threat to the skinheads? Why do you think Jenny is so committed to Alfred

Kaplan's cause? Over what do she and Jonathan disagree, and why is this significant? What makes Jonathan decide to help her?

Chapters 15-19. Who is Jed Ward? How are Carl and Mitch alike? How are they different? What do Mitch's songs tell you about him? Where do they take Jonathan? What happened to Mitch's brother? How did this affect Mitch?

Chapters 20-22. How has Jonathan been affected by the secrets in his family? What do you think is the problem with his mother and grandfather? What are Carl's strengths? What doubts does Carl plant in Jonathan's mind? Does he "get to" Jonathan at all?

Chapters 23-25. Mitch suggests that Jonathan's grandfather "thinks like" the skinheads. How does Jonathan react to this idea? Describe Mitch's brother: Was he like Mitch? How does Mitch feel about Carl? Why does he follow him? What are Mitch's strengths? What is important to him?

Chapters 26-27. How is Jed Ward associated with Carl and Mitch? How does Jonathan get Carl to confess to the murders of Alfred Kaplan and Mitch? Why does he threaten Carl so aggressively—do you think he really is as violent as Carl? Why is Detective Ward both depressed and motivated by the skinheads?

Chapters 28-31. What startling truth does Jenny reveal to Jonathan? Why does he have trouble admitting the truth about his grandfather? What truth? Why does Jonathan call his grandfather a murderer? Do you think he is exaggerating? Why does Jonathan leave his grandfather? What would you have done?

• *Activity D: Reading Quizzes.* Although regular reading quizzes are impractical if students read at widely differing speeds, it is still a good idea to give students a chance to succeed at simple reading quizzes. Every 100% grade gives all students (especially poor readers) a shot of confidence and can improve their self-esteem. Schedule short, easy quizzes to keep students up-to-date in their reading and to accustom them to feeling in control and on top of their reading assignments.

• *Activity E (Group Work): Creating Story Maps.* When students have read on their own enough to get a sense of plot and characterization (through at least Chapter 5), divide students into small groups. Distribute HANDOUT 5: STORY MAP. Story maps help students get basic stated information straight and encourage a type of casual reflection on theme (which some students find "too hard" to focus on). See INSTRUCTORS' NOTES Q: STORY MAPS (Chapter 4). Students also may work on this handout alone if desired. Here is a student's sample story map:

STORY MAP

NAME OF BOOK: *SKINHEAD*   CHAPTERS 1 to 2

Main characters: Jonathan Atwood
                                                       Sergeant T. Ward
                                                       Dying man

Setting:	Jonathan's bedroom in Southampton, LI [Long Island, New York] and the car
Main events:	1. J. is woken at night by a call from Seattle 2. Man in Seattle hospital wants to see J. before he dies 3. J. goes to airport
Themes:	Fear of the unknown in Seattle J.'s distance from his family J.'s wealth and privilege

• *Activity E (Group Work): Creating Discussion Questions.* Divide students into small groups. Distribute HANDOUT 6: CREATING DISCUSSION QUESTIONS. Discussion sheets help students recognize their own powers of interpretation and insight as readers. Teachers can use HANDOUTS 5 and 6 to direct class discussions or can modify them into quizzes or tests. The following sample comes from a small group:

CREATING DISCUSSION QUESTIONS

Name: <u>James</u>   Other students in group: <u>Irene, Liza, Janice</u>

Book: <u>*SKINHEAD*</u>   Section for discussion: <u>Ch. 19-20 (pp. 77-87)</u>

1. Why does Mitch hate Jews?
2. Whose hate is stronger, Carl's or Mitch's?
3. Would you hate your grandfather or your mother more, if you were Jonathan?
4. Is Jonathan brave or just fronting?
5. Is Carl brave or just fronting?

• *Activity F: Essay Questions/Important Issues in **Skinhead**.* Change the phrasing of students' responses on HANDOUT 6 to create more reflective questions. These questions can address the power of hatred, stereotyping, prejudice born of fear, and intolerance of people's differences. Students also can write answers to these questions. Sample questions:

1. What stereotypes do the skinheads believe?
2. What is the most powerful emotion in the book, love or hatred?
3. Why does Mitch become a skinhead?
4. Why does Carl become a skinhead?

• *Activity G: Final Test on **Skinhead**.* When students have finished reading and the class has discussed the important issues in the book, prepare students to take a final test. I use questions generated in group discussions and make sure that the test contains simple, factual questions for those students whose skills are so low that they have trouble making inferences and recognizing complex relationships. Here are some questions from a student-written test on *Skinhead.* Students were exempt from questions that they devised; each question in the test was written by a student.

1. How would the story have been different if Jonathan's family had been able to communicate better?
2. Did Jonathan's infatuation with Jenny hurt anyone in any way? Explain.
3. Who is the greatest bigot in the story? Explain why.
4. Who is the weakest character in the story? Explain.

HANDOUT 5: STORY MAP

Name(s) _____

Name of book _____ Chapters ___ to ___

Main characters:

Setting:

Main events:

Themes:

HANDOUT 6: CREATING DISCUSSION QUESTIONS

Name _____   Other students in group:

Book _____   Section for discussion _____

To the group: Your job is to create a few questions that you think are interesting. The best way to do this is to hold the book open to the part that you are dealing with and skim over what you already have read. As you do this, think about these characters and their problems, and develop some questions that reflect your concerns and your point of view.

Questions:

1.

2.

3.

4.

5.

Sample Questions:

What was the best part of this section and why? Has something such as this ever happened to you? What would you say to the main character? Were you surprised by these events? How do you think the story would have changed if the author had not let _____ happen? How are the characters developing or changing? How is _____ different from _____? What do you think is _____'s best quality? What is his or her worst trait? Why?

LESSON 10: RACISM IN STUDS TERKEL'S *RACE*
(for higher level readers)

Objectives

- To begin to become familiar with civil rights struggles and related sociopolitical movements of the last 30 years

  - To analyze the features of good presentations

  - To read selected chapters of a longer work critically and independently

  - To prepare presentations of one character's perspective and experiences

  - To evaluate peers' presentations

Materials

- Terkel, Studs, *Race: How Blacks and Whites Think and Feel About the American Obsession*

Procedures

Depending on class size, reading the text and preparing and making presentations may require as few as 8 or as many as 20 class periods.

- *Activity A: Introducing* **Race** *and Current Assignment.* Present Studs Terkel's book *Race,* showing it to students and explaining Terkel's interviewing and writing methods. Make the lesson's objectives clear to students. Explain that they will be working independently—reading and preparing presentations on real people's perspectives found in the book.

This book also can be read in entirety by the whole class, or excerpts can be assigned in conjunction with other works dealing with racism (i.e., Art Spiegelman's *Maus* (1986), Ralph Ellison's *The Invisible Man* (1952), and works by James Baldwin).

- *Activity B: Model Presentation of a Sample Chapter.* Select one chapter from *Race* with which to work. Distribute copies of this sample chapter. Have students read this on their own and then ask them what information it contains and what was important about it. Determine with students what information is necessary for a report on any given character. Prepare a "necessary information sheet" with students for them to use as they prepare to give presentations on one character from their section.

Prepare a sample presentation on this chapter yourself. Your presentation will serve as the model for students' presentations. For this reason, it is best to make clarity your prime objective. Although Terkel's characters' reminiscences are nuanced and complex, it is best to keep the sample presentation fairly simple. It is all right to set the formal standards high. Relate basic information on the narrator and identify story highlights. Pick a short section to read aloud. Students should take notes on your presentation in preparation for the notes they will need to take on each other's. Here are sample notes for a presentation on a section in a chapter from *Race:*

NECESSARY INFORMATION SHEET ON: Diane Romano
Sections to read aloud: Paragraphs on pp. 42, 46-47

1. Who is this? (name, race, age, $)

   Diane Romano, White, middle class, 35 in 1965. In 1990 she's 60 and makes good money.

2. What questions does she or he raise about racism?

   Why was she less racist when younger? Does age make people racist? Weaker? Why didn't civil rights make a bigger difference for Blacks?

3. What sources of racism are evident?

   Desire to be accepted. When you're exposed to the worst in people, you think everyone's bad. "The neighborhood" has a stronger influence on kids than parents do. It's human nature to look down on people of a different culture.

4. Is she or he racist?

   She "fights with herself" not to be, but she is, now. Even though she used to stand up against intolerance, now she goes along with it, because she "doesn't want to have bad feelings with anybody."

5. How has racism progressed? How will it progress?

   It's gotten worse, like her own cowardice. She thinks it will take 100 to 200 years to eliminate White superiority.

6. My feelings in relation to this perspective:

   Her desire to avoid bad feelings is understandable, but she's perpetuating hate and stereotypes. Her professed earlier tolerance seems halfhearted: Her convictions couldn't have been so strong if she's abandoned them, and her kids all turned out to be racists.

• *Activity C: Independent Projects.* Assign one section to each student to read and present. There are 30 sections in the book; each section contains one to seven characters' stories. Students can read entire sections and then choose to present whichever character's story they find most compelling.

• *Activity D: Independent Reading.* Each student should devote time to reading his or her sample chapter at home and in class. On the days when students are reading in class, stress critical reading and encourage students to take notes. Pair students to discuss and process their reading. With a partner, students can sketch out the "necessary information" on one or more of their characters and help each other select the story they will present to the class.

• *Activity E: Presentations.* When students have read and discussed their reading, they can prepare their presentations. Each student will give one presentation unless the class is very large. In that case instructors may need to vary the exercise, assigning presentations only to some students or to groups.

Class members will need to record facts and information on each presentation, using the format the class established for the teacher's presentation. I have found that most presentations need at least 10 minutes; teachers should gauge the class's pace and break up long days of presentations with other activities (i.e., skip ahead to Lesson 11).

• *Activity F: Evaluation of Presentations.* You can use a format similar to the one in Lesson 11 or try a freer reflective exercise. For example, you could ask the students what they learned from presentations in terms of:

— preparing your own presentation?
— presenting your own presentation?
— listening to classmates' presentations?
— determining whose worked well and why?
— examining the sources of racism?
— exploring the history of racism in this country?
— discussing the future of racism in this country?

LESSON 11: THE ECONOMIC ROOTS OF RACISM

Objectives

- To consider the impact competition has on racism

- To reflect on personal experiences of competition and hatred

Materials

- UNIT MATERIALS: "The Roots of Economic Violence"

Procedures

- Write the following sentence on the board: "Competition breeds hate." Ask students to respond to the following questions, which generally leads into a discussion of human nature in general:

    1. Do you agree with this statement? Disagree? Is this statement too strong?
    2. Are all people naturally competitive?
    3. What are types of competition besides and beyond sports?
    4. For what else do people compete?
    5. If people are competitive, does it follow necessarily that they are mean-spirited?

- Ask students to consider competition and racism together. Explore how the two are related and how the sentence on the board fits into the work they have just read. Discuss the rise of hate groups (such as the Nazis and the Klan) in times of social change and/or economic recession.

- Distribute the short, abridged article, "The Roots of Economic Violence." Read it aloud in class and discuss.

    1. Are hatred and race-based violence motivated by economics? By competition for jobs and resources?
    2. What types of competition exist in students' worlds that spawn hatred?

- (For lower level readers only) Consider the action and motivation in the novel *Skinhead*. Ask students to add to the book by writing another chapter for it, a chapter that orients *Skinhead* to economic reality and cites competition for economic resources as a source of racism. Students might create background scenarios: Maybe Carl lost a job to an African American or to a Jew. Or maybe Jed Ward and his Latino friend both tried to get into the police academy, but only the friend was accepted. . . .

• Ask students to consider the sentence on the board in relation to their own experiences. Write Journal Assignment 4 on the board: Write about a time you competed, and tell how this competition affected the way you viewed your rival(s).

As always, I gave students the option of keeping their journal entries private. A large number of the boys in the class did not want me to read this particular entry. When I asked them why, in class, they exchanged looks with one another but did not divulge their reasons. After class, one student came up and told me that as a gang member, he did not feel comfortable sharing his true feelings about his rivals. He said he had written a paragraph about the rival gang in which he said things such as "we're all just the same." He said that some of the other gang members in the class might not have confessed this truth; probably, he said, they had just written insults about the rival gang. The next day in class, we discussed conflicts between races and conflicts between gangs. "Aren't both rooted in competition?" "Are both essentially the same?" "Are gangs contrived races?" A heated argument followed: Most of the girls said gang rivalry was just like racism, although most of the boys said it was different.

UNIT MATERIALS

The Roots of Economic Violence: Dim Economic Prospects for Young Men

What is the connection between racist skinheads and lack of economic opportunities for whites? Do young, white, male skinheads blame blacks and immigrants for getting the jobs they think they ought to get? If the economy does not improve, and new jobs are not created, will more whites join the skinheads? Will we see more racial violence?

Young men in 1984 earned 30 percent less than young men did 11 years earlier, after adjusting for inflation. Between 1973 and 1984, average earnings for 20- to 24-year-old men fell from $11,572 to $8,072 (in constant 1984 dollars).

The decline in young men's earnings results from a change in the types of jobs now available to them. Beginning in the 1970's, the economy began losing thousands of higher wage manufacturing jobs as corporations closed plants and relocated production overseas to take advantage of low-wage labor in the third world. These economic shifts, combined with an attack on unions by employers and the Reagan administration, have decimated the unionized manufacturing sector, especially durable goods industries such as autos and steel. This drop in well-paying manufacturing jobs chiefly affects young men without extensive education, who have traditionally moved into these jobs.

As manufacturing jobs become scarce, young men have turned to the lower paying but rapidly expanding service sector for work. Service employment generally pays low wages, offers few benefits, and provides limited opportunities for career advancement. While the jobs are still predominantly held by women, more and more men—particularly young men—are entering sales and service jobs because they find few openings elsewhere.

While all young men in the 1980's are earning less than young men in the 1970's, inequality among them is growing. In 1973, the average earnings of a 20- to 24-year-old male high school dropout were three-quarters of the earnings of a college graduate. By 1984, this fraction dropped to two-thirds. This inequality is exacerbated by the fact that fewer low-income men are going to college.

The downward trend in real income for young men has important implications. Reduced earnings for young men today may signal a drop in the standard of living over a lifetime. The prospects for wage growth over time are dim—and the hope of a lifetime job has become unrealistic for many young people.

The long-term solutions to the income decline for young men are more complex. Raising the minimum wage, creating more meaningful and better paying jobs, unionizing the service sector, and improving non-wage benefits such as health insurance are among the issues that working people and the government need to address.

SOURCE: "THE ROOTS OF ECONOMIC VIOLENCE: Dim Economic Prospects for Young Men" as excerpted in the *Utne Reader* (May/June 1989) from *Dollars and Sense* (November 1987), p. 84. Reprinted with permission.
NOTES: *Dollars and Sense* is a progressive economics magazine published six times a year. First-year subscriptions cost $18.95 and may be ordered by writing to *Dollars and Sense*, One Summer Street, Somerville, MA 02143.
The opening remarks are based on the Editors' Note from the *Utne Reader*, May/June 1989. The *Utne Reader* originally excerpted the *Dollars and Sense* article.

LESSON 12: RACISM PRESENTATIONS
(for lower level readers)

Objectives

- To schedule presentations of individual choice on selected days

- To choose works that students consider educational

- To prepare presentations according to a standard format

- To evaluate each other's presentations and determine the value of this activity

Materials

- A popular song (lyrics and recording) expressing tensions between the races, for example, Paris, "The Hate That Hate Made" from *The Devil Made Me Do It*

- HANDOUT 7: NOTES ON RACISM PRESENTATIONS

- Blank calendar to be filled out by students signing up for presentation dates

- Individual works to be provided by students

- Short articles pertinent to issues that arise during student presenta-tions, such as Marriott's "Rap's Embrace of 'Nigger' Fires Bitter Debate" from the *New York Times* and Smith's "Dreaming America" from *Spin* magazine

- HANDOUT 8: EVALUATING STUDENT PRESENTATIONS

Procedures

- Distribute copies of a preselected pop song. Play the song for the students; they should read the lyrics while listening. As with every musical presentation, stress that this is still English class, still literature—not time to dance, goof around, or daydream. Explain that it is not important that students like the song or the type of music. Give them the choice of just reading the lyrics (instead of reading and listening simultaneously). If they don't want to hear the song, don't play it! See INSTRUCTORS' NOTES I: USING MUSIC IN THE CLASSROOM (Chapter 4).

- After listening to the song, analyze it. Explain to students, who will be preparing and giving presentations for the last few weeks of the unit, that this song is a model presentation. Distribute HANDOUT 7: NOTES ON RACISM PRESENTATIONS. Go through the questions on the sheet, applying them to the song and making sure each student records the answers on his or her sheet. Here are some sample notes on Paris's song:

Presenter, name of work, name of artist	What examples of racial hatred are here?	What are the reasons for racism here?	What are the consequences for the hated and the haters?
Deborah: Paris, "The Hate That Hate Made"	White man kills innocent Black man; Black man kills 10 innocent White men	Jealously and retaliation	Death and a continuation of the cycle of violence

• Assign presentations to students: Explain that they need to bring in a song, poem, or video that talks about race and racism in some way to present or teach to the class. Be clear. Tell them that they will need to do more than "push-play" on the tape player: Their ideas about what the songs are saying are most important here. In other words, students will need to know most of the "answers" to the questions on the handout for their song.

• Pass around one blank calendar page. I copy one month of a wall calendar and highlight the dates that have been slated for student presentations. In order to plan and highlight the correct number of days, figure that every student will present a 5-minute work. With stalling, disorganization, and discussion, the total presentation usually takes 15 minutes per student, that is, two presentations per class period. Tell students to sign up for days they know they will be ready. I generally plan for the first student presentations to take place a day or two after my introductory presentation. In the interim days, we work on journal revisions or other makeup work.

• Tell students that they should come to class with three things:

1. the words written out (I ask for these in advance, so I can make copies for each student in the class the next day)
2. the taped song or video, cued to the beginning of the song or section to be presented
3. HANDOUT 7: NOTES ON RACISM PRESENTATIONS, already filled out for their song

Students may feel unsure and uncomfortable giving presentations. For this reason, it is important to establish ground rules immediately and to stress them every day. See HANDOUT S: STUDENT PRESENTATION GUIDELINES; INSTRUCTORS' NOTES T: STUDENT PRESENTATIONS (Chapter 4).

• Reiterate the requirements for presenters: Songs must have written lyrics, and presenters must be willing to lead the class in a discussion of the work. Students in the audience must give presenters attention and respect and be patient with each other's differing styles. They can disagree with each other but cannot offer opinions about the type of music or particular song.

Students in my classes have brought in songs for their racism presentations as diverse as "Indians" by Anthrax (1987), "Violent" by 2Pac (1990), and "Brainteasers and Doubtbusters" by Sister Souljah (1992). Presented poems included "Let America Be America Again" by Langston Hughes (1970).

• During class discussion of the work, each presenter should list the answers to the questions on HANDOUT 7 on the board for his or her song. All students should take notes on each other's songs using this sheet. There is enough room for 10 presentations at the most; students will need to make extra pages of this handout to keep track of additional presentations.

• Presentations may suggest additional studies and assignments.

Controversy at large (and in the class) over many rappers' use of the word "nigger" led us to a lively discussion one day, and the class was very interested in the New York Times *article "Rap's Embrace of 'Nigger' Fires Bitter Debate." A "Dreaming America" column from* Spin *magazine also addresses this issue.*

• When presentations are over, distribute HANDOUT 8: EVALUATING STUDENT PRESENTATIONS. Discuss students' experiences with preparing and learning from each other's presentations.

HANDOUT 7: NOTES ON RACISM PRESENTATIONS

Presenter, name of work, name of artist	What examples of racial hatred are here?	What are the reasons for racism here?	What are the consequences for the hated and the haters?

HANDOUT 8: EVALUATING STUDENT PRESENTATIONS

1. Look over the sheet you used to keep track of everyone's presentation. Look at the first column first. Whose presentation did you think worked best and why?

2. Look at the second column. What are the most common forms of racism we heard about in students' presentations?

3. Look at the third column. List the three or four most common reasons for racism: _____, _____, _____, and _____. Does this surprise you? _____ Why or why not?

4. Look at the fourth column. List the most common consequences of racism:

What do you think about this?

5. Did you enjoy the presentations? _____ Why or why not?

6. What do you think is the value of student presentations?

7. Would you like to do it again?

LESSON 12: IS SEPARATISM A VIABLE OPTION?
(for higher level readers)

Objectives

- To explore one "solution" to the problem of racism

- To deepen understanding of characters and concepts introduced in the unit

- To determine and express position toward these concepts

- To evaluate unit informally

Materials

- Access to a video camera

Procedures

- After discussing the difficulties that arise in trying to live together peacefully, ask the class to consider the alternatives by discussing the advantages and disadvantages of integration, segregation, and separatism.

- Review the earlier discussion of integration, cooperation, and assimilation (Lesson 4). Present a hypothetical scenario such as the following:

> Chicago is already one of the most racially divided cities in the country. The city council has decided to divide it officially as an experiment for the rest of the nation to observe. South Chicago will be all Black. West Chicago will be all Latino. North Chicago will be all White. The business district in the Loop will be a separate city altogether, with businesses having the option of branching out into the three cities for commercial development and investment.

- Students will prepare to give oral opinions on the scenario and participate in a role play: an Oprah Winfrey-type panel to be videotaped. Work with students to assign roles for this exercise—story narrators from *Race*, local characters, historical figures, political figures, or entertainers whose positions on the issue can be surmised. Because this activity can feature one emcee and a panel of 10 guests at most, students who will not perform can choose roles and describe their chosen characters' opinions in writing only.

- Once the assignment is clear, each student should determine his or her "role" in class and should take notes on his or her positions. Give students the opportunity to brainstorm and confer with one another about characters' feelings about the issue. List the cast (panel members and the students playing them) on the board. The emcee (the student playing "Oprah") will need to create a list of questions and issues for the panel to discuss.

Our panel included singers from the pop group Arrested Development, Malcolm X before his pilgrimage to Mecca (Spike Lee's 1992 Malcolm X *movie had just come out), and Arsenio Hall.*

- Videotape the production the next day. Students not on the panel can direct questions and comments to panel members.

- After the exercise has run its course, assign the final exercise of the unit: Students should write a short essay delineating their characters' and their own positions regarding separatism. If the videotaping exercise was a success, these positions will be refined considerably from the previous days' ideas. If it was a debacle, students will need to work harder to arrive at trenchant conclusions.

- Play the videotape and ask the class for their evaluation of the exercise and the unit.

7

❖ Education

Some of the time when a student is messing up in school it's not his fault. It's the people around him that he can't do anything about. And even when he's doing his best, it ain't good enough for them. His family treats him wrong and his teachers treat him wrong, so he decides to keep to himself.

—Anonymous

If the teachers would teach us how to get stories like this, about racism and injustice, into the news, that would be education.

—Tony

Just hanging out in the streets and watching what goes on you could say is a school.

—Kris

RATIONALE

What Is the Topic of Study?

This unit is about education—including but not limited to "what happens at school." We will need to redefine and demystify the term: These students (some of whom have been labeled "ineducable") need to understand that they can learn and already have learned some lessons quite well. We will look at different ways lessons are taught both in and out of school. We will study what happens in classrooms—the good, the bad, the unexpected. We examine the goals of the American education system as they are and as students believe they should be. What makes a class work? What makes it fail?

Why Will Students Be Interested in This?

First, this unit will give everybody a chance to complain—and what could be more satisfying for a group of disaffected students? Students will be given structures and opportunities to evaluate the accomplishments and inadequacies of their schooling. Furthermore, students know that they learn a lot outside of school: Their educational experiences outside the classroom will be recognized and valued. As we study education and related concepts such as "lowered expectations" and "indoctrination," students will have new ways to look at what they have learned in the past.

Why Do Students Need to Study This?

Traditionally, schools may try to ignore what kids learn on the streets, even though it is this knowledge and these experiences that keep many students from achieving academic success. As a result, many students agree with assessments of their aptitude: They believe themselves to be failures, that they cannot succeed in school, and they have given up on education altogether.

This unit gives students a different sense of what education can and must be. They can begin to understand and question the labels they have received. No other unit of study affords teachers a better opportunity to increase students' self-esteem. We work to undo students' pessimism about their abilities and give them new belief in themselves and in their future educational efforts. Then, and only then, are they empowered to take control of their own education.

Why Teach This Unit Now?

Because this unit helps students recognize their educational goals and gives them support and encouragement to carry them out, I like to schedule it near the beginning of a school year or an academic semester. An instructional unit on education may be "too much" as the year's first topic of study, but it does work well as the second. Because it teaches students to approach the elements of instruction—objectives, assignments, and assessments—critically, teachers can design subsequent units of instruction to incorporate and build on these skills.

Because the unit stresses basic student skills such as note taking, students agree that it serves them best when scheduled early in the year. The unit's ongoing project—video interviews—also works well once students feel comfortable together but when they are still curious about each other's observations of the world and past experiences.

KEY QUESTIONS

1. What is education?

2. What is the purpose of school? What should it be?

3. What should be taught in school? Who should decide?

4. What is taught in school today? Why?

5. What makes a good teacher? What makes a good student?

TERMINAL OBJECTIVES

• To reflect carefully on key questions in the abstract and as they relate to students' lives

• To determine personal goals and educational agenda

• To learn and practice basic procedures of interviewing

• To improve academic skills: taking notes, keeping class papers orderly

• To distinguish between narrative and expository writing and practice narrative writing

MATERIALS

Chapters and Excerpts From Longer Works

• Illich, Ivan (1970), *Deschooling Society* (abstract of this work reprinted here with permission)

• Kozol, Jonathan (1969), "Stephen" from *Death at an Early Age*

• Kozol, Jonathan (1991), *Savage Inequalities* (pp. 51-74)

• Rodríguez, Luis (1993), *Always Running: La Vida Loca: Gang Days in L.A.* (Chapters 6 and 7)

Articles

• Carlozo, Lou (1993), "High School Drama Students Give Legislators a Tip: Act"

• Sagan, Carl (1985), "Twelve Things I Wish They Taught Me in School"

Short Stories

• Gibbs, Angelica (1961), "The Test"

Poems

- Bishop, Morris (1955/1973), "The Perforated Spirit"

- Henley, William Ernest (1908/1973), "Invictus" (reprinted here)

- Yevtushenko, Yevgeny (1991), "Lies" (reprinted here with permission)

Songs

- Paxton, Tom (1962), "What Did You Learn in School Today?" (reprinted here with permission)

Other Materials

- Copies of blank schedules used in your school

- Discipline policies or official list of rules from a local institution (I use Chicago Public Schools' Discipline Code)

- Groening, Matt (1987), *School Is Hell* (selection reprinted here with permission)

- Lauro, Shirley (1979/1980/1981/1984), "Open Admissions" (play)

- Scene from "Room 222" (1973), transcribed in *The Good Life U.S.A.: A Book About the Pursuit of Happiness*, pp. 17-19

- Williams, Robert L. (1972), The Black Intelligence Test of Cultural Homogeneity (BITCH test) (reprinted here with permission)

SAMPLE DAILY SCHEDULE

Day 1:   Lesson 1: Discuss intelligence. Use HANDOUT 1: SAMPLE INTELLIGENCE
            TEST. Define and take notes on *intelligence* as a concept.

Day 2:   Discuss *bias;* take notes.
            Use HANDOUT 2: BITCH TEST; score it.

Day 3:   Small groups design new "intelligence" test.
            Class elects editors to compile new test.

Day 4:   Lesson 2: Journal Assignment 1.

Day 5:   Read Kozol's "Stephen."
            (Test editors can work on compiling test.)

Day 6:   Discuss "Stephen"; small groups answer select questions
                in writing.

Day 7:   Editors present new intelligence test.
            Return Journal 1; read some entries aloud.
            Discuss described injustices, elements of narrative writing.

Day 8:   Lesson 3: Read "Open Admissions" in class;
            Begin to defend or refute controversial statements regarding the play.

Day 9:   Continue discussing controversial statements.
            Discuss and plan first interview using HANDOUT 3:
                INTERVIEW PLANNING SHEET.

Day 10:   Conduct and videotape interview.

Day 11:   Analyze interview in terms of both content and production.
            Small groups use HANDOUT 4: EDUCATION OPINIONNAIRE:
                WHAT'S THE POINT OF EDUCATION?

Day 12:   Discuss opinionnaire.
            Students explain select opinions in writing.

Day 13:   Lesson 4: Introduce *Always Running.*
            Read selection; finish for homework.

Day 14:   Discuss reading.
            Small groups generate discussion questions.

Day 15:   Discuss small group's questions.
            Lesson 5: Journal Assignment 2.

Day 16:   Share/read select journal entries aloud.
            Review elements of narrative writing.
            Homework: Begin Journal Assignment 3.

Day 17:   Plan next interview; continue writing Journal 3.

Day 18:   Conduct interview.

Day 19:   Evaluate yesterday's interview; compare with first interview.

Day 20:   Lesson 6: Read Sagan or Illich; finish for homework.

Day 21:   Read important sections aloud and discuss.

Day 22:   Continue discussing reading.
               Design individual educational menus/alternative
                  school schedules.

Day 23:   Lesson 7: Read and discuss poetry.
               Free writing.

Day 24:   Lesson 8: Read school's mission statement or policies
                  critically; discuss and take notes.

Day 25:   Class provides headings for HANDOUT 5: SCHOOL REPORT
                  CARD; students fill out "report cards" individually.

Day 26:   Lesson 9: Discuss motivation and money; use scenario,
                  opinion lineup.
               Journal Assignment 4.

Day 27:   Discuss journal; modify interview questions; prepare for
                  new interviews.

Day 28:   Conduct new interviews.

Day 29:   Conduct additional interviews.

Day 30:   Lesson 10: Explain final project.
               Plan student interviews at another school.
               Read excerpt from Kozol's *Savage Inequalities*.

Day 31:   Discuss reading.

Day 32:   Read and discuss background information on school to be
                  visited; prepare to conduct interviews there.

Day 33:   Visit other school; conduct interviews.

Day 34:   Watch yesterday's video footage, discuss experience.

Day 35:   Review all interviews on videotape; plan documentary.
               If classes lack necessary equipment or interest, see
                  "Additional Lessons."

Days 36-40:   Plan, write, and tape introductory remarks and other
                  commentary for documentary.

LESSON 1: INTELLIGENCE AND TESTING

Objectives

• To consider the conditions necessary for fair evaluation of intelligence and aptitude

• To begin to think of school as only one of many educational milieus

• To recognize and name cultural bias on tests

• To demonstrate command of language and social codes not traditionally valued in school

Materials

• HANDOUT 1: SAMPLE INTELLIGENCE TEST

• HANDOUT 2: BITCH TEST

Procedures

• Start by asking students to think of the most intelligent person they know. Then tell them there will be a test today. Amid their groanings and protestations, distribute HANDOUT 1: SAMPLE INTELLIGENCE TEST and ask students to write their intelligent person's name at the top of the paper. Have students take the test. While they are working, it is a good idea to work out answers that a conservative, middle-class evaluator would consider correct (i.e., 9: "Criminals are locked up so that innocent people will be safe. Criminals are locked up as punishment; this gives them an opportunity for rehabilitation so that they can become decent members of society"). Some questions are highly subjective; expect "answers" to provoke debates.

• Go over answers and discuss questions. Ask students:

1. Would the person you named do well on this test? Why or why not?
2. On which questions might she or he have the "wrong" answer?
3. Is this test a good measure of intelligence? Why or why not?

Students should try to categorize the different types of experiences and conditions necessary for a person to score highly on the SAMPLE INTELLIGENCE TEST. Discuss whether (and why or why not) this test is fair.

• Work with class to define two terms: *intelligence* (one definition: how you think, how you use what you learn, and your ability to put these together and act; another definition: the ability to express yourself verbally, social competence, and the ability to solve problems) and *cultural bias* (favoring some cultures' experiences and norms).

1. Can you be intelligent and still not score well on standard intelligence tests?
2. What do intelligence tests measure?
3. Based on the sample intelligence test, in what ways can intelligence tests be biased? (They can be biased according to culture, socioeconomic group, location, age, sex, values.)

• Discuss the notion of bias in tests. Dr. Allison Davis, an anthropologist and educator in the 1940s, and Dr. Robert L. Williams, a sociologist in the 1960s, both believed that standard tests were slanted unfairly to favor White experience. Now, in the politically correct 1990s, test questions might be skewed less obviously. Still, they most likely reflect mainstream experience, which is not shared by all test takers. All tests are biased. The issue for students is this: Have they ever taken a test that values and is predicated on their own experiences?

• Distribute HANDOUT 2: BITCH TEST. Have students take this test. When they are done and have scored themselves, they will complain that the test is totally out-of-date. They are right.

• Divide the class into groups and have them devise 10 questions that belong on an intelligence test for the 1990s. Tell them to make up multiple choice questions on current fads, slang terms, styles, and local traditions. Here is a short sample test, written, entitled, and introduced by students:

Uptown Guide to the Life of Youth: UGLY TEST

This test is designed to show you the faults in most tests. Most tests are culturally biased. If you really look at it, most of the test questions given to students are based on one certain area or culture—but these tests are given to all students. Many live outside the area, and many are outside that culture.

That's why we designed this UGLY test (Uptown Guide to the Life of Youth). This test is based on the terminology used in the Uptown area of Chicago in the fall of 1991. Our intention is to give this test to people from other cultures and other areas. Your results on this test will thus prove that tests do not test intelligence: They test background.

We want to thank you for taking the UGLY test. Hopefully you'll pass it with flying colors. But probably, unless you're a teenager from Uptown, you won't!

1. "Lampin'" means a) committing arson, b) relaxing, c) drinking heavily, d) being very successful.
2. What is a "hype"? a) someone who is easily excited, b) a drug addict, c) a dance, d) a conic section.
3. What are "jumpers"? a) shoes, b) cockroaches, c) drug addicts, d) suicide victims.
4. "Duckies" are a) people who spend time together, b) money, c) inexpensive drugs, d) stool pigeons.
5. "To gank" means to a) fight in a gang, b) kill, c) have sex with, d) cheat or deceive.
6. "Five 0's" refers to a) $5, b) $500, c) police officers, d) certain crimes.
7. If a person is "thick," he or she a) has a nice body, b) is stupid, c) is overweight, d) is drunk.

8. To "get your money" is a) to have sex, b) to rob someone, c) to become employed, d) to buy drugs.

(Answers: 1. b, 2. b, 3. a, 4. b, 5. d, 6. c, 7. a, 8. a)

- Ask a few interested students to work together to edit, introduce, and type up a similar test composed of class-generated questions. Copy this test for students to distribute to friends. In future classes, ask them for (a) informal test results and (b) test takers' reactions to the test itself and to students' studying cultural bias.

- Make sure that students keep their notes on intelligence and testing, their IQ tests, BITCH tests, and student-written tests.

Most of the students I teach do not bring books or folders to class and lose the handouts I give them. For this reason, we start fresh with the Education unit materials. I use these high-interest materials to compel students to get organized, recommending that they devote a special file, section, or notebook to Education materials. Every day I make it a point to tell students which materials they need to keep and where they need to keep them. For many, it is their first experience with devising and maintaining a system for saving papers.

HANDOUT 1: SAMPLE INTELLIGENCE TEST

Your name: _____

Who is the most intelligent person you know? _____

    1. What is the capital of the United States?

    2. Who was Shakespeare?

    3. Why do we have zip codes?

    4. If 3 candy bars cost $1, how much will 18 candy bars cost?

    5. What is the best thing to do if you cut your finger?

    6. What is the best thing to do if you lose a ball that belongs to one of your friends?

    7. What are some reasons we need police officers?

    8. Why should a promise be kept?

    9. Why are criminals locked up?

    10. What is the next number in this series? 2, 4, 6, 8 . . .

    11. What does *canal* mean?

HANDOUT 2: BITCH TEST (BLACK INTELLIGENCE TEST OF CULTURAL HOMOGENEITY)

The BITCH-100 is a culture-specific test. It is not intended to be a culture-fair or culture-common test. This culture-specific test deals with content that is familiar to the Black child. Black children already have stored away mental images of this material; because of this, they will not have to try to process foreign or unfamiliar content on the test. These dialect-specific and culture-specific questions are intended to measure accurately what is inside the Black child's head. This is the basic rationale for the BITCH-100.

Choose the correct definition as Black people use the following words and expressions:

1. *Alley Apple* a) brick b) piece of fruit c) dog d) horse

2. *Black Draught* a) winter's cold wind b) laxative c) black soldier d) dark beer

3. *Blood* a) vampire b) dependent individual c) injured person d) brother of color

4. *Boogie Jugie* a) tired b) worthless c) old d) well put together

5. *Boot* refers to a a) cotton farmer b) Black c) Indian d) Vietnamese citizen

6. *Boss* a) demanding b) the meanest c) bossy d) the best

7. *Bread* a) something to eat b) weapons c) religion d) money

8. *Heavy cat* a) fat man b) arrogant man c) depressed man d) intelligent man

9. *Cabbage* a) traveling b) friends c) money d) liquor

10. *Cat* a) man about town b) sneaky person c) thief d) untrustworthy one

11. *The claps* a) cancer b) a problem with drugs c) tuberculosis (TB) d) venereal disease (VD)

12. *Clean* a) just out of the bathtub b) very well dressed c) very religious d) has a great deal

13. *H.N.I.C.* a) Have Nothing In Common b)Head Nigger In Charge c) Holy Name in Christ d)Half Nude Italian Chick

14. *CPT* = a standard a) time b) tune c) tale d) twist

15. *Deuce-and-a-quarter* a) money b) car c) house d) dice

(continued)

16. *To dig* does not mean a) to fight   b) to understand   c) to listen
                              d) to like

17. *Do rag* refers to   a) the hair   b) shoes   c) washing   d) tablecloth

18. *Dough* is   a) money   b) dressy clothes   c) knowledge
                              d) good friends

19. *Jive*   a) important   b) worthless   c) old   d) cool

20. *The eagle flies* is   a) the blahs   b) a movie   c) payday   d) "I'm leaving"

21. *Four corners*   a) rapping   b) singing   c) the streets   d) dancing

22. *Fro* refers to a   a) suit   b) pair of shoes   c) group against something
                              d) hairstyle

23. *Funky chicken*   a) dirty name   b) dance   c) suit   d) old car

24. *Gig*   a) job   b) be discriminated against   c) car   d) jogging

25. *Gospel bird*   a) pigeon   b) chicken   c) churchgoer   d) goose

26. *Greasing*   a) oiling one's skin   b) talking   c) swinging   d) eating

27. *I know you shame*   a) You don't hear very well   b) You are a racist
                              c) You don't mean what you're saying   d) You are guilty

28. *A jackleg preacher* is a preacher   a) with a wooden leg   b) from the South
                                          c) from the North   d) without a church

29. *To get it together* is to a) go to jail   b) do something   c) invite to a party
                                d) corrupt

30. *Give me some skin*   a) to give money   b) to demand money
                              c) to shake hands   d) to run fast

ANSWERS:

1. A	11. D	21. D
2. B	12. B	22. D
3. D	13. B	23. B
4. B	14. A	24. A
5. D	15. B	25. B
6. D	16. A	26. D
7. D	17. A	27. C
8. D	18. A	28. D
9. C	19. B	29. B
10. A	20. C	30. C

SOURCE: Excerpted from *THE BITCH TEST* (Black Intelligence Test of Cultural Homogeneity), Copyright © by Robert L. Willia
1972. Robert L. Williams is Professor Emeritus of Psychology and African-American Studies at Washington University, St. Lo
Missouri. Reprinted with permission.
NOTE: Some of these answers may seem strange or even incorrect. They are reprinted as written in 1972. Times (as well as cultures) cha▶

LESSON 2: STORIES OF EVALUATION

Objectives

- To relate an educational experience that students perceived as unfair

- To become familiar with formal elements of narrative writing

- To read accounts of unjust evaluation and recognize the bias inherent in every subjective evaluation

Materials

Short story or work that presents a decisive bias on the part of an evaluator. I have used:

- Gibbs, Angelica, "The Test"

- Kozol, Jonathan, "Stephen" from *Death at an Early Age*

Procedures

- Ask students if they have ever taken a test that was, for one reason or another, unfair. Write Journal Assignment 1 on the board: Write about a time you took a test that was unfair. Before students start writing, explain two aspects of the assignment carefully:

1. Students do not have to write about a test they took in school. What is a test, anyway? Tell students to consider any time they had to meet expectations. The point of the assignment is not to indict students' previous teachers as unfair. It is, rather, to explore various reasons for and types of "failure" in educational contexts. Remind them of Lesson 1 (examination of bias in tests).

2. Unlike other journal assignments that can be any length and can take any form, students should try to spend the rest of class writing narrative. They will need to pick one incident and tell the story as best they can. Instructors should explain that this will serve as an inventory of narrative writing skills: This is not a test, but teachers need to know what type of skills students have, what needs to be taught, and so forth.

- Return journal entries after commenting briefly on them (again, journal entries are not the best assignments to correct for mechanics). Ask permission to read one or two of the better stories aloud. Focus on stories that tell of injustice in and outside of school. Try to give names to the phenomena named by students in their stories: My students' stories told of teachers' lowered expectations, cultural bias, indoctrination, and so on.

- Go over reasons why the writers "failed" at their various tests. Explore with students:

1. Did these failures teach lessons other than the ones the teachers intended?
2. What conclusions can the class reach about testing?

• Also go over the elements of narrative writing used by the writers. Read examples aloud. I have found that many students describe their feelings about testing as opposed to telling stories about actual incidents. To demonstrate the difference between commentary and narrative, read examples from students' papers or create short snippets illustrating the two types of writing (i.e., *commentary:* "I hate to take tests that I don't even have time to study for" versus *narrative:* " 'I'm not ready for this test!' I thought, as I ran out of the room"). Have the class generate criteria and take notes on elements of good narrative writing. Make sure that students save their Journal 1 entries. See INSTRUCTORS' NOTES E: SKILL INVENTORIES (Chapter 4) for examples of evaluated student-written narrative.

• Distribute copies of short works dealing with an evaluator's bias. After class reads these short works, lead a discussion around related issues. Discuss/define *subjectivity* and *objectivity*. The following questions relate to "The Test" and/or "Stephen" and should be modified to fit whatever work is used:

1. What are the biases to which Marian and Stephen are subject?
2. What do their reactions to bias tell us about human nature?
3. What are some reasons people might accept their own failures?
4. Does it matter that there might be other driving instructors or other art teachers who could appreciate Marian's and Stephen's efforts?
5. Have you (or has your work) ever been judged inadequate by someone empowered to reward or punish you? Have you agreed with this evaluation?
6. To what biases can teachers subject students' work in high school?
7. Do subjective evaluations happen in school? Where? When?

LESSON 3: WHAT IS THE POINT OF EDUCATION?

Objectives

- To define education and consider the breadth of its ramifications

- To begin to examine some of the more ambiguous issues related to urban education

- To practice interviewing skills

Materials

- Lauro, Shirley, "Open Admissions"

- HANDOUT 3: INTERVIEW PLANNING SHEET

- Access to a video camera, VCR, and TV monitor

- HANDOUT 4: EDUCATION OPINIONNAIRE: WHAT'S THE POINT OF EDUCATION?

Procedures

- Distribute copies of the short play "Open Admissions." This work raises issues such as educators' lowered expectations, racism, and "selling out." It also questions the notion and validity of equal educational opportunity. Students are to read this play aloud together. There are only two roles. After the reading, select and write a few of the following statements on the board, one at a time:

1. Alice is, in some ways, personally responsible for Calvin's dilemma.
2. The system has victimized Alice as much as it has victimized Calvin.
3. Alice is right: All the liberal education in the world won't help Calvin unless he learns to talk like a White man.
4. As Alice says, Black students who "were no better" than Calvin but who were "perceived as better" got into Ivy League graduate programs. In other words, because of a type of reverse discrimination, it actually is easier for Blacks and other minorities to make it in our society.
5. Calvin cannot do what Alice wants him to because of his economic and social reality.
6. Alice should start grading Calvin on his actual performance, not on his effort.

- After writing the first statement on the board, ask students if they agree or disagree. Have them state and defend their stances. Continue with other selected statements. This activity can be designed as a debate, informal small group discussions, or individual writing exercises. This lesson closes with a more personal series of controversial statements relating to education; for this reason, I do not like to sustain a long debate on these issues now.

- Prepare students to plan and conduct a sample interview. Students should predict how Alice and Calvin might answer questions such as "What is education?" and "What is the point of education?" The interview should be videotaped if possible. Using audiotapes to record the proceedings is another option.

Ask students to name preparatory steps for interviewing. They may believe that all they need is a list of prepared questions. Make sure they understand the interviewer's responsibilities: She or he also must introduce the interviewees, invite them to tell stories, inspire dialogue around an issue, and so forth. This first interview most likely will focus on expectations of education. The interviewees will be Calvin and Alice.

- Instructors should plan the specifics of the interview with the class, distributing HANDOUT 3: INTERVIEW PLANNING SHEET. Alternatively, a student producer can lead the class in this activity. Each student should have a copy of this handout so that she or he can use it for future reference.

- Pick two students and ask them to play the two characters in the interview. (If they enjoy role playing, instructors also can assign two students to play Marian and Stephen, characters from stories read in the last lesson. This a stretch, though.) Assign other roles for the exercise; make sure that there is a student willing to play host and that there are camera operators if the interview is to be videotaped. The host will do the actual interviewing and will need a list of the best questions compiled by the class on their Interview Planning Sheets.

- Have students conduct the interviews and videotape them if possible. Students in the audience (if the interview is not being videotaped) should take notes on the interview.

Make sure you do both an audio and video test if you are going to videotape the interview. I cannot stress this point forcefully enough. Most of my students (even the articulate, talkative ones) do not speak clearly and loudly enough on videotape. As a result, we have spent long sessions conducting brilliant interviews that have turned out to be totally inaudible.

- Optional: Assign selected interview questions for students to answer in writing, according to their own opinions and experiences.

- When the interviews are over, have students analyze this first effort:

    1. Were "Alice" and "Calvin" comfortable?
    2. Were the questions well written, or did they provoke only short answers?

3. Did the interviewer make interviewees feel comfortable enough to answer questions with stories? Did they relate and react to each other's comments?

Ideally, after the interview, students who were in the audience now should know more about the characters' and their own opinions on the meaning and the objectives of education.

• Next, ask students if their opinions about education are being affected by these activities. Distribute HANDOUT 4: EDUCATION OPINIONNAIRE. Divide students into small groups to discuss these controversial statements and come to group consensus. Reassemble the class. Go over the opinionnaire. Ask students to defend their opinions. Assign written explanations for selected (particularly heartfelt or ambivalent) opinions. Make sure students save these papers.

HANDOUT 3: INTERVIEW PLANNING SHEET

1. On what issue will this interview focus?

2. Name your interviewee(s):

3. Where will your interviews take place?

4. If the interviews are to be videotaped, how will you arrange the interviewer and the interviewee(s)?

5. What introductory questions will you ask to make sure your interview contains all necessary background information?

6. What do you want to make your audience think or feel after they read or see your interview?

7. List four or five questions you will use to prompt your interviewee(s):

Stern. *Teaching English So It Matters.* © 1995 Corwin Press, Inc.

HANDOUT 4: EDUCATION OPINIONNAIRE: WHAT'S THE POINT OF EDUCATION?

Names: _____

Directions: Read each statement aloud, and discuss it with your group. You will need to defend your opinions later in class discussion.

1. Young people need school so that they can learn two important skills: reading and writing.

TRUE   or   FALSE

2. Young people need school so that they can learn one important skill: reading.

TRUE   or   FALSE

3. Young people need school to learn skills that will allow them to make money.

TRUE   or   FALSE

4. Young people need school to keep them off the streets.

TRUE   or   FALSE

5. The most important skill young people learn in school is how to compete against others.

TRUE   or   FALSE

6. The most important skill young people learn in school is how to cooperate with others.

TRUE   or   FALSE

7. School exists so that young people can learn to value themselves and their own opinions.

TRUE   or   FALSE

8. School exists so that young people can learn to "fit into society."

TRUE   or   FALSE

9. School is the place where young people get educated.

TRUE   or   FALSE

LESSON 4: SCHOOL AND EDUCATIONAL CONTROL

Objectives

- To read accounts of a teenager's struggles with standard prescribed curriculum in school

- To consider larger issues underlying control and regulation in school

Materials

Selections from a novel or biographical work in which a teenager's education is determined by forces outside and unsympathetic to him or her. I use:

- *Always Running* by Luis Rodríguez (excerpts from Chapters 6 and 7)

Procedures

- Briefly introduce and set up characters from work to be read. Here is some background on Luis Rodríguez, author of *Always Running: La Vida Loca: Gang Days in L.A.*:

Luis J. Rodríguez grew up in Watts and East Los Angeles in the late 1960s and early 1970s. He joined a gang at age 11. By the age of 18, he had lost 25 friends to gang warfare, police killings, drug overdoses, and suicide. He was active in the gang throughout his youth but began to question the violence and death in this crazy life—*la vida loca*. He moved to Chicago, and when his son, Ramiro, joined a gang at age 15, Rodríguez began writing *Always Running*. This book tells Rodríguez's story.

Explain that the class will be reading parts of the work. If students enjoy this reading, they should read the whole book (*Always Running* is available in paperback) and also can check out Rodríguez's poetry: *Poems Across the Pavement* (1989) and *The Concrete River* (1991).

- Distribute reading material. Students can read in class or for homework. Assign small group activities in which students are to confer on events of importance in the reading and generate discussion questions based on these key passages.

- In discussions of the readings, be sure to address the issues of control in education. For example, ask class to cite passages in which Rodríguez lost interest in school and see if they can infer reasons for this.

   1. How was his education affected by mainstream curriculum?
   2. Why did he begin to take control of his own education? How did he do this? What were the results?

LESSON 5: CONSIDERING EDUCATIONAL WRONGS: PERSONAL EXPERIENCE

Objectives

- To consider larger issues underlying control and regulation in school

- To further develop narrative writing skills

- To further develop interviewing skills

Materials

- HANDOUT 3: INTERVIEW PLANNING SHEET

- Access to video camera, VCR, and TV monitor

Procedures

- Ask students to consider the questions raised by the last lesson's discussions in light of their own experiences. Assign Journal 2: Write about a time you wanted control over your education. What happened when you tried to make decisions about your own education?

- After reading the journals students choose to share, the teacher should have some of them read aloud (always with the writer's permission). After noting the basic events of the story on the board, ask the class to brainstorm about how this story could change to facilite real education. Ask students to imagine what should have happened, so that each student's experience met his or her educational needs and interests.

- Ask each student to consider his or her Journal Assignment 2 and Journal Assignment 1 also (in which each wrote about a test they took that was in some way unfair). Assign Journal 3: Retell Journal 1 or 2 so that the experience becomes an example of optimal education. Ask students to include what should have happened. Explain that this is not mere make-believe: Students will be describing the factors and conditions they need to be present in their own education.

One student, Dinh, wrote a piece for the Journal 2 assignment, "Unfair Test," in which he talked about his experience in freshman Algebra, when he missed and failed a test because he was out of school celebrating the Vietnamese New Year with his family. He was not allowed to make up the test.

In Dinh's Journal 3: "A Better Idea" his teacher gives him enough time to study and make up the test. After he takes the test, she has him write a report on the Vietnamese New Year. The whole class decides to write reports and learn about each other's family traditions and holiday celebrations.

• Review elements of good narrative writing (Lesson 2). Have students retrieve their notes and teach this review session. They should copy their notes on the board and list formal criteria for Journal 3. Here are notes two students in my class wrote on the board for this assignment:

Good narrative writing

1. has dialogue, is indented in separate paragraphs
2. describes action
3. tells what the characters are feeling
4. starts at an interesting moment

Journal 3 needs *at least*

1. ten lines of dialogue
2. one paragraph that gives details about what's happening
3. three times where feelings are described
4. an exciting start

Make sure students save journals entries and notes.

• Next, have students try another interview—this time, with a student playing Luis Rodríguez and one or two students playing themselves. Help students plan to experiment with different interview formats and modify and refine questions:

1. Is it better to conduct group interviews or to interview characters one at a time?
2. What types of questions prompt simple *yes*'s and *no*'s?
3. What types of questions invite interviewees to launch into stories and reminiscences?

Refer to or distribute another copy of HANDOUT 3: INTERVIEW PLANNING SHEET. These are the questions my students developed in conducting their interviews:

Questions for Student Interviews

1. What do you feel are teachers' attitudes toward students?
2. Have you ever had a teacher whom you felt was negligent?
3. Have you ever been in a class with no teacher? What happens when your teacher is absent? What happens in study halls?
4. What's the average number of students in each of your classes?
5. What is the racial make-up of your school?
6. What conditions are the facilities (gym, library, computers) in?
7. Are there enough books and supplies to go around?
8. How often do you cut classes?

9. Do you think you learn anything in classes? Do you think the teachers care?

10. Do you want your children to have the same education you have had?

11. Given your education, where do you think you will be in ten years?

• If the interview is to be videotaped, do not tape over the first ("Alice and Calvin") interviews. Have students conduct the interview, then review and compare this second effort with the first try. Be sure to save and file all written work.

LESSON 6: WHAT SHOULD BE TAUGHT? WHO SHOULD DECIDE? (for lower level readers)

Objectives

• To read unconventional commentary on the purpose and priorities of education

• To consider personal priorities and devise an individual educational agenda

• To learn and practice effective note taking

Materials

Any work that presents an alternative to conventional school curriculum. I use:

• Sagan, Carl, "Twelve Things I Wish They Taught Me in School"

• Copies of blank schedules used in your school

Procedures

• After reading and writing accounts of problematic educations, ask students if they have any ideas about reorganizing school and what they learn there. Distribute copies of Carl Sagan's "Twelve Things I Wish They Taught Me in School." Recommend that students highlight ideas and important sections as they read.

• Go over main points of readings with class. Present suggestions for a definite note-taking technique. See HANDOUT G: NOTE TAKING (Chapter 4).

• Students may have trouble with Sagan's style and vocabulary. Be sure to devote enough time to this work so that students are able to grasp its finer points. Make sure that students have understood both the author's ideas and his reasons for rethinking traditional educational approaches. Ask the class if they agree with Sagan. Discuss whether they think that every high school student could figure out his or her own objectives as Carl Sagan did and set up a schedule to meet them.

• Distribute schedules. It works best to obtain actual blanks of the format and type used at your school. Students are to think about what they need to learn and devise their own daily educational schedules. Review these as students think appropriate. They may be bashful about revealing their wishes; they may be eager to demonstrate their individuality.

My students have typically jumped right into this exercise. One of my classes, reading at a seventh grade level, read Sagan's piece and could not wait to get started on their own schedules. Students assigned themselves classes in the following areas: Hairstyling, Auto Mechanics, Child Care, Guitars, Snakes, Dance, Cooking, Personal Money Management, Writing Poetry, Reading Poetry, Fashion, Getting Along With Family, "Baloney Detection" (Sagan's term), Music, Self-Defense, and some traditional high school offerings (Science, Math, English).

Instruction in some of these areas is available to affluent teens—but my students do not have the resources. This exercise helped them look around a bit, consider their likes and dislikes and their strengths and weaknesses, and expand their educational horizons. It helped me see them as multifaceted people with needs and tastes beyond the big issues and skills we work on in English class.

LESSON 6: WHAT SHOULD BE TAUGHT? WHO SHOULD DECIDE? (for higher level readers)

Objectives

- To read unconventional perspectives on the purpose and priorities of education

- To consider personal priorities and devise an individual educational agenda

- To learn and practice effective note taking

Materials

- UNIT MATERIALS: Abstract of Ivan Illich's *Deschooling Society*

- Copies of blank schedules used in your school

- HANDOUT G: NOTE TAKING (Chapter 4)

Procedures

- After reading and writing accounts of problematic educations, ask students if they have any ideas about reorganizing school and what they learn there. Distribute copies of UNIT MATERIALS: Abstract of *Deschooling Society* by Ivan Illich. Recommend that students highlight ideas and important sections as they read.

- Go over main points of readings with class. Present a definite note-taking technique. Refer to HANDOUT G: NOTE TAKING (Chapter 4).

- Make sure that students have understood both the author's ideas and his reasons for rethinking traditional educational approaches. Ask the class if they agree with Illich:

    1. Could his proposals work?
    2. Could these proposals work for you personally?

- Distribute schedules. It works best to obtain actual blanks of the format and type used at your school. Students are to think about what they need to learn and devise their own daily educational menus. Review these as students deem appropriate. They may be bashful about revealing their wishes; they may be eager to demonstrate their individuality.

- It may be difficult to make the stretch from the familiar class schedule to Illich's unconventional model. This activity might need some prefatory remarks such as the following:

Ivan Illich has some radical ideas about education and schools. In the section titled "Prescriptions for Change," his proposals get specific. Using his model, your assignment is to figure out your own educational plan: What do you want to learn? Where do you want to learn it? Who do you want to teach you?

Start with your schedule of classes. Using this familiar format, replace the classes you have now with skills and subjects you want to learn. List these skills and subjects, say where the session will be taught (specify the store, stadium, theater, etc.), and name the instructors.

Using Illich's model, students assigned themselves days in theaters, hair salons, and laboratories as apprentices. They named local disc jockeys and mechanics as mentors.

Abstract of *Deschooling Society* by Ivan Illich (1970)

Introduction

Illich begins his book by discussing some common misconceptions about school. He draws some distinctions between terms that you might think have the same meanings. For example, he says:

> Many students, especially those who are poor, intuitively know what the schools do for them. . . . The pupil is . . . "schooled" to confuse teaching with learning, grade advancement with education, a diploma with competence, and fluency with the ability to say something new. (p. 1)

In Illich's opinion, schools in the United States have become just factories through which young people must pass. Kids are kept off the streets, are taught to play by specific rules, and are rewarded at the end of 12 years with a piece of paper. This piece of paper says they are ready to assume an appropriate position in the adult world. And we call this "education."

Obviously, Illich thinks our schools and entire educational system need revision. He does believe, however, that everyone—rich, poor, male, female— should have the same, fair opportunity to go to school—if he or she wants to. One of the main problems in the United States educational system, as Illich sees it, is that school is compulsory. He says:

> Equal educational opportunity is, indeed, both a desirable and a feasible goal, but to equate this with obligatory schooling is to equate salvation with the church. (p. 15)

> Every one of the modern school's problems can be traced back to the enormous amount of control that the government exercises over it. There should be no such central planning and control.

> Two centuries ago the United States led the world in a movement to disestablish the monopoly of a single church. Now we need the constitutional disestablishment of the monopoly of the school, and thereby of a system which legally combines prejudice with discrimination. (p. 15)

Not everyone needs or benefits from the same kind and amount of schooling. "Most people acquire most of their knowledge outside school . . . [and nowadays, if people learn a lot while they are in school, it is only because school] has become their place of confinement during an increasing part of their lives" (p. 18).

This, then, is the basis of *Deschooling Society:* Illich spends the next hundred pages analyzing what is wrong with the education system as it exists and then offers prescriptions for its improvement.

What's Wrong With Schools?

"The search for alternatives in education must start with an agreement on what it is we mean by 'school.' [Activities performed by the school include] custodial care, selection, indoctrination, and learning" (p. 37). What does each of these functions mean? "Custodial care" is simple: School acts as a parent/babysitter/police officer, dictating and enforcing rules. After all, young people do not always act within socially acceptable boundaries.

Second, schools act as social selectors. Students are divided according to age, race, gender, ethnicity, socioeconomic level, and intelligence. A student's future success or failure is always highly affected (often, is even determined) by these variables. School is the first place in which society sits in judgment of who you are. School is where you begin to feel the wheels of the system turn.

What about indoctrination? At school, students are conditioned into believing that they must meet certain requirements if they are going to be educated. The emphasis is on meeting those requirements—"earning credits"—rather than on learning. This is very confining, according to Illich. "It is not liberating or educational because school reserves instruction to those whose every step in learning fits previously approved measures of social control" (p. 17).

Finally, school is for learning. But realistically, school is not the only place where people get educated; "most learning happens casually" (p. 18). This may sound obvious to you, but it is a strange new consideration to some educators who believe that school is the only place in which real learning occurs. True, school is the place in which a great deal of skill mastery goes on: People learn how to read, write, and compute there. Ideally, they also should learn how to use these skills effectively.

But school manages to mess up these two modes of learning by linking them together, awkwardly, in irrelevant ways, to the detriment of both. There you are, struggling to read graphs—in the middle of history class! You don't know whether to figure out the pie chart or think about the lives of the people represented on the charts. Which is more important here—skill mastery (reading the graph) or critical thinking (considering other lives and other realities)?

You can flip the discussion around, too, and think about all the problems that get in the way when you are given the opportunity to think about juicy topics at school, in "liberal education." It can be hard to get involved in interesting discussions at school, for a number of reasons. First, you have to be there. It's the law. The teacher is requiring you to think about this issue. Your grade depends on your answers. Finally, if you suspect that your conclusions differ from the accepted (teacher's) conclusions, you run the risk of criticism, punishment, or failure. Not one of these obligations or possibilities is very liberating or exciting.

Prescriptions for Change

As stated in the last section, Illich recognizes that two distinct kinds of learning are necessary to a person's education. First, people need to acquire certain skills. Second, people need to examine those skills on a deeper level and learn how to put them to good use. Education continues throughout your life: Exercising these two processes leads to specialization and concentration on certain skills, depending on individual interest, choice, opportunity, and ability.

How do we learn these two processes? Illich says we learn by having access to (a) things, (b) models, (c) peers, and (d) elders. The institution of public school as it exists today does not use all four resources. It is no wonder, says Illich, that most students do not learn both processes effectively. What, then, can be done?

For teaching skills, he says, use peers, models, elders, anyone who cares and who knows how. You don't necessarily have to use teachers. Illich says a teaching certificate does not guarantee anything but continuation of the system and, in fact:

> Most teachers of arts and trades are less skillful, less inventive, and less communicative than the best crafts-men and trademen . . . Experiments conducted by Angel Quintero in Puerto Rico suggest that many young teen-agers, if given the proper incentives, programs, and access to tools, are better than most teachers at introducing their peers to the scientific exploration of planets, stars, and matter, and to the discovery of how and why a motor or radio functions. (p. 22)

Do you think this idea would work? Could a friend or relative effectively teach someone how to read?

And what about using these basic skills? How would we get together with people who wanted to discuss the same ideas, who wanted to think, who could teach us those more specific things we want to know? Illich proposes a kind of "educational matchmaking." People, he says,

> should meet around a problem chosen and defined by their own initiative . . . The most radical alternative to school would be a network or service which gave each man the same opportunity to share his current concern with others motivated by the same concern. . . . Let me give an example . . . each man, at any given moment and at a minimum price, could identify himself to a computer with his address and telephone number, indicating the book, article, film, [idea] or recording on which he seeks a partner for discussion [or instruction]. Within days he could receive by mail a list of others who recently had taken the same initiative. (p. 28)

(Illich wrote this before personal computers and modems made the last step of this vision—waiting for a letter—obsolete.) His plan does link us up with peers and elders. Skill exchanges such as these would work fine for people who know what they are interested in, who already have a good idea of their abilities and concerns. What about those people who don't yet know what interests them?

These people need access to things and models. We need to give young people, less-specialized learners, a chance to take things apart, to visit shops and factories that interest them and get their hands on much of the world that is currently kept "secret." These areas now are open only to the privileged few who have paid money, received appropriate educations, and thus have learned the "secrets" (mechanics, air traffic controllers, telephone repair persons, chefs, dry cleaners, etc.). Illich wants to "deschool" the potentially educational objects and processes of the world and make them available to people who are interested in them. Open up the railroad yard, for example, provide for safety there, and let those children and adults who are interested come in and observe.

> There could be tool shops, libraries, laboratories, and gaming rooms. Photo labs and offset presses would allow neighborhood presses to flourish. . . . [There could be] office equipment for use and repair . . . jukeboxes . . . film clubs . . . museum outlets . . . [for all who wanted to get involved in these various arenas] . . . The professional personnel needed for this network would be more like custodians, museum guides, or reference librarians than like teachers . . . they could refer their clients to . . . the next showing . . . could furnish guides . . . could refer those who needed advice to "elders" who could provide it. (p. 121)

How would all the expensive instruments fare in this plan? Realistically, could we allow valuable instruments, machines, and tools to be so available to the public? Why are they so expensive in the first place? Illich says that his ideas "could empower the individual to reclaim the right to use [these things] for education" and could free us from the tight corporate control that makes machines like these so rare and expensive (p. 125).

Conclusion

Certainly, replacing the modern school with skill exchanges and reference services would require radical social change. But this is absolutely necessary, says Illich. One of the reasons society is such a mess is because of the types of people our schools keep producing. If we can work to change that reality, the larger social picture that emerges will necessarily change (for the better), too.

> [Currently,] the creature whom schools need as a client has neither the autonomy nor the motivation to grow on his own . . .
> Inevitably the deschooling of society will blur the distinctions between economics, education, and politics on which the . . . stability of the present world order . . . now rests. Our review of educational institutions leads us to a review of our image of man. (p. 150)

Do you agree?

SOURCE: Abstracted from Ivan Illich, *Deschooling Society*, 1970 (New York: Harper & Row). Copyright © Ivan Illich. To be republished by Austin and Winfield, San Francisco. Excerpted and abridged by D. Stern with permission from the author.

LESSON 7: INDIVIDUALITY AND HYPOCRISY IN SCHOOL

Objectives

- To read poems addressing education-related issues

- To become familiar with rhyme scheme

- To practice new note-taking technique

- To practice freewriting or write in a creative style of students' choice

Materials

Short poems or songs dealing with education-related issues. I use:

- UNIT MATERIALS: "Lies" by Yevgeny Yevtushenko

- UNIT MATERIALS: "What Did You Learn in School Today?" by Tom Paxton

- UNIT MATERIALS: "Invictus" by William Ernest Henley

- "The Perforated Spirit" by Morris Bishop

Procedures

- Distribute poetry. The first two poems are written in a simple and direct style and make a case against hypocrisy in school. Ask students to underline the profound truths in Yevtushenko's poem and the lies in Paxton's song. The second two poems can be read as a pair commenting on the struggles to maintain individuality ("The Perforated Spirit" is a light, ironic update of the classic "Invictus").

- Take notes on the poems' meanings and significance regarding education. Discussions can follow questions devised by the teacher or the students. Stress new note-taking format.

- Also introduce and have students note rhyme scheme. The poems (all except the translated "Lies") follow a simple, regular rhyme scheme. Show students how to mark end rhymes with *a*'s and *b*'s to arrive at simple rhyme formulas, that is, "What Did You Learn in School Today?" = *abab-ccdd-ab*; "Invictus" = *abab*; "The Perforated Spirit" = *abab*. Ask for volunteers to write excerpts from songs or other poetry on the board. Have the class practice analyzing end rhyme scheme for these works, too.

- After naming the main themes and issues in the poems, practice freewriting with the class. Explain that in freewriting students must write continuously, putting whatever comes into their heads on the paper and paying no attention to mechanics if that tends to slow them down. It is a prewriting exercise designed to get at students' own truths.

There are many ways to conduct a freewriting exercise. Instructors will need to experiment to see what works best with the class. One way is to assign freewriting immediately after discussing the poetry to give students an opportunity to express their reactions. Freewriting tends to work well if assigned following good, heated discussions; in this case, instructors should cut off class dialogue when there are still plenty of hands up and ask the class to take out paper and freewrite.

• When students are done freewriting, let them work with what they have expressed in any way they choose. They can incorporate lines from their freewriting into rhyming poetry or rap lyrics (have them note rhyme scheme). They can polish their freewriting into more coherent but still free-form pieces. Students with artistic bents may want to illustrate their ideas or make a collage expressing their observations about individuality and truthfulness in school.

I had the class report the parts they liked best from their freewriting and had one student write all reported phrases on the board. We worked together as class to weave students' contributions together into this composite poem, which contrasts two students' feelings about their experiences in school:

I never knew they were lies
    I knew they were lies
I didn't learn anything in school today
    Everybody expected me to fail
The teacher learned to hate my guts
    I learned to hate my teacher's guts
My teacher thinks she is the captain of my fate
    I am the master of my soul
When you try to stick up for yourself,
    They send you to the principal
        You are just a number to this school
            They're set to make you fail
                I didn't have a chance—

    The black night is every night

I dropped out
    I kept reading

Lies

by Yevgeny Yevtushenko

Telling lies to the young is wrong.
Proving to them that lies are true is wrong.
Telling them that God's in his heaven
and all's well with the world is wrong.
The young know what you mean. The young are people.
Tell them the difficulties can't be counted,
and let them see not only what will be
but see with clarity these present times.
Say obstacles exist they must encounter,
sorrow happens, hardship happens.
The hell with it. Who never knew
the price of happiness will not be happy.
Forgive no error you recognize,
it will repeat itself, increase,
and afterward our pupils
will not forgive in us what we forgave.

SOURCE: "Lies" by Yevgeny Yevtushenko, in *Yevgeny Yevtushenko: The Collected Poems 1952-1990*, translated by Robin Milner-Gulland and Peter Levi, 1991, New York: Henry Holt & Co. Reprinted here with permission.

UNIT MATERIALS

What Did You Learn in School Today?

by Tom Paxton

What did you learn in school today,
Dear little boy of mine?
What did you learn in school today,
Dear little boy of mine?
I learned that Washington never told a lie
I learned that soldiers seldom die,
I learned that everybody's free,
That's what the teacher said to me,
And that's what I learned in school today.
That's what I learned in school.

What did you learn in school today,
Dear little boy of mine?
What did you learn in school today,
Dear little boy of mine?
I learned that policemen are my friends,
I learned that justice never ends,
I learned that murderers die for their crimes,
Even if we make a mistake sometimes,
And that's what I learned in school today.
That's what I learned in school.

What did you learn in school today,
Dear little boy of mine?
What did you learn in school today,
Dear little boy of mine?
I learned that our government must be strong
It's always right and never wrong.
Our leaders are the finest men,
And we elect them again and again,
And that's what I learned in school today,
That's what I learned in school.

What did you learn in school today,
Dear little boy of mine?
What did you learn in school today,
Dear little boy of mine?
I learned that war is not so bad,
I learned about the great ones we have had,
We fought in Germany and in France,
And someday I might get my chance,
And that's what I learned in school today,
That's what I learned in school.

UNIT MATERIALS

Invictus

by William Ernest Henley

Out of the black night that covers me,
    Black as the pit from pole to pole,
I thank whatever gods may be
    For my unconquerable soul.

In the fell clutch of circumstance
    I have not winced nor cried aloud.
Under the bludgeonings of chance
    My head is bloody, but unbowed.

Beyond this place of wrath and tears
    Looms but the horror of the shade,
And yet the menace of the years
    Finds and shall find me unafraid.

It matters not how strait the gate,
    How charged with punishments the scroll,
I am the master of my fate:
    I am the captain of my soul.

SOURCE: "Invictus" by William Ernest Henley, in A. Daigon & R. T. LaConte (Eds.), *The good life U.S.A.: A book about the pursuit of happiness,* p. 10, New York: Bantam. (Original work published in London in 1908 in *Works of William Ernest Henley.* Reprinted by AMS Press, New York.)

LESSON 8: WHAT MAKES A SCHOOL WORK FOR STUDENTS?

Objectives

• To consider and name the instructional approaches and philosophies that students find most conducive to their own learning

• To evaluate students' past educational experiences in light of these realizations

Materials

• Copies of the rules, policies, or mission statement of your school (or of another similar institution)

• HANDOUT 5: SCHOOL REPORT CARD

Procedures

• Distribute copies of the rules, policies, or mission statement of an educational institution. I used the "Uniform Discipline Code" of the Chicago Public Schools. Read these with the students. Have them take notes on the information, adding critical commentary and questioning underlying assumptions where appropriate.

My class took issue with the rights and responsibilities delineated in the document. They felt that certain student "rights" (i.e., students could expect "reasonable, fair, courteous, and consistent treatment that does not violate their rights") were not actually respected by the schools. They also felt that some "responsibilities" (i.e., students should conduct "activities in a gracious manner that provides for due respect and dignity") were so subjective as to be virtual setups for faculty who wanted an excuse to discipline certain students. They were required to provide experiential evidence for these claims, and we noted their objections in our notes.

• Ask students to consider what they would do differently if they were going to start their own school. For example:

1. How would it look?
2. What courses would be offered?
3. How would students get evaluated?
4. What approach would the faculty take to classroom teaching, discipline, establishing rules and regulations?

If students want to work with these questions as a complete assignment, let them work in pairs or teams to design the perfect school.

- Distribute HANDOUT 5: SCHOOL REPORT CARD. The class should work as a whole to supply the criteria for each subtopic. After the report card is ready, let students grade their individual teachers, classes, and educational experiences. Assemble the class and report "grades."

HANDOUT 5: SCHOOL REPORT CARD

Criteria:

Teachers:	Has patience with students			
1.				
2.				
3.				
4.				

Comments:

Criteria:

Administration:	Listens to both sides of story			
1.				
2.				
3.				
4.				

Comments:

Criteria:

Courses:				
1.				
2.				
3.				
4.				

Comments:

Other evaluations
Equipment:
Facility:
Other:

Stern. *Teaching English So It Matters.* © 1995 Corwin Press, Inc.

LESSON 9: WHAT MAKES STUDENTS WORK IN SCHOOL?

Objectives

- To examine motivation as a concept and relate it to education

- To consider the relationship between bribery and motivation in school

- To continue developing interviewing skills

Materials

- Transcribed scene from "Room 222" (pp. 17-19 in *The Good Life U.S.A.: A Book About the Pursuit of Happiness*)

- HANDOUT 3: INTERVIEW PLANNING SHEET

- Access to video camera, VCR, and TV monitor

Procedures

- Ask class if they are surprised by the school report card grades. Review the idea of the utopian school—the one that would get straight A's on yesterday's report card. Discuss with class if all students would be successful in such a school and what students would need to do to keep their end of the bargain. In the ensuing discussion, the idea of *motivation* is bound to come up. Ask students what they think about this term and record responses on board:

    1. Is every student motivated in some way? Why or why not?
    2. What motivates people outside of schools and classrooms?
    3. What has motivated students in school?

- I use a transcribed scene from the early 1970s TV show "Room 222" for the next procedure. Distribute copies of this scene or paraphrase the situation: A high school teacher and his principal are talking about the teacher's latest effort to motivate his students to read—he has been giving them money. The principal argues that this is bribery. It will make students materialistic. They will want to work for money only. Grades should motivate students. The teacher maintains that grades are meaningless to his students, most of whom will not be going to college. He says he didn't teach them to be materialistic; he's just trying to use their value system so they will educate themselves.

- After acting out the scene (or relating its thrust), ask the students where they stand on this issue. Arrange an "opinion lineup." Ask the student who most strongly agrees with the principal ("We should not pay students to come to school and learn!") to stand on one side of the room. Ask the student who most strongly agrees with the teacher in the scene ("You've got to make education valuable in a way students understand!") to stand opposite the first student, at the other end of the room. Tell the rest of the students in the class that they need to arrange themselves according to their positions on the money-as-motivation issue. Students are to stand in a line across the room, ranged from one extreme position to the other. They will need to find out their peers' positions and stand to the left or right accordingly. This gets unwieldy with groups above 20. Use your judgment: With larger (or sedentary or excitable) classes, choose a smaller group of students (10-15) to discern and demonstrate their relative positions.

- Next, ask students to consider what motivates them.

    1. Is it always money?
    2. What else has made you act or work for something?

Write Journal Assignment 4 on the board: Write about a time you really were motivated to do something, in or out of school. For what were you working? Why did you feel like working?

- When students are done writing, discuss Journal Assignment 4. Ask the class to consider whether the motivation named in this journal entry could work in a school setting and what teachers can do to help students get in touch with what motivates them.

- Amend topics first specified on HANDOUT 3: INTERVIEW PLANNING SHEET, adding questions on motivation and teachers' perspectives. Plan and carry out additional interviews (interview as many students as possible by the end of the unit). In addition to continued peer interviewing, this is a good time for students to interview the teacher. Again, if the interviews are being video-taped, make sure that you do not erase past interviews as you conduct new ones.

LESSON 10: ARE ALL EDUCATIONS EQUAL?

Objectives

• To become more aware of the relationship between economic status and educational opportunities

• To learn about educational experiences in other sociocultural groups

• To become aware of similarities and disparities among different sociocultural groups

• To practice interviewing skills with strangers

• To develop directorial, editing, and other decision-making skills in creating a video comparing educational experiences: a "High School in the 1990s" documentary (if the necessary equipment is available)

Materials

• Excerpts from Jonathan Kozol's *Savage Inequalities* (pp. 51-74)

• Permission to visit a classroom in another part of the city or community and to interview (on videotape, if possible) students there on their educational experiences

• HANDOUT 3: INTERVIEW PLANNING SHEET

• Access to a video camera, VCR, and TV monitor

Procedures

• Teachers will need to prepare for this lesson beforehand:

1. Set up interview dates with the teacher and school administration of the school to be visited in another area.
2. Get permission and arrange transportation to the other school.

• If video camera, VCRs, and TV monitor are available (or if you have access to video editing equipment), explain that the final project of the Education unit will be a documentary-type video and that students have been working on it for the past few weeks. If no such equipment is available, explain that the students will expand the scope of their interviews by traveling to another area and interviewing students from another school in another community.

• Distribute excerpts from *Savage Inequalities* (pp. 51-74) or other information that details and compares the various services and resources that are available to schools in affluent and poor communities. I supplemented the excerpts from Kozol with copies of a school newspaper, a recent annual report, and a calendar from the well-furnished school we were to visit.

• Analyze and discuss the reading and whatever other supplemental material you use. Let the students generate discussion questions based on the information they read. Remind them that they will be visiting and interviewing students from this other community. What are their expectations? How do they feel about visiting these classes? Students may be uncomfortable (inadequate, envious, out of place) about the coming visit. Although individual students' feelings cannot be anticipated, teachers must try to prepare students for their visit by providing sufficient background information and lots of assurances.

My students, many of whom are gangbangers and cannot travel to other parts of the city freely (they fear for their lives on enemy turf), were at first opposed to the idea of visiting another school. I had set up a visit to Niles North High School, in Skokie, Illinois, a prosperous suburban community just north of Chicago. I worked hard to convince my students that they would be in no danger in this school. I advised them to wear no hats or other gang identification. After they read excerpts from Kozol's Savage Inequalities, *some were willing to admit that there might be communities in which their gang affiliations would be unknown and largely irrelevant. Not all students went to Niles; their fears could not be assuaged.*

• Students should prepare, as always, for interviews with HANDOUT 3: INTERVIEW PLANNING SHEET. By this time, all questions should be refined to elicit willing and expansive response on the part of the interviewed subjects. Students also should select the interview format they feel works best: one-on-one, group or panel conversation, question-and-answer, and so forth.

• Conduct interviews of visited class members. Videotape interviews if possible and if permission has been secured.

• Review interviews in class. Discuss the similarities that are apparent in all educations, and the differences that exist between them. Student can write short pieces comparing elements of interviewed students' educations.

• If you have been videotaping and students are interested in producing a finished product, review all interviews and choose the footage appropriate for your documentary on "High School in the 1990s" (or whatever the class decides they want to call it). Have the class work in teams to sketch out and videotape introductory sections or whatever they need to make the video flow. This work is done best by a team of committed students (working with the teacher and/or an experienced video specialist), rather than by the whole class.

ADDITIONAL LESSONS

Objective

- To prepare additional projects reflecting both student experiences and their hopes for the future

Materials

- Selections from Matt Groening's *School Is Hell* (one selection reprinted here with permission)

- Lou Carlozo's article "High School Drama Students Give Legislators a Tip: Act" in the *Chicago Tribune*

Procedures/Activities

- Continue designing the perfect school as suggested in Lesson 8. Depending on individual talents and interests, teams or groups of students can concentrate on various aspects of the plan. Tasks include designing the school's physical layout, constructing a scale model, preparing a student handbook, writing a school philosophy, creating an evaluation system, listing the course offerings, designing the daily schedule and disciplinary procedures, and so forth. Students may present the finished plan to administrators.

- Discuss recent debate over school choice:

  1. Will choice "deschool society"? Or will it increase the "monopoly of the school"?
  2. Should schools compete with one another for students? How would this plan affect students?

- If students are interested in the school choice issue, have them devise advertising campaigns for their school and for the ideal school. They can create commercials, print ads, radio spots, and so on.

- Discuss other current educational controversies in your state or community. Students can write letters and articles and attend meetings or demonstrations supporting the causes in which they believe. For example, see the *Chicago Tribune* article "High School Drama Students Give Legislators a Tip: Act."

- Students can create comics and cartoons depicting their educational experiences. For inspiration, distribute selections from Matt Groening's *School Is Hell* (see Figure 7.1). Students will recognize Groening's style (he is the creator of *The Simpsons*) and will appreciate these funny, thought-provoking cartoons. You can choose one cartoon style (the diagram, the classroom exchange, the illustrated list) as a model for students' cartoons or let them create their own format.

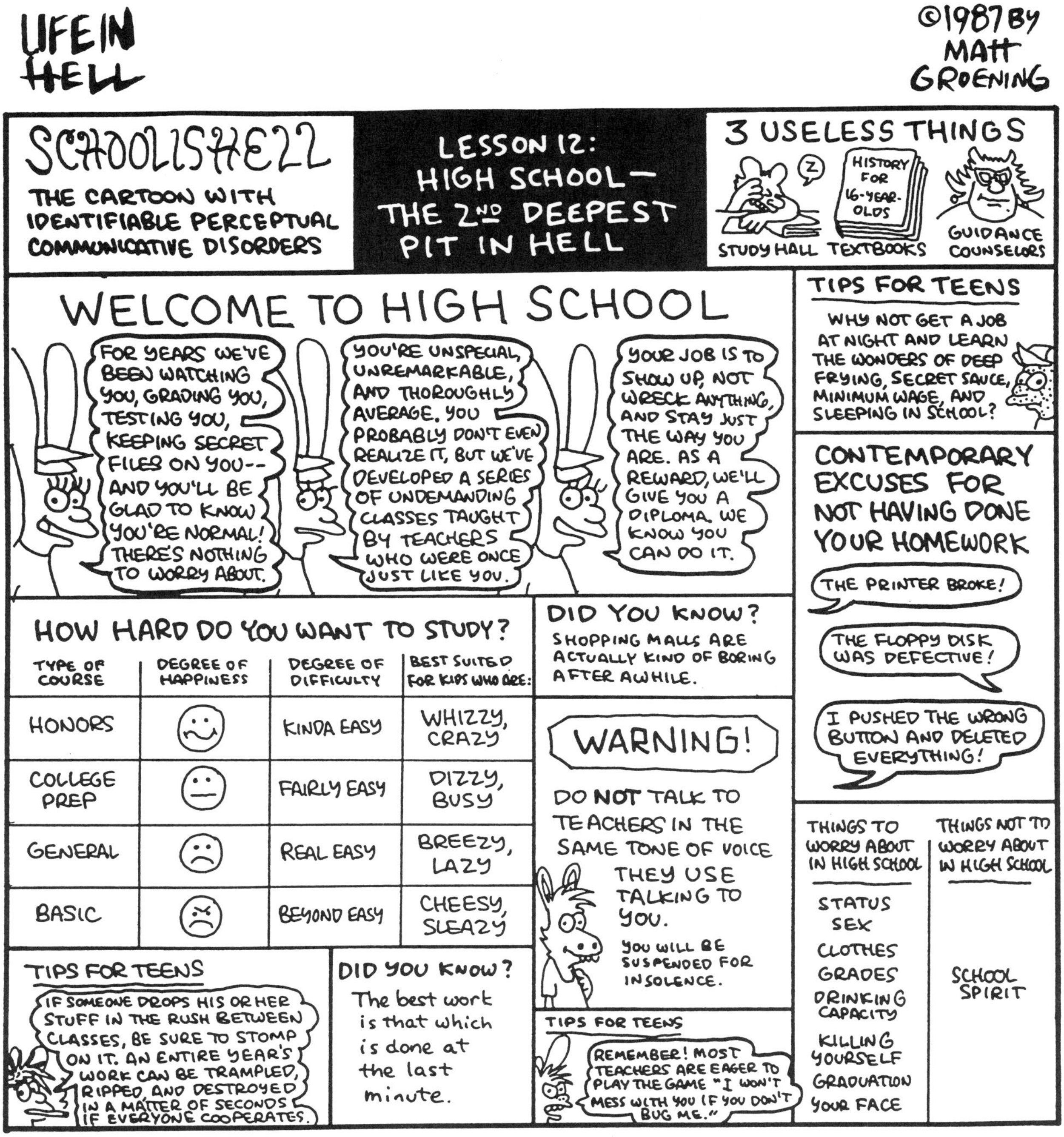

Figure 7.1. *School Is Hell* Cartoon

SOURCE: From *School Is Hell* © 1987 by Matt Groening. Reprinted by permission of Pantheon Books, a division of Random House, Inc., New York.

8

❖ The Streets

Before long, the streets became my home, my food, my money, and my bed. They have saved my life, and almost ended it. I've been in and out of hospitals, jails, drug treatment centers, and different people's homes and lives. The streets have given me knowledge, wisdom, fear, sensitivity, strength, made me weak, strong, happy, pissed off, and sad.

—Simon

Everything I really need to know, I learn on the street.

—Martin

RATIONALE

What Is the Topic of Study?

Every year, my students say they want to study "the streets." When pressed to explain, they say they want to read and write and talk about the reality they know. It does not resemble the picture of America—White, middle class, and replete with opportunity—that is painted by so many of their textbooks. Nor does it square exactly with the picture currently sensationalized by the media: constant drive-by shootings, Nike-motivated murders, and "wilding." They want to examine issues that matter to them personally: peer pressure, fighting, taking risks, families, crime, drugs, and coming of age under fire.

Any honest definition of the streets requires firsthand knowledge. The best way for instructors to open the unit is to ask students to articulate their conceptions of "the streets." Let students wrestle with definitions and big questions: What are "the streets"? How is life on the streets different from life off the streets? Is it different now from how it used to be? Does it always involve drugs and crime? How do the roles of kids and adults differ? Are the streets different for boys and girls? How? What role does ethnicity play? Are the streets a strictly urban condition? If your family has money, can you grow up on the streets? Is it as bad as recent magazines and TV specials say? Is it worse? Is there any way off the streets?

Why Will Students Be Interested in This?

This unit has been designed by and for urban teens; it gives them a chance to be incontrovertible experts. The recent explosion of urban culture regarding music, dance, and fashion may create a demand for this topic of study in other environments.

Students will identify subtopics that they think the class should cover. These include traditional teen concerns—"hanging out," popularity, and independence. In studying teen life on city street corners, a few grim additions lengthen that list: desperation, replacing family with friends, and early death. Adolescence is hard enough without these perils. Teenagers who face them will welcome a chance to speak out about them and to read of other teens' experiences under these pressures.

Why Do Students Need to Study This?

When we consider the mixed messages teenagers receive about life on the streets, it is clear why they need to start looking carefully at these images. Recent movies and songs portray the "gangsta" lifestyle in all its gritty brutality. Are these images supposed to deter teens in some way? Hardly. It's pretty exciting stuff for most teenagers, many of whom are positively besotted with media violence. They need to learn about the hardships and tragedy connected with street life—that is, if they don't already know.

For those students caught up in life on the streets themselves, nothing could be more important for them than to start looking critically at their lives. If they have become deadened to the tragedy of real-life violence, a unit on life in the streets—maybe—can reawaken their sensibilities. They must see and believe that they deserve a life free of high-risk activity, unemployment, and murder. They must begin to see that life on the streets is a conscious choice, not an inevitability.

Why Teach This Unit Now?

This is another good unit with which to begin a year or academic semester. The energy will be high and it establishes a pattern of cooperative planning between teacher and student right away. This unit provides urban instructors with a perfect opportunity to teach something *with* the students, instead of *to* them. We can show students that we will not ignore their reality, preach, or inundate them with reporters'-eye view, lurid stories of teen murders and violence. Instead, we will trust them to define the topic. Then, perhaps, they can learn to trust us.

Instructors do need to have a rough idea of where the unit will go—if only to see to the major work. There are wonderful books about growing up on the streets. I recommend either Piri Thomas's *Down These Mean Streets* (1967/1991) or Luis Rodríguez's *Always Running: La Vida Loca: Gang Days in L.A.* (1993).

Both works are substantial enough to make long lists of supporting materials and activities unnecessary. However, the unit should be scheduled to allow adequate time for Lawrence Kohlberg's theory of moral development. It also is important that students can spend a good deal of time talking and writing about their own experiences.

KEY QUESTIONS

1. What are "the streets"?

2. How is growing up "on the streets" different from growing up off the streets?

3. What impact does gender have on one's experience on the streets?

4. What is the relationship between racism, poverty, and the streets?

5. Is there any way off the streets? Is individual choice a real possibility or an impossible luxury?

TERMINAL OBJECTIVES

- To think critically about personal involvement with the streets, if applicable

- To read major work in entirety

- To reflect on unit concepts as they are presented in the major work and as they impact students' own lives

- To write and evaluate a formal essay with central thesis, textual citations, and conclusion

MATERIALS

General References (for instructors)

- Duska, Ronald (1975), *Moral Development: A Guide to Piaget and Kohlberg*

- Kuhmerker, Lisa (1991), *The Kohlberg Legacy for the Helping Professions*

Major Works

- de Jesús, Carolina María (1962), *Child of the Dark: The Diary of Carolina María de Jesús*

- Rodríguez, Luis (1993), *Always Running: La Vida Loca: Gang Days in L.A.*

- Thomas, Piri (1967/1991), *Down These Mean Streets*

Chapters and Excerpts From Longer Works

- Bing, Léon (1992), "Gang Class" from *Do or Die* (pp. 120-127)

- Price, Richard (1992), *Clockers* (pp. 345-349)

- Sheffield, Anne, and Frankel, Bruce, Editors (1988), *When I Was Young I Loved School: Dropping Out and Hanging In by Children's Express* (selections by instructor)

Articles

- Bing, Léon (1988), "Reflections of a Gangbanger" (reprinted here with permission)

- Gelman, David (1993), "The Violence in Our Heads"

- Levi Strauss, David (1991), "The Youngest Homeless: A Threnody for Street Kids"

Poems

Students' choice; I suggest selections from:

- Rodríguez, Luis (1989), *Poems Across the Pavement*

- Rodríguez, Luis (1991), *The Concrete River*

Films

- *American Me* (1992)

- *Boyz N the Hood* (1992)

- *Just Another Girl on the IRT* (1993)

- *Straight Out of Brooklyn* (1991)

SAMPLE DAILY SCHEDULE

Day 1: Lesson 1: Demonstrate "Kill-Die" equation from *Do or Die;* distribute reading and reading inventory.

Day 2: Review final question(s) from reading inventory.
Lesson 2: Small groups work on HANDOUT 1: STREETS OPINIONNAIRE.
Student(s) lead discussion on group work.

Day 3: Lesson 3: HANDOUT 2: TEENAGERS TALK ABOUT THE STREETS.
Discuss.
Journal Assignment 1.
Invite a team of students to lead a discussion on a film of their choice.

Day 4: Lesson 4: HANDOUT 3: KOHLBERG'S THEORY OF MORAL DEVELOPMENT.
Discuss.

Day 5: Small groups work on HANDOUT 4: MORAL DILEMMA SCENARIOS.

Day 6: Review Kohlberg handouts.
Homework: Lesson 5: Journal Assignment 2.

Day 7: Work with partners to review entries à la Kohlberg.
Volunteer teams of students present analyzed entries.

Day 8: Begin watching film of students' choice.

Day 9: Continue viewing film.

Day 10: Finish viewing film.
Team of students leads discussion using questions from Lesson 3 and Kohlberg's stages.

Day 11: Lesson 6: Introduce *Down These Mean Streets.*
Read prologue; draft "letter" to Piri Thomas.

Day 12: Independent reading.

Day 13: Discussion. Solicit students' questions.

Day 14: Short reading quiz.
Read selected passages aloud.

Day 15: Small groups generate discussion questions.

Day 16: Independent reading.

Day 17: Answer select small group's discussion questions in writing.

Day 18:   Analyze Piri's actions using Kohlberg's stages of moral
           development.
           General discussion.

Day 19:   Journal Assignment 3.

Day 20:   Short reading quiz; introduce team teaching projects.

Day 21:   Independent reading; prepare team teaching projects.

Day 22:   Teams of students present activities/assignments.
           Use HANDOUT 5: NOTING SIGNIFICANT PASSAGES.

Day 23:   General discussion; read selected passages aloud.

Day 24:   Teams of students present activities/assignments.
           Use HANDOUT 5.

Day 25:   Short reading quiz.
           Teams of students present activities/assignments.
           Use HANDOUT 5.

Day 26:   Independent reading.

Day 27:   Small groups create discussion questions.

Day 28:   Read excerpt from *Clockers*. Discuss; try to generate theses for
           final essay.

Day 29:   General discussion of *Down These Mean Streets* using students'
           questions and the previous day's theses.

Day 30:   Read "Reflections of a Gangbanger."
           Discuss; try to generate theses for final essay.

Day 31:   General discussion. Apply Kohlberg's theory to characters and
           events in *Down These Mean Streets*.

Day 32:   Lesson 7: Begin organizing and drafting essay.
           Use HANDOUT 6: BOXES PLANNING SHEET FOR ESSAY WITH SAMPLE NOTES

Day 33:   Continue writing essay.

Day 34:   Continue writing essay.

Day 35:   Rough draft/boxes worksheet (HANDOUT 6) due; peer editing using
           HANDOUT 7: PEER EDITING SHEET.

Day 36:   Essay due.

Days 37-40: Additional lessons, unit evaluation.

LESSON 1: STREET MENTALITY

Objectives

- To demonstrate reading comprehension skills

- To begin examining widely held conceptions of kids involved in street gangs

- To determine personal moral code and to contrast this mentality with that of gangbangers

Materials

- "Gang Class," a short excerpt from Léon Bing's *Do or Die* (pp. 120-127)

- Prepared reading inventory (see procedures)

Procedures

The following procedures effectively introduce the specified excerpt from Do or Die. *Instructors are advised to read the excerpt carefully before beginning—to become acquainted with the exercise and also to determine if the explicit language in the excerpt renders this reading inappropriate. If this is the case, an alternative reading should be substituted. I suggest short pieces from* When I Was Young I Loved School: Dropping Out and Hanging In *by Children's Express. If an alternative to* Do or Die *is used, instructors will need to modify the introductory procedures as well.*

- Write the word *kill* on the board. Ask the class to supply good reasons to kill someone. Of course, responses to this request will vary depending on the community, the students, and the mood in the classroom. Write any responses offered by students on the board. If no responses are forthcoming, you can try to cajole students into supplying reasons such as "self-defense." If no one in the class can name a reason to kill anyone, note that and skip the next procedure.

- Follow the model established by Mr. Jones in "Gang Class" as depicted in Léon Bing's *Do or Die*. Cross out (but do not erase) the reasons to kill that students have suggested but for which they would not die. Explain his "kill-die equation"; define *irrational* and *normal/sprung* if desired. Using his terminology, engage the class in a discussion of their responses.

- Ask the class if they think everyone shares their moral code. Introduce the concept of growing up on the streets:

    1. How could this affect a young person's kill-die equation?
    2. Does it have to? In your opinion, should it?

Explain that students have just begun examining concepts central to the unit and that over the next few weeks they will analyze their own initial impressions and other people's perspectives on surviving city street life.

• Distribute reading. Explain that students will be given questions on this reading and that their answers will provide you, the instructor, with information about how developed their reading skills are.

• Prepare and distribute a reading inventory, or graduated series of questions on the reading. These questions progress from very simple to more difficult and are designed to measure a student's ability to make inferences, determine authorial intent, and so on. I use this inventory to help select reading materials for the rest of the unit and to gauge the analytical level at which the unit should operate. For another example of a reading inventory, see Chapter 5: "Sex Roles, Power, and Identity" (Lesson 6). See also INSTRUCTORS' NOTES E: SKILL INVENTORIES (Chapter 4).

1. What type of boy is assigned to "Gang Class"?
2. What does Mr. Jones ask the boys to do once he writes the word *kill* on the board?
3. What role do the O.G.s play in the class?
4. How do the students relate to Mr. Jones? Be specific.
5. Mr. Jones uses the red/white/blue pants scenario to make a point. What is his point, and why do the boys struggle with it?
6. What do you think are the author's feelings about the class? In answering this question, you should quote a specific line or two from the story that you feel illustrates the author's viewpoint, or explain how you can read between the lines to determine how the author feels.
7. How are these boys different from people you know? How are they the same as people you know?

• If time permits, go over questions in class. Focus on the final question, which directs students toward a more personal involvement with the topic.

LESSON 2: WHAT DOES IT MEAN TO GROW UP ON THE STREETS?

Objectives

- To begin considering unit concepts both objectively and subjectively

- To refine unit's key questions and make them reflect class's interests

- To encourage and model student leadership

Materials

- HANDOUT 1: STREETS OPINIONNAIRE

Procedures

- Open class by (re)focusing on the question designed to encourage individual reflection on the street mentality displayed in the previous day's reading (Question 7: How are these boys different from people you know? How are they the same as people you know?). Continue with more complex questions:

    1. Are these boys victims or predators on the streets?
    2. Is growing up on the streets synonymous with gangbanging?
    3. Are all experiences of the streets the same?

- Divide students into small groups. These groups should be as heterogeneous as possible. Distribute HANDOUT 1: STREETS OPINIONNAIRE. Students should try to engage each other in sincere discussions of the questions. Specify how (or whether) students should record responses.

- As the groups are working, circulate and try to assess individual students' involvement with the activity. Choose one student—one who is either very interested in the exercise or one whom you suspect has a lot to say, although she or he might not be working too effectively in the group. While the other students are working, ask this student to suggest ways to lead class discussion on the opinionnaire. If this student is unwilling to lead discussion, ask him or her to suggest other ways students could take control of this activity.

- Reconvene the class and follow student's suggestions for going over group responses. Provide a rationale for this instructional technique: I have said that students have the experience and the information to teach the class in this particular exercise. I take this opportunity to stress that we will be building a unit around teenagers' experiences and feelings, not around grown-ups' memories or preaching.

• Ask students if they think the opinionnaire missed any important issues. Solicit ideas for other topics students feel should be included in an examination of life on the streets. Use their responses and suggestions to write or refine the unit's key questions. Make sure that students copy these notes for future reference.

HANDOUT 1: STREETS OPINIONNAIRE

Directions: Discuss the following questions in small groups. It is not necessary for the group to reach consensus (agreement). It *is* necessary for all opinions to be heard. Note answers as instructed.

1. What do you learn on "the streets"? Does everyone learn the same thing?

2. What makes life "on the streets" different from life off the streets?

3. Are the streets different for boys and girls? In what ways?

4. Do you think the streets are substantially different now from how they used to be? How?

5. If your family has money, can you grow up on the streets? In other words, what role does money play?

6. What role does race or ethnicity play?

7. What are kids' roles on the streets compared with the roles of adults?

8. Are the streets strictly an urban condition? What about a kid growing up in a small town, messing around with the same stuff—is she or he living on the streets?

9. Is there any way out of or off the streets? Explain.

This lesson can be skipped if pressed for time; it is an expansion of Lesson 2.

LESSON 3: WHAT LEADS PEOPLE TO THE STREETS?

Objectives

- To further refine conceptions of "the streets"

- To continue examining individuals' experiences on the streets

- To theorize about possible motivations and consequences of living on the streets

Materials

- HANDOUT 2: TEENAGERS TALK ABOUT THE STREETS

- Popular films dealing with teens who have rejected or are not able to access traditional avenues to success (possible titles: *Straight Out of Brooklyn, Boyz N the Hood, Just Another Girl on the IRT, American Me*, etc., and/or articles:

  - Levi Strauss, "The Youngest Homeless: A Threnody for Street Kids"

  - Gelman, "The Violence in Our Heads"

Procedures

- Ask the class if their understanding of the concept "the streets" has changed over the last few days. Distribute HANDOUT 2: TEENAGERS TALK ABOUT THE STREETS. This may be read in small groups. Lead the class in a discussion of the generalizations that can be made about teens' experiences on the streets.

The pieces in Handout 2 are excerpted from my students' writing over the years. Based on these assignments, we have defined street life (strong allegiance to and reliance on groups of organized friends and places outside the home), identified reasons motivating teenagers to live on the streets (adolescent stress, boredom, and a search for thrills, acceptance, structure, stability, understanding, status, and money), and discussed all possible outcomes (lower grades and a decline in schoolwork, injury, death, jail, destruction of family ties, guilt, getting trapped, loss of self-respect; thrills, acceptance, status, money).

- Write Journal Assignment 1 on the board: What are your responses to teens' stories of life on the streets? Write about your own experiences if you can.

This is a vaguely worded assignment, but it is one to which my students responded positively. There is enough leeway for all students—gangbangers as well as kids who have no personal experience on the streets—to voice their opinions and viewpoints.

- If the class's reading level is high, assign articles by Gelman and/or Levi Strauss. These use sophisticated vocabulary and syntax to address adolescent street crime (Gelman) and teen runaways on the streets (Levi Strauss). Both are useful in that they lead the discussion around to personal responsibility and moral decisions, the next area of study.

- If students are not able to read these short but difficult articles, you can show any of several popular films depicting adolescent street life. Discuss the issue of personal responsibility and the various decisions that the main characters make in these works, using questions such as these:

1. What motivates them to hang out on the streets?
2. To what extent is each individual responsible for his or her own actions and decisions?
3. Who has the most power in the film and why?

I like to assign a team of students to lead discussion around the issues they find most compelling in the film. I sit in the class and participate. If none of the students' questions focus on responsibility, I ask questions that bend discussions in the direction of moral choice and individual power.

HANDOUT 2: TEENAGERS TALK ABOUT THE STREETS

What has led each person to the streets?

What does each person say she or he can get from the streets? Why?

1. Growing up is hard. You have so many decisions to make. Should you go to school and be a "nerd"? Should you join a gang and be "tough"? Or maybe you should have sex with a lot of girls and be "cool." Teenagers spend most of their time "hangin' out" with their friends, and when you do this, you end up out on the streets, and are bound to run into some problems.

My experience on the streets started with being in a gang. For four years I thought that I was "the shit." Girls liked me, I was popular, I was in the scene, and I loved every bit of it. But I got tired of it, and a little scared by all the B.S. I became frustrated, dropped out of school, and did absolutely nothing. Then I met a graffiti artist . . . I started messing with it a little and got really good. Now I'm running down railroad tracks, the elevated train lines, jumping across buildings and painting stuff. I love everything about it and I'm a happier person. (Maurice)

2. The streets have been a major part of my life. When I was just a kid, the streets were my playground. They've always been home to me. I guess that's because I never wanted to stay in the house when I could be out. It's only natural that I would stay out even more as I got older.

As time went by the streets meant a totally different thing to me. I started to meet new and interesting people. I started to get into new and interesting music. I started learning about drugs. I started selling drugs.

Before long, the streets became my home, my food, my money, and my bed. They have saved my life, and almost ended it. I've been in and out of hospitals, jails, drug treatment centers, and different people's homes and lives. The streets have given me knowledge, wisdom, fear, sensitivity, strength, made me weak, strong, happy, pissed off, and sad.

To me, the streets aren't just asphalt. To me, the streets are people, ideas, home, life. It's a reality that's sad but true. (Simon)

3. The streets are an environment, a dangerous environment. Some teenagers who want to be accepted by their friends spend a lot of time there. Even when you're in a gang, when it comes down to it, it's you on your own. You and your homies may have fun, and reject society together, but the price you pay in the end—jail, death, or no future—is yours to pay alone. (Tina)

4. I think the streets refers to a "bad area." A person growing up there doesn't have to be bad herself. It's more of a matter of money. And then, people who have power and influence in these areas may make "bad" look pretty damn "good."

Whether you follow the crowd or not, growing up on the streets can make you more cautious and more aware of what's going on around you. Never knowing what could happen is a very scary feeling. That's what I think is the main thing about the streets. You never know what might happen to you or around you. If you get caught up in a gang like I did, you never know what could happen because of you. (Lissee)

5. For some people, life on the streets is about gangbanging. For me, it was different. I couldn't live with my mom and dad anymore. Two years ago, I ran away from a sheltered home, and then from juvenile hall, and ended up on the streets. I have learned and tried much more

than I ever knew I could. I started out living in a one-bedroom apartment, already occupied by 11 teenage runaways and drug addicts. I suppose that they weren't all addicts, but they all used. I remember how I felt when I would lay down on the dirty hardwood floor to sleep, and find a used syringe just below my ear.

The apartment was rented by an 18-year-old ward of the state. I think his name was Mike. Not that I really cared. I didn't know him, anyway. And yet I lived in his apartment. That's the type of situation it was. I remember the stale smell of tobacco that hit you like a Mack truck when you walked in the door. And at night, coke was cooked and shot regularly. The floors were the beds and whatever you had on was your blanket.

I finally left when the shower fell apart, and now, I no longer live this way. The tension and fear of living on the streets taught me to respect myself and my body. For my associates who are still in that tiny, dirty drug shack (and there still are a few), I wish you good luck. Sincerely. Good luck. (Geri)

6. "Shorty, are you sure you want to join us?" said the chief of the gang.

I said, "Yeah, I'm sure. I want to be a part of this." Then he told three of the boys to give me my violation in. Those boys beat me up for three minutes. Then they all gave me their hand and told me welcome to the Raza.

After a couple of weeks, they started to tell me what to do, and when to pay fees.

Then I started not to like the idea of getting told what to do. One day I started to have a problem with one of the older boys. He tried to take my money.

So I told him, "What is your fucking problem?"

He said, "Are you talking to me, you little punk?"

I said, "Just don't fuck around with me. You think I'm a little punk? Look what this punk could do." I grabbed a bat and hit him in the head. He fell to the ground and started screaming and bleeding.

Since that happened I got my respect, and the older boy stopped telling me what to do. But I wish I had known more information, like when you join a gang it is easy to get in, but to get out is hard. Sometimes you're in for life. Or you could end up dead or in jail. I wouldn't join a gang if I would have known that. That's why I say I suffered for this, because ain't no way out. And I been with them for a long time. And if I try to get out I'll end up dead. (Chris)

Stern. *Teaching English So It Matters.* © 1995 Corwin Press, Inc.

LESSON 4: KOHLBERG'S THEORY OF MORAL DEVELOPMENT

Objectives

- To become familiar with Lawrence Kohlberg's theory of moral development

- To apply Kohlberg's theories and terminology to real-life scenarios

Materials

- HANDOUT 3: KOHLBERG'S THEORY OF MORAL DEVELOPMENT

- HANDOUT 4: MORAL DILEMMA SCENARIOS

Procedures

- Review Journal Assignment 1 and materials studied in Lesson 3. Ask students if they think some people are more responsible than others on the street. Explain that you will begin studying one theory that tries to break down the different stages people evolve through as they grow up and make decisions about right and wrong. Introduce Lawrence Kohlberg, an American psychologist who advanced a theory of moral development in the 1950s and 1960s (see Duska, 1975; Kuhmerker, 1991).

- Distribute HANDOUT 3: KOHLBERG'S THEORY OF MORAL DEVELOPMENT. Read it through with the class. For those unfamiliar with Kohlberg's work, the handout is for the most part self-explanatory. Kohlberg considers young children to be at the lowest stage of moral development because they have not yet developed a sense of responsibility. People who make moral decisions based on social examples and rules are at the next level of moral development, a level he labels "conventional." People in the highest stages of moral development reflect on human rights and responsibilities in order to make moral decisions. He divides each of the three levels—preconventional, conventional, and postconventional—into two stages.

- Discuss the different stages and levels of moral development. Go over any difficult sentences or explanations. If students disagree with Kohlberg, ask them to try to articulate their dissatisfaction specifically. Stress that this is only a theory and that in the years since its development, several psychologists have refined or rejected it. Try the five examples at the bottom of Handout 3 (Answers: cookie = 1; eye = 2; teenager = 3; Ten Commandments = 4; cheating = 1; just saying no = debatable; different reasons for saying no will locate an individual at different stages). Continue until students seem to have a firm grasp of the separate stages and until they can create scenarios illustrating individuals at different stages of moral development.

• Distribute HANDOUT 4: MORAL DILEMMA SCENARIOS. Let students work in small groups to classify the examples of reasoning as belonging to one of Kohlberg's six stages. When students are done working, reassemble class and go over answers.

(ANSWERS FOR HANDOUT 4:   A. 4, 2, 6, 1, 3, 5
                                             B. 1, 5, 2, 6, 4, 3
                                             C. 4, 3, 5, 2, 6, 1
                                             D. 6, 3, 5, 4, 1, 2, 4/5)

HANDOUT 3: KOHLBERG'S THEORY OF MORAL DEVELOPMENT: A BRIEF OUTLINE

LEVELS

STAGES/CHARACTERISTICS

PRECONVENTIONAL:
At this level the individual responds to a moral decision as good or bad, right or wrong, only in terms of pleasant or unpleasant consequences (punishment, reward, exchange of favors) or in terms of the physical power of those who might punish him or her. The level is divided into the following two stages:

1. Punishment and Obedience:
Something is good because you won't get hurt for doing it. Something is bad because you will get hurt for doing it. Unquestioning respect for power; avoidance of punishment.

2. Personal Usefulness:
Something is good because it satisfies one's needs. "I'll do for you if you'll do for me"; "I'll scratch your back if you scratch mine."

CONVENTIONAL:
At this level, maintaining and supporting the individual's family, group, or nation is seen as valuable in its own right, regardless of the individual's immediate and obvious needs. The attitude is one of conformity and loyalty to the group. There is also concern for actively maintaining, supporting, and justifying order and stability in the group. The individual's moral choices must necessarily conform to the expectations of the group. At this level, there are the following two stages:

3. Conforming to the Will of the Group:
Pleasing or helping others to win approval or avoid disapproval. Conformity to standard ideas. Trying to earn majority approval by being "nice" or acting appropriately.

4. Law and Order:
Rules are important. Doing something because the law says so. Maintaining order and laws (which do not change). "Doing your duty." Showing respect for authority and maintaining the social order for its own sake.

POSTCONVENTIONAL (INDEPENDENT JUDGMENT):
At this level, there is an effort to define principles that seem generally true or valid apart from the personal authority of the group. Individuals try to consider a greater good, beyond selfish concerns. This level also has two stages:

5. Social Contract:
Solving moral issues by reaching consensus; for example, creating democratic values and constitutionalism. Right is a matter of reconciling individual values in a group context. Laws tend to serve society; laws change as society changes.

6. Personal Conscience:
Based on abstract, ethical principles, that is, the Golden Rule. Basing decisions on justice, mutual dependence, cooperation, equality, human rights, and respect for the dignity of all people, all cultures.

Into which stage do the following examples fit?

A toddler sneaking a cookie when Mommy isn't looking ___
"An eye for an eye" ___
A teenager calling her friends to see what everyone else is saying about the accident ___
The Ten Commandments ___
Cheating when the instructor leaves the room ___
Just saying "no" ___

HANDOUT 4: MORAL DILEMMA SCENARIOS

Directions: Read each of the following scenarios aloud. With your group, identify the stage reflected by each of the responses according to Lawrence Kohlberg's theory of moral development.

A. You're driving down an ice-covered road through a terrible winter storm. Up ahead, you see a person hitchhiking. It's illegal to pick up hitchhikers. What do you do?

___ I'm not going to break the law to give a poor fool a ride.

___ I may skid out of control if I try to stop, and it's not worth the possible injury to me or my car.

___ I don't care what the law says, there's a human being out there suffering.

___ I might get a ticket if a policeman sees me. Maybe the hitchhiker will harm me.

___ Everybody else is passing the hitchhiker by, so I'd better do the same.

___ Well, I know it's illegal, but I guess this is an instance where it could be justified to pick up a hitchhiker.

B. You're at a party. Someone lights up a blunt (a cigar filled with marijuana) and passes it around the room. It's getting closer to you. What do you do?

___ What if I get caught or the party gets busted? I'd better not take it.

___ I know it's against the law, but it's really not that harmful. Besides, it's a bad law.

___ Why not? It may give me enough nerve to ask somebody to dance.

___ I don't care about the law. No one has a right to tell me to do something or not. It's my decision.

___ The law was made for the good of all people. I'm not above the law. No one is.

___ I guess it won't hurt. Everyone else is smoking it.

C. You didn't have time to study for the final exam and you need to do well to be eligible for a scholarship next year. The person next to you obviously is having an easy time with the exam. The instructor leaves the room. Should you copy the answers you don't know?

___ The rule is for everyone in this school. What would it be like if everyone cheated?

___ Everyone else cheats. Why shouldn't I do the same?

___ I think it's a fair rule. I'm going to respect it.

___ I'll never get caught. Besides, I really need that scholarship.

___ It is better to be honest. Even if I don't get the scholarship, at least I did my own work.

___ If I get caught, I'll get expelled and be in a lot of trouble.

(continued)

D. You are faced with the issue of capital punishment. Label the following rationales according to Kohlberg's stages of moral development.

___ Society does not have the right to destroy human life, no matter what the situation is.

___ Opinion polls show that 80% of Americans favor capital punishment: I'll go with the majority.

___ All citizens have the right to be protected from destructive criminals. I have to vote for capital punishment.

___ God's commandment says, "Thou shall not kill."

___ I'm not going to cast a vote at all. No one will know if I voted or not.

___ What if someone I knew got convicted? I wouldn't want them to die.

___ The Constitution guarantees all citizens "life, liberty, and the pursuit of happiness."

LESSON 5: MORAL DEVELOPMENT AND PERSONAL EXPERIENCE

Objectives

- To relate Kohlberg's theory to personal experience

- To begin looking critically at individual decisions (made on the streets or in other social contexts)

Materials

- None

Procedures

- Write Journal Assignment 2 on the board: Tell a story that shows yourself and others facing a moral dilemma.

Explain that this story should be based on experience but cannot be so private that students mind sharing it with at least one other person in the class. Stress the types of stories that work well for this assignment: situations where the students and their friends were faced with difficult decisions. *Make sure that students know they should talk about the reasoning behind their decisions.* They cannot say just that they decided to "do x or y"; they need to trace their thinking processes. Decisions made by characters in journal entries will be analyzed to demonstrate different levels of moral development.

- After students write this piece in class or for homework, ask them to exchange papers with a partner and read each other's work. If students are willing, they can present their moral dilemmas in teams. Teams are to choose the stories they want to present and explain to the class. They can read the stories aloud or give a brief summary of the situation. Then they are to label each other's reasoning as examples of stage 3 moral development or stage 5 moral development, etc.

- If students are unwilling to share their personal accounts or if they enjoy this type of work, you can ask them to bring in artistic works depicting characters in various stages of moral development. Have students present these works and analyze characters' actions in them as they were directed to do with Journal 2.

I offered this assignment to students who were in need of extra credit. One girl brought in a song by Arrested Development, "People Everyday" (1993), and took the class through the lyrics that showed examples of preconventional and conventional moral reasoning. Another boy brought in "The Language of Violence" by The Disposable Heroes of Hiphoprisy (1992) and delineated examples of every one of Kohlberg's stages of moral development. The whole class was excited to see this theory applied to works and actions they recognized; this made the theory legitimate.

LESSON 6: INVESTIGATING STREET LIFE IN *DOWN THESE MEAN STREETS*

Objectives

- To read long novel in entirety

- To apply unit concepts and questions to major work

- To work constructively and cooperatively in groups

- To develop and experiment with different teaching activities

- To compile evidence for use in writing an expository essay

- To conceive a thesis for final essay

Materials

- Thomas, Piri, *Down These Mean Streets,* or another work that describes the trials of growing up on city streets outside mainstream culture. Powerful and affecting alternatives to Thomas's work include autobiographical works such as Luis Rodríguez's *Always Running: La Vida Loca: Gang Days in L.A.* and *Child of the Dark: The Diary of Carolina María de Jesús.*

- HANDOUT 5: NOTING SIGNIFICANT PASSAGES

- Excerpt from Richard Price's *Clockers* (pp. 345-349)

- UNIT MATERIALS: "Reflections of a Gangbanger" by Léon Bing

Procedures

- *Activity A: A Letter to Piri.* Distribute copies of the novel. Let students thumb through *Down These Mean Streets.* Direct their attention to the opening prologue. Ask for a volunteer to read Piri's passionate declaration. Briefly discuss this passage, stressing Piri's tone and general frame of mind.

Ask students to draft letters to Piri framing the questions they would like to ask him, based on the prologue. Divide the class into small groups to do this (students may do this exercise individually).

Next, ask groups or individuals to volunteer to read their questions out loud. Have a student at the board draft a composite letter made up of the more searching questions posed by letter writers. Students should copy this final letter into their notes for later use.

The following composite letter was written by one of my classes:

Dear Piri,

What happened to you to make you so angry? You've got a good imagination, but you seem to be a little crazy. OK, you've had a hard life. But haven't you adjusted?

Maybe drugs are the problem. Are you always high? What kinds of drugs do you use? Do you know what makes you want to get messed up all the time? Why do you feel so alone and bitter? So crammed with hate?

It almost seems like you're mad at the whole world. What is your real attitude about your race? Your nationality? Where are all your friends? What about your family?

What are you hoping for? What makes you feel so dissatisfied? What will you do to get what you want? Do you want to stay on the streets forever? Are you still in school? What would make you happy? Until you figure out some of these questions, you will just stay an angry young man. And everyone has to grow up sometime.

Sincerely yours,

3rd Period

• *Activity B: Discussing **Down These Mean Streets**.* Questions should be open-ended; that is, do not ask students to recall facts. Invite them, rather, to offer their own insight and understanding of events and characters in the work. The following questions can be used to start general class discussions:

"Harlem"

Chapters 1-3. Describe Piri's home life. What are Piri's father's concerns? What lessons do the Thomas children learn from their mother? From their father? What happens that changes the financial situation of the Thomas family? How does Piri feel about the war? On page 22, Piri reflects on his relationship with his father. Do you think his doubts are normal? Is he too sensitive? How does he resolve his doubts? (See page 23.)

Chapters 4-5. Why does Piri start having trouble on the streets? What street protocol do the boys follow? What gives Piri the greatest feeling of pride? How and why does the Thomas family's situation change in Chapter 5? How does Piri feel about asking for aid or relief?

Chapters 6-8. Is Piri in a gang? Why do they fight other Puerto Ricans? Is Piri gay? Homophobic? Who is in control? Why does Piri go along with Alfredo? Why is the scene at Concha and Antonia's so distasteful? Why do you think Thomas included this scene in the book? Why does Piri hit a teacher? How does Piri make money? Why, when, and how does he commit his first theft?

"Suburbia"

Chapters 9-10. Where does the family move, and how does Piri feel about it? What is Piri's response to the prejudice he encounters in Long Island? How do the kids in his new school treat him? What is his response? What three crises does Piri face in Chapter 10? Why is he ambivalent about Betty?

"Harlem"

Chapters 11-16. Why does Piri leave home? Where does he stay? How old is he now? Describe Piri's attitude toward his girlfriends. What does Piri's job search teach him? How does he support himself? Who is Trina? How does Piri try to control her? How do her looks figure into his attitude? Is Piri immediately addicted to heroin? What plans do Piri and Brew make? How is Piri "prodigal," and what "funeral" is he talking about (Chapter 16)? Has Piri made peace with the color of his skin? What is his mission in Chapter 16?

"Down South"

Chapters 17-19. Who is Alayce? What effect does Brew's attempted rape and Alayce's account of her gang rape at 15 have on Piri? Why is this a change for him, and why is it significant? In what way is Piri practicing self-deception? What are your feelings about Gerald? Why is Piri's attitude about him different from Brew's? Explain: *"Como es, es como se llamo."* How is Piri just being born (Chapter 19)? Has Piri found peace? Do you agree that he has learned a lot on this trip?

"Harlem"

Chapters 20-24. Why does Piri's mother's death intensify the conflict between Piri and his father? In what ways are Piri and his father alike? In what ways are they different? Why does Piri become a heroin user and addict? Who helps him kick his habit? Why does Piri decide to take up a life of crime? Is he doing it to be "down"? To be equal to his White partners? What would you have done if faced with a situation similar to Piri's when he was ready to start school at Howard University? Why does the "big job" in Chapter 24 fail?

"Prison"

Chapters 25-29. What is Piri's attitude about his jail sentence? What is most important to him when he first arrives at Sing Sing? Is it difficult for Piri to accustom himself to jail? Does he want to become accustomed to jail? What does he do to occupy himself? Do you think he and Trina would have gotten married if he hadn't gone to jail?

Chapters 30-32. How does the chaplain help him when Piri is denied parole? What conflicting impulses does Piri struggle with when there is a riot in the prison? How does studying Islamic principals and the *Quran* change Piri? Why did Piri become so much more reflective and curious about the world? In your opinion, what is the most critical lesson or truth Piri learns in jail?

"New York Town"

Chapters 33-35. What conflicting emotions does Piri feel when he is released from prison? Why can't he just go home? What do his prayers at the Bronx Tombs give him and why? How does he keep from going back to his old ways? Do you think he will slip back into them?

Another way to organize discussions is around students' questions. Because these questions are not always forthcoming, I sometimes stop discussion of a scene or chapter in midstream and ask students to write down one or two of their own questions on a small card or piece of scrap paper. They then pass these forward, and I shuffle through the pile and pose selected questions to the class as a whole.

When students are not caught up in the reading, discussions become impossible; I usually ask the class what they think we should do about this. Their responses vary: Sometimes they say we should have a catch-up reading day. Sometimes they prescribe temporary separation of the students into two groups—those who are caught up on the reading and those who are behind—each with different class activities and homework assignments. Occasionally some students vote to punish the students who are behind. In general, however, they usually are sensitive to each other: They can differentiate between the chronic slackers and students who are only occasionally remiss in their responsibilities.

- *Activity C: Reading "Good Parts" Aloud.* Although students may be at different places in their reading, I have found that they are more willing to do their reading homework when we interrupt in-class reading to read "good parts" aloud. Suggested sections: pages 22-23; 48-51; 54-63 (some explicit descriptions of sexual activity); 102-104; 144-148; 176; 207-210; 231-234; 255-258; 280-283; 298-299.

- *Activity D: Short Reading Quizzes.* To help students stay on top of reading assignments, give frequent short quizzes. Ask simple questions designed to check students' reading progress.

Reading Quiz, Chapters 27-32:

1. Who is Little?
2. Who is Tico, and how does Piri help him?
3. What bad news does Piri's family bring him when they come to visit?
4. Studies of what two disciplines teach Piri about dignity and self-preservation while in jail?

- *Activity E: Small Groups Generate Discussion Questions.* Have students who are at the same approximate place in their reading form small groups. In these groups, they create four to five original questions, which can be incorporated into discussions and reading quizzes.

• *Activity F: Taking Kohlberg "Down These Mean Streets."* Use Kohlberg's stages of moral development to analyze characters and events in the work. Ask students to trace Piri's developing moral consciousness. (For example, as a child, Piri was hungry for/relied exclusively on parental approval: stage 1. As a youth, Piri followed street protocol, sought group status—had to be a "down stud": stages 3-4. After his jail sentence, he started educating himself, evaluating street life: stage 5. Now he reflects on all codes and experiences, writes the book: stage 6.) Ask questions about moral stages evident in specific episodes. This can be done in discussion, in quizzes, or as separate writing exercises.

• *Activity G: Depending on Others' Approval.* Discuss with students how at home, at school, and in the street, Piri is always struggling to prove he is *hombre* and how other people's opinions—his father's, his friends', White people's—motivate him more strongly than any inner impulse. Ask students if they ever have cared about winning the approval of others and what it felt like. Assign Journal 3: Write about a time in your life when nothing mattered as much as other people's (or another person's) opinions of you.

• *Activity H: Team Teaching Projects.* After a week or two of reading—once students have gotten involved with the protagonist's life—assign a teaching project to be completed in small groups or with partners. First, ask students to choose their coworkers. It is best to limit the groupings to four students maximum to ensure good participation. Next, distribute or write the following list on the board:

Race	Drugs	Concept of Women
Family	Money	Peer Pressure
Taking Risks	Crime	

Tell students that their assignment is to work with their group or partner to create an activity or assignment that investigates one of these issues in *Down These Mean Streets*. Suggest assignments. The simplest project is to choose a scene in the book, plan to read it aloud, and prepare discussion questions around it. Other ideas: A group can identify a scene in the book that addresses one or more of the issues specified above; they then can assign a journal entry asking their peers to relate this scene to their own lives. They can stage a role play using characters in the book. They can make a controversial claim ("Piri is a born criminal"; "Piri is racist") and stage a debate. The activity they create must involve the whole class and must address one or more of the issues listed.

A group in one of my classes could not decide how to address the issue of peer pressure. I worked with them to create the following scenario (based on *Down These Mean Streets*, Chapter 12), and they led the class in a discussion to identify the six responses as indicative of Kohlberg's six moral stages. We decided to include profanity, to mirror Thomas's voice, and to make the sentiments seem authentic. All quotations are from *Down These Mean Streets*, page 112. Answers are provided.

You are Piri. You are hanging with your homies one night, when one of them holds out a capful of heroin to you and says, ". . . we've got some bad stuff, real down and we're going high. Cop some." What do you do?

2____ *If I do it, Carlito will tell Trina, and she'll think that I'm a man who can make my own decisions. This will be good-o for me.*

6____ *Fuck it, I don't need to prove I'm* hombre *by snorting up some nasty shit. I got enough* corazon *to teach these fearful, fronting motherfuckers something here. Maybe they can cop some of my attitude.*

4____ *I'm gonna follow the rules of the street and say, "I've used this stuff before. But some wise motherfucker don't seem to know that I did and maybe like punks gotta be shown."*

1____ *If I don't do this, all my friends will think I'm not down. No one will stand by me on the streets anymore, and I'll get my ass kicked.*

3____ *All my boys are doing it, so I'm going to do it, too.*

5____ *This* tecata *is bad news, but I can handle it for this once and show these motherfuckers there ain't no shit on earth can get the better of me.*

After making this assignment, set aside one day for students to work on their projects in groups. Set reasonable limits as to the size and scope of the projects, so that students do not bite off more than they can chew. If they need more time to finalize their activities, let teams work quietly while other students are engaged in independent reading. When students are ready, use student projects to break up regular classroom activities such as in-class reading, quizzes, and instructor-led discussions. Distribute HANDOUT 5: NOTING SIGNIFICANT PASSAGES. Have the class keep track of notable quotations in each other's presentations.

Students' activities probably will require instructor-led follow-up or summary questions. After a group of students have presented their projects, take the time to ask the class what conclusions they have been able to draw about Piri and race, money, women, crime, and so forth. Review textual evidence for these claims.

• *Activity I: Introducing and Prewriting for an Essay on "Life on the Streets."* As students prepare and complete their own and each other's assignments, they will be examining significant sections in the book. Explain that they can use these quotations to write the final project for this unit: an expository essay discussing life on the streets. Remind them to use HANDOUT 5 to note these key passages about money, family, race, and peer pressure. For example:

Page Numbers, Quotation, and Basic Situation	What Issues Does This Address?	What Does This Say About the Protagonist?
Piri has sex with White woman, says "I hate you . . . your damn color . . . why am I in the middle?" (p. 90)	Racism, women	He's ambivalent about race, wants to be White and hate Whites, both.

Tell students that as they might expect, there are no right or wrong answers to the final essay/final project on "The Streets." Students will write a paper expressing their own perspectives on street-related issues. This must be a coherent essay on the different ways race, class, adolescence, machismo, or moral reasoning impact people who live on the streets. List legitimate sources for students' evidence: the major text, excerpted works read in class, movies, and students' own experiences.

Go over the formal requirements of the essay. If students are unacquainted with the constituent components of argumentation (making claims, supporting these claims with evidence, and warranting the evidence), see Chapter 5: "Sex Roles, Power, and Identity" (Lesson 10, HANDOUT 8). Adapt other prewriting exercises—Chapter 5, Lesson 10, HANDOUTS 9 and 10—as necessary. See also HANDOUT N: BASIC ESSAY ORGANIZATION (Chapter 4). If students already are familiar with these processes, I make the following points clear: "There is no need to give a summary of either the book or your life in this essay. It is crucial that you do some focused reflection, arrive at some conclusions, and then substantiate your findings with precise references."

• *Activity J: Writing a Thesis (drawing conclusions about life on the streets)*. Clarify the first step of the essay writing process: formulating a thesis. Students can formulate theses by reviewing and reflecting on their journal entries. Or instructors can introduce extremely evocative and informally reflective readings in which a literary character strives to formulate a thesis or make sense of life on the streets him- or herself.

If desired, these selected literary pieces can be read in class, as a break from *Down These Mean Streets*. Distribute excerpt from Richard Price's novel *Clockers* (pp. 345-349). Instructors should review this selection carefully before assigning it: It uses unexpurgated language. Tell students that this piece is from a longer novel about street life in a small city outside of New York City and that in this scene a police officer is telling what happened to him one day when he was out on the streets.

Have students read the selection aloud. Make sure that students understand the street slang in the scene from *Clockers* ("raising up five-oh" = signaling that police officers are approaching; "Hambone's" = fictional fast-food restaurant; "Fight the power!" = Public Enemy rap song, popularized as a rallying cry against oppression in Spike Lee's 1989 movie, *Do the Right Thing*). Draw their attention to the long paragraph on page 349 (this is the last paragraph we read) about "dis" and "heart." Ask students if they agree with what Thumper says about the inevitability of street conflict and misunderstanding: "them's the rules . . . everybody did what they had to do." Ask students to assess the mood and identify the narrator's overriding concern.

After reading the excerpt from *Clockers,* pose the following situation to the students: "You are the narrator of this piece. What, in your opinion, is the main characteristic of street life?"

Write their comments on the board, and work to refine them into sample essay theses. Ask students to confirm, refute, or refine these comments into theses that reflect their own opinions.

Another piece—UNIT MATERIALS: "Reflections of a Gangbanger" by Léon Bing—also can be used effectively here. After reading this piece, say to students: "You are the interviewer of Racketeer. What have you learned about street life?"

Again, write their comments on the board, and work to refine them into sample essay theses. Ask students to confirm, refute, or refine these comments into theses that reflect their own opinions.

HANDOUT 5: NOTING SIGNIFICANT PASSAGES

Directions:

1. As other students direct your attention to different places and passages in the book, use this sheet to write down phrases and page numbers in the first column. Note the main issues addressed in the second column.

2. In the third column, make claims about the main character based on the actions and thoughts noted in column 1.

3. You can use the quotations, issues, and claims when you write your essay on life on the streets.

Page Numbers, Quotation, and Basic Situation	What Issues Does This Address?	What Does This Say About the Protagonist?
Example: Piri's crowd is going to visit friends who are homosexuals. Piri doesn't want to go but feels he must: "I don't wanna go—but I gotta, or else I'm out, I don't belong in. And I wanna belong in! Put caro palo on, like it don't move you." (p. 55)	*Machismo, reputation, fitting in, playing it cool*	*It is more important to Piri to be true to the crowd than it is for him to be true to himself.*

Stern. *Teaching English So It Matters.* © 1995 Corwin Press, Inc.

Reflections of a Gangbanger

by Léon Bing

Racketeer (not his real street name) is 18 years old. He is a member of one of the sets that make up the Crips, a gang with about 20,000 members in Los Angeles. At the time of this interview, Racketeer was on probation for attempted murder. He was interviewed by Ms. Bing at the Kenyon Juvenile Justice Center.

Why did you get into a gang?

I wasn't in it at first. I was just young, about twelve years old, and I started talking about gangbanging and all that. Then they started breaking my stuff and all that, you know, so you figure, well, what's the use, it's protection. So you thinking about it and then somebody sock you when you not looking and then you fight 'em back and you end up in their set.

What if you want to leave the set?

That's really hard. They probably kill you or catch your mother, something like that. When they think you don't want to be from their set no more they probably wind up killing you.

When I was younger I didn't even think people did that—I thought it was just on TV, like with the Mafia and all that, biggest gang in the world, and they get hit men and do that. But you ain't got no friends out in L.A. Not even in your own set. You by yourself.

Do a lot of guys feel that way?

Lot of guys.

Why?

They fight against each other every time they get loaded. And that's why a lot of homeboys be getting killed, because after they fight they got a grudge against each other, you know. So then they thinking: "I'll get him—I'll *let* him get killed. I'll *let* somebody shoot him." So that person can't trust the other person no more and the other person can't trust him, there ain't no trust left and when they get out there, they both get shot up.

What makes you feel bad?

When somebody get killed who you feel close to. That make me angry enough to go kill somebody.

How do you feel afterward?

You see, sometimes after you kill somebody, you feel like, "Why did I do that? I should not have done that, that wasn't even called for. What made me do this?" You be thinking all that, then you see somebody look just like the person you killed. Then you be thinking, "I probably didn't even kill him—he probably coming back to get me."

I used to "jack" people—you know, with a gun or your hand, just catch 'em and go into their pockets—because I thought it was fun. But, you know, you get to the point where you wouldn't like nobody doing you like that when you get old, and you wouldn't like nobody just coming around you mother and just snatching her purse and lapping her, you know, so I start thinking, I can't be doing this no more, because somebody who do my mother like that make me ready to kill anybody. I started to be, like, sorry for things that I done, started to think that if I had stayed in school maybe I wouldn't have been into some of the things that I done. What I done in my life ain't so bad, maybe—the problem is, I done it.

Do you ever feel bad because you killed somebody who was somebody's son, somebody's brother, somebody's boyfriend, just like you are?

See, if you friend get shot, you will get somebody. You don't care who it is, you will get somebody, just to let your friend know, if he was still here, that's what you would do, you know. Like most of the times the set be down and stuff, they take off they head rags, put 'em in the casket with the bullets they killed people with—let the friend know they did this for him. Right now I'd say our set be cooled down, we ain't been killing nobody, we ain't been doing nothing but kickin' it. But that's hard because we been fighting each other.

How do you get involved in a drive-by shooting?

See, like when one of your homeboys get killed, you think you gonna go kill somebody—you gonna do it because he died—you gonna do it for him, just to let him know you really miss him.

What if somebody in the set says, "I can't do that"?

You don't. See, when a homeboy says, "Come on!" and you say, "No," that's like saying you don't want to be from the set. You ain't really down for your set if you ain't ready to die for the set. Then they probably kill you. You can't say no to your set.

What does your sister think about you being in a gang?

She into the Lord. That's what got me thinking. She be playing that gospel music, all that stuff, and I be sitting at home listening to it and she be telling me the Lord ain't gonna keep letting me get away with the crimes I been doing. He ain't gonna keep helping me out. Day before yesterday my cousin got shot in the chest in a drive-by.

Who do you think shot him?

We got so many enemies we don't know which one done it.

Who is your worst enemy?

Bounty hunters [a Blood set].

Do you have Crip enemies?

P.G.s, 60s.

Would you kill another Crip?

Bloods kill bloods. Crips will kill Crips. That's why I don't even know why it's Bloods and Crips, because they be killing each other.

If you didn't have Bloods or 60s or some other enemies to fight, who would you turn your anger on?

Just fight our own selves.

Do you think gangs are moving east?

Yeah—I don't know how far. I'm thinking all over the world. I think Crips will rule the world—that's what they trying to do.

If you could be anybody you wanted to be, who would you be?

Somebody rich. Somebody famous, like the rappers. You know, make a lot of money. But you know, the rappers, they got the same problems we all do: They got to think, like, they up on there on the stage one day and they be saying the wrong thing and somebody just shoot 'em from the crowd.

If you could change the world, how would you do it?

I wouldn't know what to do. Because if I take all the guns away, the, you know, you can just use a knife. I would not know what to change.

Are other gangbangers starting to think about stopping the killing and shooting too?

Most of 'em. They think about it, but they try not to show it. Like me—I think it, but I try not to show it.

What makes you happy?

When all my homeboys is just kickin' it, like we all just go somewhere, like a big old park—we be going to a picnic or something, and there just be a long line of cars, you know, like a funeral—only we going to a picnic and we just get up there and we just be kickin' and having fun, and then the police come and they run everybody off the place, and we come back to our 'hood and we be talking about how much fun we had, and then the next thing you know, somebody just drive by and start shooting, and somebody get hit and somebody get killed, so that just spoil all the fun that we done had, and now you ready to go do the same thing, but you ain't gonna do it that night, because you know the police is gonna to be out so you gonna try to find a night the police ain't gonna be out. But you ain't gonna do it when you're sober; you will get like all tipsy and you will start talking crazy, like saying, "Fuck Blood!" and all of that, and then there's gonna be another homeboy saying, "What you-all want to do? You-all want to go get 'em?" And you will just be so drunk and all of that, you just say, "Come on!" and everybody start getting guns and stuff. And the next thing you know, we drove over and shot them up.

What do you think you'll be doing in ten years?

I don't think I'll be alive in ten years.

LESSON 7: ESSAY WRITING

Objectives

- To outline a supporting argument for prepared thesis

- To organize textual evidence

- To work cooperatively in groups

- To work constructively as and with peer editors

- To write an organized, coherent, and honest essay

Materials

- HANDOUT 6: BOXES PLANNING SHEET FOR ESSAY WITH SAMPLE NOTES

- HANDOUT 7: PEER EDITING SHEET

- HANDOUT O: BLANK BOXES FOR ESSAY PREWRITING (Chapter 4)

- HANDOUT P: PEER EDITING/ESSAY REVISION (Chapter 4)

Procedures

- Distribute HANDOUT O: BLANK BOXES FOR ESSAY PREWRITING (Chapter 4) and HANDOUT 6. Using these and HANDOUT 5 (from Lesson 6), students can start outlining their formal essays.

For an example of a student-written thesis and introductory paragraph to this essay, see the student writing sample cited in Chapter 1, page 7.

I let students outline, write, and edit their drafts with peers in class. They can "share" quotations; I am comfortable with students calling out and responding to comments such as, "Did anyone find anything good to use for Piri and peer pressure?" Students will spend most of their writing energy completing the boxes worksheet. The writing that follows the worksheet is just as important, but they will treat it as mere fine-tuning and polishing.

- Specify due dates for completion of boxes worksheet, and/or for rough drafts. Some students like to squeeze a lot of writing onto their boxes worksheets so that they become virtual drafts (as opposed to brief outlines).

Typically, my students want to write their papers only once. Period. They hate revising. I try to encourage sloppy boxes worksheets and/or rough drafts so that they will not mind so much when their peers make comments and mark the drafts in peer editing sessions. Also, students do seem to be less resistant to revision when they know they have to "copy it over" anyway.

- When students have completed their rough drafts, dedicate one day to in-class peer editing. Use HANDOUT 7: PEER EDITING SHEET or HANDOUT P: PEER EDITING/ESSAY REVISION (Chapter 4). The editor's tasks on this sheet are more concrete than those on Handout 7. Students should work in pairs (or in trios, if all three students in the group care enough about each other's work to do justice to each essay). They can write their final drafts in class the next day or for homework. It is critical that essay writers use Handout 7 and their partners' comments on their rough drafts when writing their final drafts; this is as much a revision exercise as it is an editing task.

HANDOUT 6: BOXES PLANNING SHEET FOR ESSAY WITH SAMPLE NOTES

Directions: Notes you take on this sheet are the outline of your essay. When you copy this into paragraphs for the final draft of your essay, you will need to add phrases, sentences, and missing information to make it flow smoothly and make sense.

THESIS: *All actions on the street hinge on public reception. No word, no attitude, no gesture can escape public scrutiny. This fact directs and changes Piri Thomas's life in his autobiography,* Down These Mean Streets. *It also holds true in Richard Price's novel* Clockers.

CLAIM 1	CLAIM 2	CLAIM 3
Piri's search for identity centers on others' perceptions of him.	*For Piri, public opinion is stronger than pain and common sense, almost stronger than the will to survive.*	*Thumper's need to maintain superiority in public supersedes his sense of duty, justice, and humanity.*

CLAIM 1: *Piri's search for identity centers on others' perceptions of him.*
EVIDENCE: (with page numbers) " 'Como es, es como se llama' " (173)
"Goddammit, can't he see the whole white world don't care what he feels inside?" (150)
" 'I'm Puerto Rican.'
'You think that means anything to them Jim Crow paddies?' " (123)
WARRANT: *Down south, Piri learns that no matter how he sees himself, he cares most about what he is called: Black. He argues with his father's stubborn refusal to be Black, to accept his looks and his racial heritage. He also struggles with mixed Puerto Rican-Black identification—all because of how he looks to others.*

CLAIM 2: *For Piri, public opinion is stronger than pain and common sense, almost stronger than the will to survive.*
EVIDENCE: (with page numbers)

WARRANT:

Stern. *Teaching English So It Matters.* © 1995 Corwin Press, Inc.

CLAIM 3: *Thumper's need to maintain superiority in public supersedes his sense of duty, justice, and humanity.*
EVIDENCE: (with page numbers)

WARRANT:

HANDOUT 7: PEER EDITING SHEET

EDITORS: Use this sheet to check your partner's rough draft thoroughly. Read through the essay and use this sheet to check over the form, the argument, and the mechanics. You can write on this sheet and/or on your partner's draft. If you have trouble finding a thesis or if some quoted evidence makes no sense to you, it's not your fault. You need to point these things out to your partner, who then will be able to make clear revisions.

First, check the form.

<u>In the first paragraph,</u>

- Is there an indented paragraph starting off the paper? YES ___ NO ___

- Is there a thesis? Copy it here:

- Are the sources (book titles and authors, movie titles) correctly named and punctuated? Mark on draft if an author or a source is missing.

- Are there three claims stated clearly in this opening paragraph as a preview? What are they?

1.

2.

3.

<u>In the body of the paper,</u>

- Is each of the next paragraphs indented? YES ___ NO ___

- Is every claim restated in a separate paragraph? Mark draft if writer needs to correct this.

- Is all evidence quoted with quotation marks? Mark draft if writer needs to correct this.

- Are page numbers given? Mark draft if writer needs to correct this.

<u>Is there a final section of the paper with concluding remarks?</u>
YES ___ NO ___

<u>Does the paper have a title?</u> Is it a good title? Copy it here:

Then check the argument.

<u>In the first paragraph,</u>

- Does the thesis make sense? It should be clear and direct.

- Are three claims listed there that relate to the thesis?

<u>In the following paragraphs,</u>

- Is each claim supported with quoted, warranted evidence? Mark on draft if evidence is insufficient in some way: missing, incorrectly quoted, unrelated to claim, or in need of further explanation or warrant.

<u>Does the conclusion</u> address the thesis and the claims? Make appropriate comments on draft.

Last, try to check the mechanics.

Are the punctuation and spelling correct? Look up and ask questions about correct spelling, title, and quotation punctuation if you aren't sure.

Based on your findings . . .

This essay needs

___ minor revision
___ some major revision
___ complete revision

Thank you!

ADDITIONAL LESSONS

Objectives

- To continue examining unit's key questions and applying them to characters and situations in poetry

- To refine earlier conceptions of life on the streets

- To evaluate unit

Materials

- Rodríguez, Luis, *Poems Across the Pavement*

- Rodríguez, Luis, *The Concrete River*

Procedures

- Set up a role play exercise. When essays have been written, let the class "interview" the protagonist of the major work read, posing questions (from Lesson 2's opinionnaire) to a student playing Piri.

- Ask students to pay special attention, in a discussion or in writing, to the final question of the opinionnaire: Is there any way off the streets? Ask:

    1. How would Piri have answered this question at the age of 16?
    2. How would he have answered it at the age of 35?
    3. How did Piri get off the streets? Did he really ever leave them?

- Ask a student who finished his or her essay early to select a few of Rodríguez's poems for the class to read. Depending on time, these poems can be read by students, discussed, and used to inspire final journal assignments or other creative writing exercises.

- Students also can look back at the early opinionnaire on the streets (Lesson 2) and see how their own impressions have changed.

- Evaluate the unit's readings, activities, and general content. Discuss with students what should be changed if this unit is to be taught again in coming semesters. Ask them their opinions about what should not change. Students can answer these questions aloud, in writing, anonymously—any way that will yield truthful, expansive responses.

9

⚏ The Hero

I believe in doing this I will be a tragic hero. I was born strong but the environment is stronger than me. I don't really have any special powers to help me. Only my mind and those who support me.

—Tina

I'd like to make a drastic change in the way society works. I would like to make life easier, less complicated, and more equal, more fair. At least I believe that there's hope for the next generation, which would be our children. But it's not gonna happen until we get some kind of equality established among all of us. There are no simple answers for this. I feel it messing with my head every day in day out. In ten years, I'd like to be stable, in a job that I would be happy and proud of doing. Something I love like writing. Will this make me a hero? What do you think?

—Anonymous

RATIONALE

What Is the Unit of Study?

Students will study the evolution of the hero and also will analyze the concept of heroism. How do heroes reflect a society's needs and beliefs? Are heroes for children only? After Superman, what? What types of heroes are possible in a jaded modern age such as ours? Can today's values define a new type of heroism, or do they preclude it? Has every hero's asset—physical strength, beauty, intelligence, moral integrity—become tarnished by technological manipulation and materialism? Do today's would-be heroes stop in midheroic journey—becoming marginalized fanatics, languishing as political prisoners, suffering violent martyrdom?

Each student will read a novel or biography of his or her choice and will analyze the hero within it. Students will study Joseph Campbell's heroic cycle and also will learn to categorize heroes according to a progression delineated by Northrop Frye in *The Anatomy of Criticism* (1957). They will generate their own definitions of heroism and apply all three of these analytical tools to the literary hero they have chosen. Presentation of this work and of the protagonist as "a hero" will be the final project for this unit.

Why Will Students Be Interested in Studying This?

Students will welcome the chance to express both their own emerging values and their cynicism. First, they enjoy figuring out what makes a character heroic, what distinguishes the people they admire. As adolescents, they are busy discriminating between and modeling themselves after various exemplars. Whether or not they can name a role model, they all will be able to point to sports figures, entertainers, relatives, and neighborhood legends who are everything they want to be.

Some students maintain that they have no heroes, that they respect only those characters who are succeeding by any means necessary—including walking all over everyone else. When these students define heroism, they maintain that it cannot guarantee survival; on the contrary, it invites doom and failure. Can heroism stand up against self-preservation? In the course of this unit, these students will come to appreciate and understand different types of heroes. They will find meaning and take solace in the more complex realistic or ironic heroes as described by Frye. They will learn to recognize true heroism in a modern guise, which can include failing before the shibboleths of an elite. In doing so, they come to a fuller understanding of their own heroes, values, and goals.

Why Do Students Need to Study This?

If we do live in an age bereft of heroes, what of it? Joseph Campbell says that people in every age have a need to believe in heroes, that heroes provide a crucial paradigm. Their stories are a universal model for human maturation: Each of us must go on a heroic journey of a sort, which includes a departure (from childhood), a series of trials (adolescent rebellion/alienation and search for our own identity), and finally, fulfillment and enriching return (to familial and/or social interdependence).

At first glance, this progress does seem to be an ideal that is unrealized for much of modern humanity. Instead, life is seen as an unresolvable struggle. Few people—especially those handicapped by dissolved families, poverty, and dysfunctional communities—find that fulfillment, that certainty, that wholeness. And yet, this is exactly what we need to do. In any culture, under any condition, a life so lived is the essence of human prerogative. It is totally and ultimately heroic.

As teenagers, as disenfranchised peoples, as young adults scared about survival and determining their own priorities—what could serve these students better than a course designed to help them recognize the heroic in the human experience?

Why Teach This Unit Now?

This unit works well as a final year-end project. The suggested readings are all stimulating and short, and class discussions around them are usually lively. Students also enjoy the two critical theories—Campbell's cycle and Frye's sociohistorical progression—even though they may seem at first too sophisticated for teens in high school. Individual pacing is possible with this unit: Students determine their own schedules and deadlines and devote much of their time to independent reading. It also accommodates instructors' busy spring schedules. The final presentation, in place of a test, allows instructors to attend to the more idiosyncratic tasks and scheduling needs of the final weeks of school.

KEY QUESTIONS

1. What is heroism? What are the characteristics of the hero?

2. What is their purpose in society?

3. Are heroes viable in our society today?

4. What is the relationship of power to heroism?

TERMINAL OBJECTIVES

- To read and present a "hero" book of student's own choosing

- To determine individual reading and written project deadlines for this work

- To write an extended definition of heroism with various popular textual references

- To reflect on unit topic and key questions in relation to students' own lives

MATERIALS

General References (for instructors)

- Campbell, Joseph, with Bill Moyers (1988), *The Power of Myth*

Major Works

- Individual students choose their own major work

Chapters and Excerpts From Longer Works

- Hamilton, Edith (1940), "Theseus" from *Mythology* (pp. 149-157)

- Hayton-Keeva, Sally (1987), "Karla Ramirez" from *Valiant Women in War and Exile: Thirty-Eight True Stories* (pp. 1-6)

- Terkel, Studs (1974), "Herb Goro: A Fireman" from *Working* (pp. 446-449)

Poems

- Levertov, Denise (1985), "The Altars in the Street"

- Updike, John (1957/1984), "Ex-Basketball Player"

- Yevtushenko, Yevgeny (1966), "Conversation With an American Writer"

Songs

- Lennon, John (1970), "Working Class Hero"

- Springsteen, Bruce (1980), "Pointblank" and "Glory Days"

Films

- *The Terminator* (1984)

SAMPLE DAILY SCHEDULE

Day 1: Lesson 1: Use HANDOUT 1: POPULAR HEROES?
Discuss heroism. Assign Journal 1.

Day 2: Lesson 2: Use HANDOUT 2: CAMPBELL'S CYCLE.
Discuss, analyze personal hero.

Day 3: Use HANDOUT 3: FRYE'S PROGRESSION OF HEROES.
Discuss, analyze heroes.

Day 4: Lesson 3: Read and discuss "Theseus."

Day 5: Discuss "Theseus" in groups.
Analyze myth using Campbell's cycle. Use HANDOUT 4: THESEUS'S
HEROIC JOURNEY.

Day 6: Lesson 4: Read "Karla Ramirez."
Assign HANDOUT 5: KARLA RAMIREZ: ARCHETYPAL HERO; have students
finish this for homework.

Day 7: Discuss HANDOUT 5.
Read "Herb Goro: A Fireman" from Terkel's *Working*.

Day 8: Discuss reading in small groups.

Day 9: Lesson 5: Begin explaining how to classify various items.
Play Categories Game.
Homework: HANDOUT 6: GENERAL CATEGORIES WORKSHEET (Part I).

Day 10: Go over HANDOUT 6.
Discuss next step in the extended definition process: differentiating
related terms.
Differentiate underlined terms from other members of the same
general category.

Day 11: Lesson 6: GO OVER HANDOUT 7: EXTENDED DEFINITION SAMPLE
AND WORKSHEET.

Day 12: Distribute HANDOUT 8: PLANNING AN EXTENDED DEFINITION OF
HEROISM; students work alone or with partners.
Homework: Students begin writing rough draft for extended definition.

Day 13: Work on rough draft in class.
Homework: Finish rough draft.

Day 14:   Work with peer to edit rough draft using HANDOUT 9:
             PEER EDITING CHECK SHEET.
             Work on extended definition in class; finish writing independently.

Day 15:   Lesson 7: Read Yevtushenko and Levertov poems; discuss.

Day 16:   Extended definition due.
             Assign Journal 2.

Day 17:   Lesson 8: Use HANDOUT 10: SAMPLE READING AND ASSIGNMENT
             SCHEDULE and HANDOUT 11: SUGGESTED READINGS FOR "THE HERO"
             to explain independent reading project.
             Discuss possible works; tell students to choose a work by a
             specific date.

Day 18:   Lesson 9: Discuss current events and clippings depicting antiheroes.
             Listen to/read antihero lyrics.

Day 19:   Read Updike's poem. Use HANDOUT 12: ANTIHEROES.
             Assign "Glory Days" creative writing (see Sample Student-
             Written "Glory Days" Poems).

Day 20:   Lesson 10: Complete HANDOUT 13: "THE HERO" READING AND
             ASSIGNMENT SCHEDULE.
             Determine individual reading schedules and assignments.

Day 21:   Students read independently in class.

Day 22:   Students read independently and work on independent writing
             assignments.

Day 23:   First reading and assignment due date.

Day 24:   Students finish all delinquent written work and work on
             independent writing assignments.

Day 25:   Small group informal reports; independent reading.

Day 26:   Second reading and assignment due date.

Day 27:   Students read and write independently.

Day 28:   Book talks with partners.

Day 29:   Third reading and assignment due date.

Day 30:   Students read and write independently.

Day 31:   Fourth reading and assignment due date.

Day 32: Explain final presentation assignment.
Use HANDOUT 14: PRESENTATION GUIDELINES.

Day 33: Lesson 11: See *The Terminator.*

Day 34: *The Terminator.*

Day 35: *The Terminator.*

Day 36-end Lesson 12: Written hero analyses or presentations due. Use
of unit   HANDOUT 15: PRESENTATION EVALUATIONS.
Assign Journal 3.

LESSON 1: WHAT IS A HERO?

Objectives

- To begin discussing the concepts of heroes and heroism

- To name some popular heroes

- To distinguish between heroism and fame

- To reflect on a personal hero

Materials

- HANDOUT 1: POPULAR HEROES?

Procedures

- Open the discussion of the hero by asking students to name some heroes they believe in now or used to believe in as children. Distribute HANDOUT 1: POPULAR HEROES? Have students work on these individually.

- Discuss student responses together.

1. Did students name famous figures, heroic figures, or some of each?
2. What characteristics distinguish the famous people from the heroic ones?
3. Is fame the same as heroism?

- Discuss the concept of heroism as an altogether dubious proposition in this modern age of dollars, co-optation, and corruption in high places. Some students may voice cynicism about "heroes," claiming that it's all cartoons and naive fantasy; no one is really a hero anymore. If they do take this tack, pursue it with searching questions:

1. Why do there seem to be no more heroes?
2. What one quality are all modern candidates for heroism missing?
3. What is this quality that seems to define heroism? Integrity? Unselfishness? Conviction? The ability to appeal to many disparate groups?
4. Do heroes have to please everyone in the world or just certain segments of the population?
5. Is a hero really a hero if only a few people think so? If only the hero thinks so?

If students do not engage readily in active discussions of heroes and heroism at this point, it is useful to play a devil's advocate role. Instructors might begin by suggesting the following thesis: There are no heroes anymore;

there can't be. Continue with the types of questions outlined in the above procedure.

- Assign Journal 1: Write about a hero you had as a child. What could this hero do? Why did you admire this hero? Did you want to be like this hero? How did you feel when you were in his or her presence?

HANDOUT 1: POPULAR HEROES?

Directions: Fill in the boxes with names and qualities of the following types of heroes.

TYPE OF HERO	NAMES	HEROIC QUALITIES
Sports Heroes		
Historical Heroes (explorers, cowboys, outlaws, statesmen, military leaders)		
Cult Heroes (figures special to one group of people; usually possess outstanding vision or talent)		
Fictitious Superheroes (characters from movies, comics, cartoons)		
Personal Heroes (role models, family members, friends)		

LESSON 2: THEORIES OF THE HERO

Objectives

- To become familiar with two theories associated with heroism

- To practice applying these theories to personal heroes

Materials

- HANDOUT 2: CAMPBELL'S CYCLE: THE ARCHETYPAL HEROIC JOURNEY

- HANDOUT 3: FRYE'S PROGRESSION OF HEROES

Procedures

- Briefly introduce Joseph Campbell (1904-1987) as a scholar, storyteller, writer, editor, and teacher:

In his work Campbell tried to explain the relevance and power that myths still hold for people today. Campbell said that myths are clues to certain experiences and spiritual truths. All cultures have stories and rituals that describe human struggle with disaster, triumph, heartache, and knowledge. These common human experiences, or archetypes, pervade the mythologies of every time and culture. Today as we struggle with modern disaster, triumph, heartache, and knowledge, we can recognize and learn from the mythological archetypes described by Campbell. (See Joseph Campbell with Bill Moyers, *The Power of Myth*, 1988.)

- Define *archetype:* a model or original version of a form. An archetype has significance because it is the first, most perfect, and most true example of a form. Calling something an *archetype* confers gravity and importance.

- Distribute HANDOUT 2: CAMPBELL'S CYCLE: THE ARCHETYPAL HEROIC JOURNEY. This handout describes the archetypal heroic journey. Every hero departs one environment or condition, finds an "answer" through various experiences and trials, and brings a richer condition to the world and him- or herself. Campbell breaks down every hero's journey into the four stages shown on this sheet:

1. Departure
2. Testing
3. Fulfillment
4. Return

- Flesh out the sketch on the handout with commentary. Students should add notes to their handouts based on instructor's commentary:

Stage 1: Departure. The hero may not be aware of his or her true identity. The hero experiences some type of loss or privation. She or he recognizes a personal need or a larger environmental problem and sets out to try to find answers. This is a call to adventure. Often the hero is met by a helper at this stage.

Stage 2: Testing. The hero faces many trials and adventures. Typical trials include fighting a monster of some sort, battling a brother, abduction, crossing the sea, crucifixion, going into the belly of the whale, loss of limbs, and so forth. These experiences are an induction: The hero crosses a threshold, leaving ordinary experience behind. She or he enters the belly of the beast in preparation for the "big one."

Stage 3: Fulfillment. The hero slays the dragon or otherwise achieves his or her goal. Fulfillment can take many forms. The hero can literally slay a minotaur or other grisly beast, come back from the dead, find and forgive a father figure, enter into a sacred marriage, or obtain a special curative elixir. This fulfillment usually ends with the hero in flight.

Stage 4: Return. The hero returns to the world with what has been lost or with some other life-giving quality. This return/resurrection/rescue is accompanied by deep sadness. The hero enriches the world but always sacrifices something that she or he loves. Each heroic journey makes the world a better place. In the process, the hero gains maturity and finds him- or herself.

• Encourage questions and commentary from students on Campbell's cycle. Discuss the progress of a few popular heroes through the cycle, applying Campbell's stages to watersheds and events in their stories. Suggested heroes: Moses, Jesus, Luke Skywalker from *Star Wars*, and so on.

• Once students are comfortable with Campbell's cycle, ask each to write a short paragraph that applies the cycle to the hero he or she named in Journal Assignment 1. This exercise can be done for homework. If students do not feel that their privacy is invaded, they may try this activity with a partner, reading each other's journals and discussing how Campbell's cycle applies to each other's heroes.

• Next, introduce Northrop Frye's progression of heroes. Distribute HANDOUT 3: FRYE'S PROGRESSION OF HEROES. Northrop Frye says that you can tell a lot about a culture by the type of heroic literature it generates. Again, flesh out information on the handout with commentary. Students should add notes to their handouts based on instructor's commentary:

Different cultures and eras produce different types of heroes.

Ancient Greeks' stories of supernatural gods and their powers explained the workings of the universe. Their *mythological heroes* were capable of miracles; their exploits accounted for mysteries and forces of the natural world.

As time passed, people began to see men, aided by gods, as the center of the universe. Special people, such as kings and churchmen, ruled the lives of others with their considerable, divine powers. Legends arose around the great deeds of *romantic heroes*.

With the Renaissance and the Reformation, science rose to preeminence. People no longer accepted heroes with special powers and supernatural abilities. It seemed that some people were just better than others. *Tragic heroes*—people of superior capabilities who failed only because of an inability to rise above some aspect of their environment—became popular.

In the beginning of the modern age, we believed that some people could rise to the occasion and be capable of greatness: *realistic heroes*. We have valued soldiers, great leaders, and people who are able to put others' safety before their own.

Now it seems we are not in control of our lives at all. Technology has taken over, and we are at the mercy of all-powerful institutions and environments. We do appreciate people who can rise above this reality, but we are most drawn to people who cannot. These *antiheroes*, or *ironic heroes*, make us feel a little better about our own impotence. We're not so bad; everyone is struggling.

Individuals of different ages relate to different types of heroes.

Mythological heroes satisfy children because kids are comfortable with the idea that there are beings powerful enough to read minds and stop the world from turning. These heroes answer a child's need to see someone in control. Kids also suspend disbelief easily; they accept and enjoy flying caped crusaders and giant turtles who speak.

Many teenagers are baffled or angered by their lack of control. They appreciate others who "rage against the machine" and recognize them as antiheroes. When teens find artists and musicians trying to express the same feelings, their own sense of alienation and heroic struggle is given voice and confirmed.

• Encourage questions and commentary from students on Frye's progression. Ask students to fill in the blanks with other examples. Name a few heroes and ask the class to categorize them. For example: Hercules (mythological or romantic); Rambo (romantic); the late Kurt Cobain of the band Nirvana (ironic).

• Once students are comfortable with Frye's progression, ask them to categorize the heroes they named on HANDOUT 1. Also ask into which category the hero they named in Journal Assignment 1 falls. If desired, students can write a short paragraph that explains the categorization of their hero.

HANDOUT 2: CAMPBELL'S CYCLE: THE ARCHETYPAL HEROIC JOURNEY

Stern. *Teaching English So It Matters.* © 1995 Corwin Press, Inc.

HANDOUT 3: FRYE'S PROGRESSION OF HEROES

Mythological Hero

- Different from other people

- Superior in ability and intelligence

- Can control the environment

- Divine or semidivine

- Often believed in by children

Mythological heroes: Superman, Thor, _____

Romantic Hero

- Human—but like a superhuman, is still special and can control environment

- Gets help from enchanted weapons, talking animals, witches

- Requires a stretch of the imagination; natural laws are slightly suspended

- Sometimes gets help from another, supernatural world

Romantic heroes: King Arthur, Rambo, _____

Tragic Hero

- A superior human but flawed in some way (not perfect)

- Still subject to environment and to "cruel fate"

- Born special in some way

- A leader (often eloquent)

- Fits many military men who have ascended to "bigger than life" status

Tragic heroes: Martin Luther King, Malcolm X, Macbeth, _____

(continued)

Realistic Hero

- One of us; definitely human

- Momentarily transcends the environment

- Made special—brave, courageous, determined—for a short time

- Fits some athletes and rescuers

Realistic heroes: Michael Jordan, firefighters, _____

Ironic/Antihero

- Inferior human, totally at the mercy of the environment

- Makes us recognize the frustration or the absurdity of modern life

- Makes us feel superior to him or her because of the situation she or he is in

- Often a loser who prevails due to sheer guts, not ability

- Is this all we have left in modern times?

Antiheroes: Rodney King, Rocky, _____

LESSON 3: THE MYTHOLOGICAL HERO

Objectives

- To read a classic mythological heroic journey

- To analyze this myth according to the theories presented in Lesson 2

Materials

- "Theseus" in Hamilton's *Mythology*

- HANDOUT 4: THESEUS'S HEROIC JOURNEY AS ANALYZED WITH CAMP-BELL'S CYCLE

Procedures

- Distribute "Theseus" and have students read on their own. When they are done reading, discuss the story by asking students basic questions about the events, characters, and heroic archetype:

    1. Why did Theseus take the land route instead of the sea route? (Theseus wanted to prove self; to go by the more difficult route would be more heroic.)
    2. How was Theseus's identity in question? (Theseus did not live with his father; he could claim Aegeus as father only if he was strong enough to roll the rock off the sword and shoes.)
    3. Who was Theseus's helper? What did she or he provide? (Ariadne gave him thread to trace his way out of the labyrinth.)
    4. Why was it obvious or likely that Theseus would forget to take down the black sails? (Many possible reasons: a. he wanted to kill and succeed his father, Aegeus; b. this is the one flaw in his otherwise perfect character; c. the myth needed to account for the name of the Aegean sea; d. he was distracted by the loss of Ariadne.)
    5. What does Theseus give to his city that had never been tried before? What part of the trip does this represent and why? (Theseus gives Athens democracy, the elixir that changed and enriched the world.)
    6. It is said that the hero's journey takes him somewhere—psychologically as well as physically. How does Theseus change from the beginning of his journey to his return? (Theseus left with no conscious moral objective; he just wanted to be a hero. He returned as a selfless adult with a noble purpose: bringing democracy.)

- Divide students into groups to discuss and/or write answers to the following reflective questions:

    1. What deficiency prompts Theseus's journey? What does this tell you about his psychological state?

2. Do you think Theseus was destined to be a hero? Why or why not?

3. Why did he want to "get in good" with Athenians once he was recognized as Aegeus's son? What did he decide to do?

4. What is a labyrinth, and why is it a particularly appropriate place for Theseus to slay the dragon?

5. How did Ariadne help Theseus? How did she challenge him? Did he meet this challenge?

6. Classify Theseus according to Frye's progression. (He is a classic mythological hero.)

• Draw a circle on the board to represent Campbell's archetypal heroic journey, and take Theseus through Campbell's cycle with students. Distribute HANDOUT 4: THESEUS'S HEROIC JOURNEY AS ANALYZED WITH CAMPBELL'S CYCLE to students if desired.

• If instructors have easy access to copying, they should distribute another copy of HANDOUT 2: CAMPBELL'S CYCLE: THE ARCHETYPAL HEROIC JOURNEY and ask students to note details from Theseus's journey on the sheet where they fit into the cycle. Otherwise students can sketch their own versions of the cycle and take notes on their "homemade handouts."

Tell students that this analysis provides a model: As students now are analyzing Theseus's story, so too will each student in the class need to analyze another hero's journey. Theseus (and other readings in subsequent lessons) will give the students practice.

HANDOUT 4: THESEUS'S HEROIC JOURNEY AS ANALYZED WITH CAMPBELL'S CYCLE

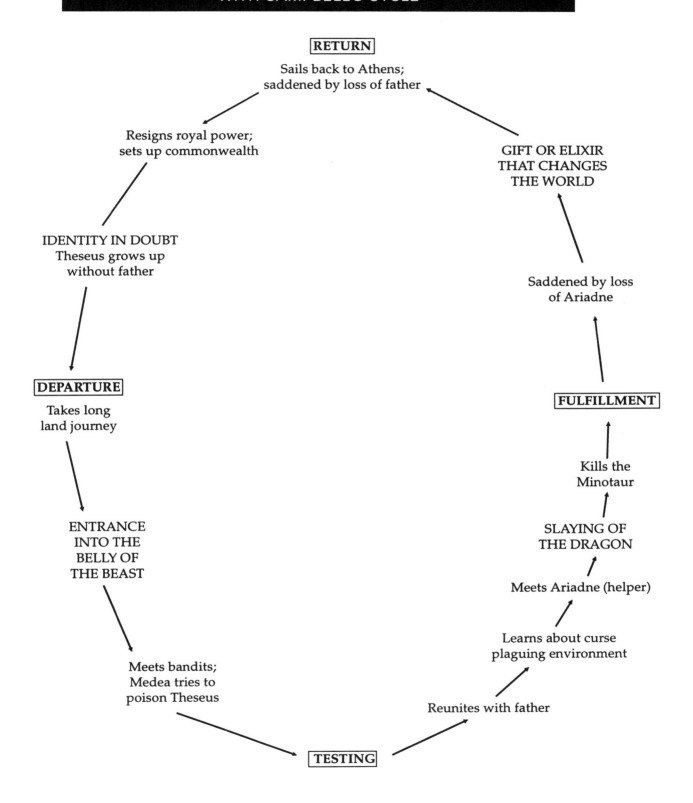

RETURN
Sails back to Athens;
saddened by loss of father

Resigns royal power;
sets up commonwealth

GIFT OR ELIXIR
THAT CHANGES
THE WORLD

IDENTITY IN DOUBT
Theseus grows up
without father

Saddened by loss
of Ariadne

DEPARTURE
Takes long
land journey

FULFILLMENT

ENTRANCE
INTO THE
BELLY OF
THE BEAST

Kills the
Minotaur

SLAYING OF
THE DRAGON

Meets Ariadne (helper)

Learns about curse
plaguing environment

Meets bandits;
Medea tries to
poison Theseus

Reunites with father

TESTING

Stern. *Teaching English So It Matters.* © 1995 Corwin Press, Inc.

LESSON 4: THE REALISTIC HERO

Objectives

- To read accounts of realistic heroes

- To analyze these accounts according to the theories presented in Lesson 2

- To reflect on personal feelings and other current attitudes toward heroes

Materials

Short accounts of realistic heroes. I use:

- "Karla Ramirez" from Hayton-Keeva's *Valiant Women in War and Exile* (pp. 1-6)

- "Herb Goro: A Fireman" from Terkel's *Working* (pp. 446-449)

- Yevtushenko's poem "Conversation With an American Writer"

- HANDOUT 5: KARLA RAMIREZ, ARCHETYPAL HERO

Procedures

- Distribute Karla Ramirez's story, found in the collection of first-person tales *Valiant Women in War and Exile*. This short account works well when read aloud.

At this point, it is a good idea to tell students that they will be responsible for choosing their own major work to read for the unit. They can start thinking about books they would like to read or can at least get used to the idea that the teacher will not be reading with the class all together.

- Also distribute HANDOUT 5: KARLA RAMIREZ, ARCHETYPAL HERO. If students feel comfortable with the analysis of Theseus's story, they may complete this sheet for homework. Students may enjoy discussing Ramirez's story in small groups informally as they work together on completing this handout.

- Go over HANDOUT 5: KARLA RAMIREZ, ARCHETYPAL HERO. Answers may vary on this sheet. Encourage discussion and analysis of the events in Ramirez's life.

- Distribute excerpt ("Herb Goro: A Fireman") from Studs Terkel's *Working*. Students can read this short work aloud or to themselves. As they are reading, write the following questions on the board:

1. How does the firefighter feel about doing his job?

2. How do people in the neighborhood treat the firefighter?
3. What does he say is a firefighter's job today?
4. Why do you think the people in the street do not respect him?
5. What is his attitude toward the people he serves?
6. Do you think he is a hero? Why or why not?
7. What questions would you ask Herb Goro (or any firefighter, police officer, or other public servant who has opportunities to be a realistic hero) yourself?

- Discuss these questions or have students consider them in small groups. If students talk among themselves in groups, instructors should convene the groups afterward so that students can pose their own questions (question 7) for the whole class to consider.

HANDOUT 5: KARLA RAMIREZ, ARCHETYPAL HERO

Directions: In the spaces below, trace Ramirez's account of her life using the stages in Campbell's cycle.

THE HERO	KARLA RAMIREZ
Has a question about his or her identity; senses a lack or need	
Goes on a journey that tests or challenges him or her	
Meets a helper who provides a tool, weapon, etc.	
Accomplishes a major feat or succeeds in overcoming a major obstacle	
Brings a gift or elixir to the world that heals one of society's ills	
Other features that characterize this hero's story (consider motivation, sacrifice, self-evaluation, etc.)	
What type of hero is this according to Frye's progression?	

LESSON 5: EXTENDED DEFINITION: PREWRITING

Objectives

- To become familiar with processes requisite for writing complex definitions—specifically, classifying and differentiating related terms

- To become adept at using these processes to classify familiar concepts and terms

Materials

- Prepared game sheets for Categories Game (see procedures)

- HANDOUT 6: GENERAL CATEGORIES WORKSHEET

Procedures

(Many of the terms and procedures in this and the next lesson are adapted from Johannessen, Kahn, and Walter [1982], *Designing and Sequencing Prewriting Activities.*)

- At this point in the unit, students will be ready to figure out what does and does not constitute heroism. Explain that during the next few days students will polish their defining skills. Use a demonstration to illustrate the first step in defining any object or term: naming the general class to which it belongs. Hold up a dictionary. Ask the class to define it. Hold up a banana or a boot. Ask students to try to define the item. As the class offers various definitions of these items, it will become clear that the most basic information about any of them is its *general category*. (A dictionary is a book. A banana is a piece of fruit. A boot is a shoe.)

- Divide the class into two (or three or four) teams and prepare them to play the Categories Game. Explain that they will see lists of items and that their task is two-part: First, they must add one more term that fits into the general category. Then they will name the general category specifically. If they cannot do both these things, another team may try and thus can "steal" the first team's points.

    1. After the first group of terms is uncovered, whichever team first raises a hand will have 10 seconds to confer and proffer another term in the same category (25 points). Then they must name precisely the general category to which all terms belong (25 points).
    2. If the team has completed both tasks successfully, they are to be awarded 50 points, and the play continues with the next series of terms. If students did not name a term that fit in the same general category or did not name the category correctly and/or specifically enough, they do not win any points. Even if the team correctly

deduced the general category, they must forfeit these 25 points if they first did not suggest a term that correctly belongs in that same general category. Other teams can try.

3. The other teams must correctly name a different term belonging to the correct general category. They also must name (or restate) the general category. They then are awarded 50 points.

It is important that students understand that this is not a guessing game; for that reason, I do not uncover items incrementally. Teachers may choose to do this and award more points for answers offered early (that is, when only one or two items are uncovered). This does increase the drama of the game. When we played the game like this, however, my students stopped thinking and started taking wild potshots. I felt that this did not advance the objectives of the exercise and amended game procedures accordingly.

To prepare for this game, I make nine large posters corresponding to nine general categories. On each of the posters, I list five items that fit into one general category. These categories are listed here for instructor's reference only.

SAMPLE CATEGORIES

I.	II.	III.	IV.
Tide	Zeus	puma	Arnold Schwarzenegge
Bounce	Odin	cheetah	Sylvester Stallone
Downy	Shiva	jaguar	Errol Flynn
Cheer	Mars	panther	Jean-Claude Van Damn
Spray 'n Wash	Mercury	leopard	Steven Seagal
————————	————————	————————	————————
(laundry products)	(pre-Christian gods)	(wild cats)	(action/adventure mov stars)

V.	VI.	VII.	VIII.	IX.
Vibe	march	Baldwin	adultery	lacrosse
Omni	salsa	Wright	profanity	hockey
GQ	swing	Walker	stealing	soccer
Jet	waltz	Morrison	killing	cricket
Time	bossa nova	Ellison	disrespecting parents	hurling
————	————	————	————————	————
(magazines)	(musical rhythms)	(African American novelists)	(acts prohibited by the Ten Commandments)	(sports)

• Whether students enjoy or have trouble with the game, it is advisable to distribute HANDOUT 6: GENERAL CATEGORIES WORKSHEET immediately. Help students struggling with the concept to work through a few of the series. Have students finish the sheet alone or for homework. They can create their own series for the blanks in 14-16. Make sure that all students have the worksheet in class the next day to work on the next step of the defining process.

• When students have completed the sheet, go over the answers (provided below). Students should try to refine general categories as precisely as possible. For example, when trying to define a term such as *Morocco*, stress that it is better to name the general class to which it belongs as *African countries* (as opposed to the more generic *countries*). Distinguish between a series of concrete objects (i.e., 10) and abstractions (i.e., 11). Ask for volunteers to share the series they created for 14 to 16.

• Next, draw students' attention to the italicized item in each series. Ask them what makes this item different from other items in the general category. Explain that this is the second task in defining a term. The students must identify characteristics that set it apart from other terms in the general category. In other words, they must differentiate related terms.

Answers for HANDOUT 6:

1. Chicago professional sports teams. *Bears:* professional football team in Chicago.
2. Holy scriptures of major world religions. *Quran:* the sacred book of Islam.
3. Dogs. *Jackal:* a type of wild dog found in Africa and Asia.
4. Greetings. *Hola:* Spanish greeting.
5. Sports apparel manufacturers. *Nike:* very popular brand advertised by Michael Jordan.
6. Sources of energy. *Nuclear:* energy from the inner core of the atom.
7. Countries in Africa. *Morocco:* Arab country on the north Atlantic coast.
8. Island countries. *Japan:* economic superpower in the Pacific.
9. Monetary units. *Ruble:* Russian money.
10. Cheeses. *Swiss:* pale yellow cheese with holes originally made in Switzerland.
11. Emotions. *Affection:* positive feeling of liking or warmth.
12. Inclement weather conditions. *Snow:* soft, cold flakes.
13. Rap artists. *Ice Cube:* actor and former member of NWA.

HANDOUT 6: GENERAL CATEGORIES WORKSHEET

Directions: Part I: Write the general category into which each series of items falls. In naming the category, make sure you are specific. Create your own series at the end for items 14 to 16.

One of the terms in each item is in italics. When you bring this sheet back to class tomorrow, we will work on Part II of this worksheet, which will deal with each italicized word.

1. Bulls, Cubs, *Bears*, White Sox: _____

2. Bible, *Quran*, Torah, Upanishads: _____

3. *jackal*, terrier, spaniel, bloodhound: _____

4. hello, bonjour, *hola*, guten tag: _____

5. *Nike*, Reebok, Converse, Fila: _____

6. *nuclear*, hydroelectric, natural gas, solar: _____

7. Somalia, Zaire, Mozambique, *Morocco*: _____

8. Haiti, Cuba, New Zealand, *Japan*: _____

9. peso, *ruble*, lira, pound: _____

10. *Swiss*, American, feta, Chihuahua: _____

11. jealousy, anger, *affection*, guilt: _____

12. wind, rain, *snow*, sleet: _____

13. *Ice Cube*, Queen Latifah, Ice T, Public Enemy: _____

14. _____

15. _____

16. _____

LESSON 6: WRITING AN EXTENDED DEFINITION OF HEROISM

Objectives

- To practice identifying and using processes involved in complex definitions, that is, classifying and differentiating related terms and generating defining criteria

- To adhere to a strict formula and criteria for writing an expository essay

- To use these skills to write an extended definition of heroism

Materials

- HANDOUT 7: EXTENDED DEFINITION SAMPLE AND WORKSHEET

- HANDOUT 8: PLANNING AN EXTENDED DEFINITION OF HEROISM

- HANDOUT 9: PEER EDITING CHECK SHEET

Procedures

The procedures in this lesson will vary depending on students' ability to process new information. High-skilled students may have had no difficulty absorbing the first two parts of an extended definition—determining the general category and identifying differentiating details. If this is the case, you simply can present the remaining steps of the formula and have them start outlining their definitions of heroism.

- Distribute HANDOUT 7: EXTENDED DEFINITION SAMPLE AND WORKSHEET. Read the definition together. Highlight the "general category" and "differentiating details" of greed, the concept that is being defined. Explain that there are six steps of writing an extended definition and that they already know the first two (determining the *general category* and identifying *differentiating details*). The next step is explaining and illustrating three *defining criteria*, or "necessary ingredients" of the term being defined. This third step is crucial; in it, students must struggle to get at the essence of the term or concept they are defining. Have the students highlight this information in the sample essay. Finally, go over the final step in writing an extended definition: presenting a *contrasting example*, or "gray area," in which some but not all of the defining criteria are met. The class should take notes in the margins of the worksheet in small groups, or they can complete it for homework.

- After students have completed the worksheet and have processed the components of the sample extended definition, I often have to run through some additional model definitions. *Love* and *freedom* work well:

Term	General Class	Distinguishing Features	Three Defining Criteria and Examples	Contrasting Example
Love	feeling	intense, positive	(1) Passion (Romeo and Juliet) (2) Intimacy (lovers in the film *Say Anything*) (3) Commitment (local couple who just had 50th anniversary)	A typical high school couple: Donna and Don have (1) passion and (2) intimacy but no (3) commitment
Freedom	emotional or physical condition or capability	involves another person or institution	(1) Choice (a person who is free to do volunteer work has choice) (2) Capability for action (if you have your own car, you often have capability for action) (3) Untroubled by consequences (a person who is racked with guilt is not free)	Lisa, 14 years old, wants to stay out late at a Friday night party. She (1) chooses to ignore her curfew; she says she (3) doesn't care if she gets in trouble; but her mother picks her up at 10:30 so Lisa has no freedom to act (2) on her choice.

• Explain that students can begin writing their own extended definitions of heroism. Ask them to consider characters from the unit's readings, their observations, and their own gut feelings. Distribute HANDOUT 8: PLANNING AN EXTENDED DEFINITION OF HEROISM. Students may work on these alone or may work with a partner as they determine the general class, differentiating details, and necessary ingredients of heroism. (Even if students agree on these elements, their illustrating examples will need to differ.)

As with most writing exercises, I found it helpful to fill out a planning sheet myself, outlining my own extended definition of heroism. In this way, I was able to anticipate some of the difficulties students would experience working with this challenging, subjective assignment.

• Check over students' planning sheets and have them write drafts for their extended definitions. Use peers to check these drafts. Let students pick their own partners. Distribute HANDOUT 9: PEER EDITING CHECK SHEET. Walk them through proper usage of this sheet. More advanced students can and should devise their own peer editing criteria and check sheet.

My students' ideas about heroism vary greatly. They suggest that the general class to which heroism belongs is variously a "force," a "feeling," an "attitude," a "process," or a "behavior." They distinguish it from other terms in the general class as being "very demanding" and "something you control yourself"; they say that "you need maturity to feel it." In their essays, students name such defining criteria as "a conscious moral objective," "sacrifice," "bravery," "indifference to public opinion," and "modesty."

HANDOUT 7: EXTENDED DEFINITION SAMPLE AND WORKSHEET

Directions:

1. Read the sample extended definition.

2. Underline the general category of greed and identify it as "general category" in the margin next to it.

3. Underline the differentiating details of greed and identify them as "differentiating details" in the margin.

4. Underline each of the three necessary ingredients and identify them as "necessary ingredient 1," and so forth, in the margins.

5. Find and label all examples of necessary ingredients in the margins. Underline what you think is the best part of the example.

6. Find and underline the contrasting example, and label it in the margin.

Beyond Rudeness

Greed is a type of desire. It is different from other desires because it is intense and knows no limits. Greed often is associated with money, but it is not limited to finances. A person can be greedy about lots of things, including money, love, food, and knowledge. In order to be greedy, a person must lack respect for others, have no common sense, and go too far.

The first essential ingredient of greed is nonconcern for others. Greedy people lack respect for others; in other words, they are selfish. For example, Claire was greedy at the Halloween party. She grabbed all the good candy, took three caramel apples, and had four pieces of cake. She did not care that there were people who were coming later and that there might not be enough left for them. "Too bad," she said as she stuffed her face. She definitely was being greedy because she was depriving someone of something and did not care about anyone but herself.

Another sure sign of greed is when people have no common sense about how much they need or about how much they really can use. If someone does not let reality determine the limits of what they take, then they are being greedy. For example, they were giving away free birdseed at the hardware store this weekend, and Mr. Waleed rushed over and took as much as they would give him: five pounds. He then kept on disguising himself so they wouldn't recognize him and proceeded to pick up 55 more pounds. There's no way he could use 60 pounds of birdseed. He did not use common sense. He was just being greedy.

The third important part of greed is excessiveness. Greedy people will get an idea that they need something and will not be able to recognize that they have gone too far. For example, Tony and Tina are going out, and Tony is very jealous of everything that Tina does. He wants her to call him the minute that she gets up and every hour on the hour. He even wants her to write down every single person she talks to during the day. She is supposed to hand him this report every night. She is not allowed to talk to her sisters. He will not let her talk to any of her friends. She can't go anywhere without him. He wants all of Tina's time, all of her attention. He is being greedy: It is impossible for Tina to limit her interaction with the human race the way Tony wants her to. Still, he thinks he is doing right. His greed has blinded him to practical reality.

A person must display all three of these characteristics to be truly greedy. If people are stupid and excessive but not disrespectful of others' needs, then they are not being greedy. For example, Chris wasn't thinking when she bought her brand-new baby niece a lot of stuff. She spent over $600 on baby clothes, including a teeny leather jacket. She spent hours and hours picking out stuffed animals: $400 worth. She bought tiny books, tiny toys, tiny furniture, and even tiny headphones. Altogether she spent $1500! This is too much to spend on the baby, whose parents already had bought everything she needs. The baby doesn't care what she wears, isn't aware of her furniture or toys, and can't even use half the things Chris bought. Chris is not being greedy because she isn't depriving anyone of anything. She's just being stupid and excessive. If you want to be greedy, you've got to be stupid, excessive, and selfish.

HANDOUT 8: PLANNING AN EXTENDED DEFINITION OF HEROISM

If you wanted to define heroism, you could just copy what the dictionary says. Or you could write your own, longer, extended definition of what it takes to be a hero in our time.

An extended definition is a five-part essay that defines a term and provides clear examples that illustrate that definition. This sheet will help you organize your thoughts on heroism so that you can write a coherent extended definition of this term.

THIS INFORMATION BELONGS IN THE FIRST PARAGRAPH OR SECTION:

1. What is the general class under which heroism belongs?

2. How is it different from other terms in this class?

EACH INGREDIENT AND EXAMPLE BELONGS IN A SEPARATE PARAGRAPH OR SECTION:

3. What are three necessary ingredients of heroism? Provide examples from experience, movies, or songs. Make sure that you explain the particulars of each example.

a.

b.

c.

THIS BELONGS IN THE FINAL PARAGRAPH OR SECTION:

4. Think of a contrasting example. For instance, name a character that satisfies some but not all of the criteria.

HANDOUT 9: PEER EDITING CHECK SHEET

EDITORS: As you read your partner's rough draft, look for the following things. As you find them, help the writer by checking off each item. Offer suggestions in the sections for comments.

1. An indented first paragraph __
   in which the writer clearly states the general category into which heroism falls __
   and the things that make heroism different from other things in this category (the differentiating details) __.
Comments:

2. An indented second paragraph __
   containing a clearly stated, essential ingredient of heroism __
   and a clear, complete example of a person displaying this attribute __.
Comments:

3. An indented third paragraph __
   containing a different, clearly stated essential attribute of heroism __
   and a clear, complete example of a person displaying this attribute __.
Comments:

4. An indented fourth paragraph __
   containing a different, clearly stated essential attribute of heroism __
   and a clear, complete example of a person displaying this attribute __.
Comments:

5. An indented fifth paragraph __
   that gives an example of a person who is not heroic because she or he has some but not all of the three essential attributes __.
Comments:

And: 1. Look for spelling mistakes and circle the words that you think need to be checked.
       2. Make sure the writer has used complete sentences. Each sentence needs a subject and a verb. If you see a sentence that is missing a subject or a verb, circle it.

WRITERS: Use your partner's observations to fix your rough draft. When you copy it over, change it according to your partner's suggestions.
   The whole packet—containing the planning worksheet, rough draft, this check sheet, and final draft—is due: _____

LESSON 7: INTEGRITY AND HEROISM

Objectives

- To read poetry celebrating "realistic heroes"

- To consider the issues precipitating heroism today

- To reflect on heroic action as observed in everyday life

Materials

Poems depicting characters who see nothing heroic in their simple, humane acts or moral integrity. I use:

- Levertov, Denise, "The Altars in the Street"

- Yevtushenko, Yevgeny, "Conversation With an American Writer"

Procedures

- Distribute poems. Provide background information for both works.

For Levertov's piece: On June 17, 1966, Vietnamese children built altars in the streets of Saigon and Hue, jamming traffic and impeding commerce on the busy city streets as part of the Buddhist campaign of nonviolent resistance.

For Yevtushenko's poem: During the most repressive periods of Communist rule, intellectuals, writers, and artists were punished for questioning government practices and policies. Many were imprisoned, exiled, and otherwise silenced. Some simply shut up. Others, such as Yevtushenko, continued to voice their criticism.

- Read both works aloud with class. Let students ask their own questions and pose the following questions to start discussions:

1. What are the acts of heroism described here?
2. What made the "heroes" act?
3. How do the heroes feel about their colleagues—the Vietnamese townspeople and Yevtushenko's fellow poets?
4. Are the children and Yevtushenko heroes according to your extended definition?

- Explain that in these poems people are standing up for something they believe in. Discuss with students:

1. These characters do not consider themselves heroes. Their simple actions expose the confused values of their environments. In what

situations could you take a stand like Yevtushenko's and be applauded simply for upholding your principles?

2. Have you ever been in (or seen) a situation similar to that of the
Vietnamese children in which you ignore the craziness around you
and just do what you know is right?

• Write Journal Assignment 2 on the board: Write about a time you or
someone you know was just acting with integrity, and outsiders applauded
this "heroism."

• If students cannot think of an experience or observation that fits this
assignment, they may write a creative piece or short story describing a realistic
hero whose integrity exposes the weakness of the surrounding cultural norm.

*Tina, 17, an articulate student and rapper, wrote the following poem, modeled
on Yevtushenko's, for Journal Assignment 2:*

"You're a brilliant and creative artist—"
they tell me . . .
Bull. These lyrics are not a creation
They are daily real life for many.
I hate to see my brothers so ignorant or scared to admit the truth

I don't imagine or make up the things I rap
Others rap of things like girls, money, and fame.
I rap truth.
That's all.

I try to say
Just what I see.

I defend the oppressed people
Brand the incapable
With lyrics

I do this because I have to.

Will my children remember these times
With bitter shame?
When simple truth was called "creativity?"

• If pressed for time, instructors may forego students' independent reading of a major work. In this case, classes should skip Lessons 8 and 10. In
Lesson 12, students may respond to Journal Assignment 3 in writing or by
preparing a speech.

LESSON 8: REVIEWING AND CHOOSING A WORK OF HEROIC LITERATURE

Objectives

- To choose a major work to read for this unit

- To learn expectations and assignments required for this independent reading project

- To determine individual reading schedule and other assignment deadlines

Materials

- HANDOUT 10: SAMPLE READING AND ASSIGNMENT SCHEDULE

- HANDOUT 11: SUGGESTED READINGS FOR "THE HERO"

Procedures

- Explain the independent reading project: Students will be reading a book on their own, and will complete a few assignments while they read to process information about the hero(es) in the work. When they have finished reading, they will be responsible for presenting the book orally or by written report. Specific requirements for this presentation will be made later, but students should know that their presentations must follow a strict form. Students will apply Campbell's cycle, Frye's progression of heroes, and their own extended definition to the protagonist/hero in the book.

- Show students HANDOUT 10: SAMPLE READING AND ASSIGNMENT SCHEDULE. Explain that when they choose the work they will be reading (in a specified number of days), students will be given a similar blank schedule. They will decide how much they will be reading each week, on what dates simple story maps will be due, and so forth.

- Distribute HANDOUT 11: SUGGESTED READINGS FOR "THE HERO." Make sure students know that the book selection is really up to them. Ask them if there is a book that they have been curious about that might have a heroic figure in it. Remind them of the antihero. If there are any students who ask about specific books ("My friend just read *One Flew Over the Cuckoo's Nest*. Can I read that?"), let that lead the class into a general discussion of books not on the list that might be appropriate. Tell students that they must choose their book by a given date.

I wanted to make books accessible and unintimidating for my students, most of whom do not read on their own and do not visit libraries often. I collected single copies of as many of the works as I could find and brought them to the classroom that day.

We talked about each book on the list on HANDOUT 11. Students passed the available books around, thumbing through them and seeing what looked appealing. One year we did this one week before spring break; I specified that students needed to come back from vacation with their book selected. Over break, many students had begun reading; a few came back to class having finished their chosen work already.

- Tell students that they must report which book they will be reading by a certain date. Give students at least a few days to choose their books; if this lesson falls on a Thursday, for example, give students the rest of the week and the weekend. Continue with Lesson 9 while they are selecting and finding their books. Also make sure that students know when they must bring their chosen books to school; it is crucial that students begin Lesson 10 with their books in hand.

HANDOUT 10: SAMPLE READING
AND ASSIGNMENT SCHEDULE

Name: *Jill Student*   Name of novel: *Down These Mean Streets*

Today's date: *May 2, 1995*   Author: *Piri Thomas*

                                        Number of pages: *314*

I have/have not started this book already.

I am on page *47*

	Expected Page	Short Assignment
By: *Friday, May 5*	87	*A letter from me to the main character*
By: *Wednesday, May 10*	148	*A four-question "quiz" on the book so far*
By: *Friday, May 12*	204	*A story map*
By: *Wednesday, May 17*	290	*A list of main events since last due date's readin*

I will finish the book by: *Friday, May 19*

I understand that I must give a short presentation or write a report on this book by: *May 26*

HANDOUT 11: SUGGESTED READINGS
FOR "THE HERO"

Angelou, Maya, *I Know Why the Caged Bird Sings*
Arnow, Harriet, *The Dollmaker*
Chernin, Kim, *In My Mother's House*
Dorris, Michael, *Yellow Raft in Blue Water*
Gibbons, Kaye, *Ellen Foster*
Gibson, William, *Neuromancer*
Greenburg, Joanne, *I Never Promised You a Rose Garden*
Guthrie, Woody, *Bound for Glory*
Haley, Alex, with Malcolm X, *The Autobiography of Malcolm X*
Heinlein, Robert, *Stranger in a Strange Land*
Hesse, Hermann, *Siddhartha*
Hinton, S. E., *The Outsiders*
Irving, John, *A Prayer for Owen Meany*
Keyes, Daniel, *Flowers for Algernon*
Kingsolver, Barbara, *The Bean Trees*
Least Heat Moon, William, *Blue Highways*
MacInerney, Jay, *Ransom*
Miller, Sue, *The Good Mother*
Moody, Anne, *Coming of Age in Mississippi*
Mukherjee, Bharati, *Jasmine*
Pirsig, Robert M., *Zen and the Art of Motorcycle Maintenance*
Price, Reynolds, *Kate Vaiden*
Rodríguez, Luis, *Always Running: La Vida Loca: Gang Days in L.A.*
Salinger, J. D., *Catcher in the Rye*
Tan, Amy, *The Kitchen God's Wife*
Taylor, Mildred D., *Roll of Thunder, Hear My Cry*
Thomas, Piri, *Down These Mean Streets*
Trumbo, Dalton, *Johnny Got His Gun*
Vonnegut, Kurt, *Slaughterhouse Five*
White, Edmund, *A Boy's Own Story*
Yezierska, Anya, *Bread Givers*

LESSON 9: THE ANTIHERO

Objectives

- To read accounts of ironic heroes or antiheroes

- To evaluate the heroic status of antiheroes

- To write a short poem describing a real or imagined antihero

Materials

- Newspaper clippings presenting antiheroes (see first procedure)

- Updike, John, "Ex-Basketball Player"

- HANDOUT 12: ANTIHEROES

- Lennon, John, "Working Class Hero"

- Springsteen, Bruce, "Pointblank" and "Glory Days"

- SAMPLE STUDENT-WRITTEN "GLORY DAYS" POEMS (for instructors' reference)

Procedures

- Distribute newspaper articles or clippings depicting antiheroes. These articles can describe everyday people who struggle unsuccessfully against the awesome power of "the system." Their heroism is ironic because they are unsuccessful. The articles also can be about people who act absolutely immorally or unlawfully. Their heroism is a type of criminal celebrity. They live outside the law as antiheroes.

- Discuss the antihero:

    1. Why do negative heroes have such power?
    2. Do they have more power than "good" heroes?
    3. Are they heroes at all?

Students should apply their own extended definitions of heroism to these antiheroes.

- Distribute Updike's poem and HANDOUT 12: ANTIHEROES. Read the poem aloud with students, focusing especially on Updike's use of sports metaphors to describe the ex-athlete's current actions. Ask the students about the effect of this language.

- Students may discuss the questions on the handout, or they may write out answers independently or with peers in groups.

- If instructors desire, they can play any or all of the suggested powerful songs before assigning the creative piece at the bottom of the handout. "Working Class Hero" and "Pointblank" paint profound pictures of pathos and desperation; "Glory Days" is simpler and more upbeat. By examining popular lyrics such as these, students generally come to understand the antihero's dilemma.

Against the grinding disappointments and ugly truths of modern life, we are powerless. We can't win. If we "follow their rules," we may go crazy, as Lennon warns. If we believe in promises and possibilities, we may get "twisted up till . . . [we] become just another part of it," like the destroyed protagonist in Springsteen's "Pointblank."

- After reading Updike's poem and the popular song lyrics, assign the creative writing at the bottom of Handout 12 for homework.

This assignment is one that students really have enjoyed in past years. One wrote a short poem about a former beauty queen now scrutinizing her reflection in a saucepan lid. See SAMPLE STUDENT-WRITTEN "GLORY DAYS" POEMS for other examples.

HANDOUT 12: ANTIHEROES

As children watching cartoons, we all love seeing mythological heroes do impossible things. As we grow up, our ideas about heroism and heroes change. We become more and more cynical and no longer believe in flying superheroes who will "make everything all right" and save the day.

What types of heroes are left for us as teenagers and adults? Have social institutions and technology taken over our lives so that we, as individuals, are powerless? Are we all doomed to become victims of our environments, with no hope for real, life-enriching heroism? This is Frye's "Ironic Hero" in a nutshell.

Is the antihero the only type of hero possible these days?

Questions on "Ex-Basketball Player" by John Updike

1. What facts about Flick's life can you deduce? In other words, what was he, and what is he now?

2. Examine the description of Pearl Avenue. Why are these words used specifically?

3. Think about the objects that you imagine were a part of Flick's life when he was a basketball star. Next, name four objects (mentioned in the poem) that Flick uses now. How do these two sets of objects differ?

4. What is the significance of Flick's name?

5. What is the significance of the fact that Flick plays pinball now?

6. What type of hero (according to Frye) is Flick? Why?

7. Examine the first and fifth stanzas. Both stanzas bring Flick's past and present together in a similar way. What do the two stanzas have in common?

Assignment

Consider other "has-beens" and write a poem in the style of Updike's "Ex-Basketball Player." Make sure you write about a character who lives in the shadow of the past. Try to make some active details from the past act as metaphors in your poem.

SAMPLE STUDENT-WRITTEN "GLORY DAYS" POEMS

The Ex-Runner

by Antonio, 18 years old

California Avenue speeds over Chicago Avenue,
Leaps over 13th Street, stretches to 26th Street,
And comes to the finish line at Anthony Norwood.
Most days you'll find him washing dishes
In the kitchen at Cook County jail

He quickly grabs a pot,
Hands it off to the dish rack,
Dashes to grab the dry towel,
Comes back to lift the pot
And drys it with quick ability

Once Tone ran for the high school relay
Speed racer
He was the best. Well, one of the best.
In 1978 he went All State

He used his speed well
And turned to a life of crime
He fastest thief on the streets, he left all police behind
Now he has pots and pans, forks and spoons to cheer him on.

Ex-Football Player

by Joel, 16 years old

Fullerton Avenue crashes through Kimball Street
Runs and cuts and seems elite.
Laying on Fullerton now is Frank.
Not tackling any player like a tank.
Thinking he's getting stronger
He just clings to a bottle,
Noone wants to think of him any longer.

Frank lies low under city viaducts
People stare and laugh, don't give two fucks
This is Frank's new playing field
He wears no shoulder pads,
Just some cardboard as blanket and shield.

Once he played for the Prologue Blues
He was great in every way—
Even how he tied his shoes.
People loved him when he scored the winning touchdown in the final conference game
This is how he earned his fame
Later on he was named Frank the Tank,
Cause he ran and jumped and cut like a shank.

He never thought that he would need school
But he was trapped in being a fool
People who recognized him would steal his bottles and toss them like footballs
Frank didn't like this at all
So he aimed like a tank gun, ready to fire
He got up, swung, missed, and got knocked over.
They just whipped his ass like Rin-Tin-Tin and Rover.

LESSON 10: INDEPENDENT WORK WITH THE HERO

Objectives

- To read independently a work of student's own choosing

- To complete short, simple reading comprehension assignments on this work

- To complete short assignments requiring more reflective and critical thought on this work

- To comply with contractual schedule of assignments designed in Lesson 8

Materials

- HANDOUT 13: "THE HERO" READING AND ASSIGNMENT SCHEDULE

- HANDOUT 14: PRESENTATION GUIDELINES

- Assorted handouts determined by students' choices of assignments

Procedures

- Distribute HANDOUT 13: "THE HERO" READING AND ASSIGNMENT SCHEDULE. Ask students to refer to HANDOUT 10: SAMPLE READING AND ASSIGNMENT SCHEDULE. Each student should fill out his or her own schedule and hand it in to be copied or noted by the instructor. Instructors should specify four incremental due dates and the final date by which students must be done reading. In this way all students will be handing in short assignments on the same days, and the class can continue with their work together.

- In the blank spaces for "short assignments" on this sheet, students are to list a few activities and short writing exercises that they will complete on their own. These activities give structure to the days when students will not be reading in class. Students can be creative and design assignments for which instructors might never ask—one of my students drew detailed portraits of the main characters in his chosen work. Instructors should suggest activities from which students can choose. The four activities named on the sample sheet all work well. These and other suggested activities are outlined in the following procedures.

- Lesson 10 typically will require 2 weeks or so to accommodate students' self-determined reading schedules. In a typical week students might spend 1 or 2 days reading their books independently; other class periods are spent completing written assignments and in other procedures described in this lesson.

My students know that they have to bring their books on the days that are set aside for in-class reading. If they arrive in class on reading days without their selected hero book, they must complete other work and are counted as absent.

- Suggested assignments and activities:

A letter to the main character. During the beginning of their reading, students can write short letters to the protagonist featured in their chosen work. They might ask the protagonist questions about his or her actions, motivations, past history, and future plans.

Story maps. Students are to use a prepared sheet outlining the main characters, setting, main events, conflicts, and themes in the work so far. See Chapter 6, "Racism" (Lesson 9) and INSTRUCTORS' NOTES Q: STORY MAPS in Chapter 4.

Student-written quiz. Students can create short essay questions interpreting themes and conflicts in their works. If there are students who are reading the same works as peers in their class or in other sections, they may take each other's quizzes.

Imagining personal details. Students are to make a list of all objects that most likely would be found in the protagonist's pockets/purse/dresser drawer. This also can be done for other major characters in the work.

Writing in the hero's voice. Students who are reading works narrated by a character with a distinctive narrative voice can write a short paragraph describing events in or outside the book in this distinctive voice.

Small group informal reports. Combine students in small groups of three or four and have them give short, informal oral reports on their books. Instructors can put students together who all have prepared story maps on their current reading.

Book talks. Pair up students and have them discuss their books. Students may use the following questions to structure these more reflective sessions:

1. Who do you think is the strongest character in the book and why? How does this character demonstrate his or her force?
2. Consider one or two of the more crucial situations described in the book. If you were the main character, would you have acted differently? How?
3. What to you is the single most confusing aspect of the book (so far)?
4. Has anything you have read reminded you of similar experiences that you have had?
5. What questions did you have when you finished (this section of) the book?
6. Pick one particularly eventful section or chapter. Why do you think the characters acted the way they did?
7. Add at least three questions of your own.

• As students near the end of the reading schedule, distribute HANDOUT 14: PRESENTATION GUIDELINES. Go over this sheet carefully, making sure that students understand what is expected of them. Instructors will need to decide if students will have the option of a written report or an oral presentation. Students also should know if their peers will be evaluating the oral presentations (and that it always helps to have the book in hand to hold up during an oral presentation).

• Assign or have students sign up for due dates for oral presentations and/or written reports. It is a good idea to make the first presentation due date four days after the distribution of the guidelines, to allow time for Lesson 11.

HANDOUT 13: "THE HERO" READING AND ASSIGNMENT SCHEDULE

Name: _____   Name of novel: _____

Today's date: _____   Author: _____

                              Number of pages: _____

I have/have not started this book already.

I am on page _____.

                              Expected Page Number   Short Assignment

By: _____

By: _____

By: _____

By: _____

I will finish the book by: _____.

I understand that I must give a short presentation or write a report on this book by: _____.

HANDOUT 14: PRESENTATION GUIDELINES

1. Tell the name of the book, author, basic facts about setting, and main characters' names.

2. Name the heroic figure.

3. Take this hero through your extended definition of heroism; tell us how she or he did or did not fulfill your basic requirements for a hero. You will need to give some basic information about plot at this point, but it is not necessary to tell us the whole story.

4. Categorize this hero according to Frye's progression. Explain briefly your choice of heroic type.

5. Take your hero through Campbell's cycle. Explain the stages of her or his journey.

6. Add something personal to your presentation. Here are a few suggestions from which to choose:

- Pick a short section to read aloud (you will need to set it up briefly with a little background information).

- Prepare a short review, telling why you liked (or did not like) the book.

- Give a recommendation telling what type of reader would especially like this book.

- Imagine that this book is going to be made into a movie. Cast it appropriately.

- Think of something else that will make us want to read the book.

Due date for presentation: _____

LESSON 11: ANALYZING A POPULAR HERO

Objectives

- To analyze a popular movie according to heroic archetypes

- To see a model presentation of a heroic work

Materials

- *The Terminator* or other film depicting the heroic archetype in a contemporary idiom. Suggestions:

  - *Taxi Driver*

  - *Silkwood*

  - *Norma Rae*

  - *Rebel Without a Cause*

  - *Sid and Nancy*

  - *Coming Home*

Procedures

- Introduce the film, explaining that even if students already have seen it, they will need to watch it in a different way. Show the film without interruption, but do stop it a few minutes before the end of class to discuss the day's events and to ask students what heroic elements they recognize so far.

- After seeing the whole film, ask students to refer to their HANDOUT 14: PRESENTATION GUIDELINES. Explain that you, the instructor, will model the presentation by presenting *The Terminator* as a heroic tale.

- Using HANDOUT 14: PRESENTATION GUIDELINES, analyze the character Sarah Conner as a hero.

  1. The work is *The Terminator;* the setting is Los Angeles in the "present" (1984) and the near future (2044). The main characters are Sarah Conner, Kyle Reese, and the Terminator (Arnold Schwarzenegger).
  2. The heroic figure is Sarah Conner (also Kyle Reese).
  3. One extended definition of heroism holds that heroism is a *status* (Sarah achieves status in the future: She is a legend, a veritable goddess, mother of a savior) achieved through a *process requiring personal strength* (Sarah saved and trained herself and her son) and consisting of (a) a *conscious moral objective* (Sarah knows she must survive and have a son who will save humanity), (b) *sacrifice* (Sarah pays for her initial disbelief by losing her parents, her lover, Kyle,

and her friends; she overcomes physical danger, others' opinions that she is insane, and the rigors and poverty of life in Mexico), and (c) *improving human experience* (she makes human survival possible).

4. According to Frye's progression, Sarah goes from antihero (she starts out as a passive girl, at the mercy of her environment, in the thrall of and victimized by various machines in her life) to realistic hero (she rises to the occasion and enables humanity to achieve a realistic heroic status).

5. Campbell's cycle:

   Departure: Sarah begins with no sense of her identity. She loses friends, security, and her home. She sets out in desperation, with no sense of heroic journey. She is met by Kyle, who helps her.

   Testing and Fulfillment: Sarah fights the Terminator, over and over. Each of her confrontations echoes classic heroic contests, including abduction, fighting a monster, and so forth. Her union with Kyle is an induction: In conceiving her son, she leaves ordinary experience behind. She has entered into a sacred marriage and created a curative elixir: humanity's savior. This fulfillment ends with Sarah in flight.

   Return: Sarah returns to the world with new life, which ultimately will save humanity. She deeply mourns her lover, Kyle. Sarah has found herself and her mission.

6. Add a personal recommendation of the video.

LESSON 12: PRESENTATIONS, FINAL REFLECTION, AND EVALUATION

Objectives

- To evaluate peers' presentations

- To bring personal relevance to all unit concepts

- To evaluate unit

Materials

- HANDOUT 15: PRESENTATION EVALUATIONS

- SAMPLE REFLECTIONS ON PERSONAL HEROISM (for teacher reference)

Procedures

- As students give presentations of their heroic works, distribute copies of HANDOUT 15: PRESENTATION EVALUATIONS. Explain that students are to evaluate each other's presentations—not their choice of book.

- During or after all final presentations, write Journal Assignment 3 on the board: How will you be a hero in your own life?

This entry can be written without specified guidelines, or instructors can recommend that students "take themselves" through Campbell's cycle and their own extended definitions of heroism. See SAMPLE REFLECTIONS ON PERSONAL HEROISM.

- After students finish with presentations, ask them to evaluate the unit:

  1. Did you like the materials read for the unit? Can you recommend that we add any? Drop any?
  2. Did you like choosing which book to read? Should your book be included on a future list of suggestions for students?
  3. Do you think it is a good idea to let students pick their own books? Should teachers do this more often? How often?
  4. Do you think it is a good idea to let students set their own reading pace? Did this help you get your reading done? Would you have gotten more reading done if you had to keep up with the class? Did setting your own pace make any difference to you?
  5. Was it a good idea to study "the hero"? Why or why not?
  6. Did your opinions about heroes and heroism change in any way?
  7. What was the best or most useful thing about this unit? The worst or most useless thing?

HANDOUT 15: PRESENTATION EVALUATIONS

Name of presenter: Your name:

Name of book and author: Date:

1. Did the presenter provide general facts about the book? In other words, do you have a basic understanding of the characters, setting, and main events?

(1-10 points) _____

2. Did she or he name the heroic figure?

(10 points) _____

3. Did she or he take this hero through her or his extended definition of heroism in a clear, organized way?

(1-30 points) _____

Comments:

4. Did she or he categorize this hero according to Frye's five types of heroes and explain the categorization?

(10 points) _____

5. Did he or she take the hero through Campbell's cycle and explain the stages of the hero's journey in a clear, organized way?

(1-30 points) _____

Comments:

6. Did she or he add something personal to the presentation?

What was it? Did you enjoy it?

(1-10 points) _____

General comments about the presentation:

Stern. *Teaching English So It Matters.* © 1995 Corwin Press, Inc.

SAMPLE REFLECTIONS ON PERSONAL HEROISM

How Will You Be a Hero in Your Own Life?

by Tina, 17 years old

My heroic act that I will perform as an adult is to become a lawyer. That perfectly fits my extended definition of a hero. In my extended definition I defined Heroism as, when someone unselfishly sacrifices something of value to them with determination and faith to better the world or his or her surroundings.

My unselfish sacrifice would be of my free time. It takes many years of hard work and study to become a lawyer. Though I will take shortcuts I believe it is a sacrifice just the same. I know that once I finish my high school education that my freedom will be of great value to me. But in my heart I feel that many people are being misrespresented and run over by the system. And as the hero I plan to be I cannot let that continue.

Determination and faith will no doubt be the hardest. But what is a hero without it. I will be determined to get my degree and have faith in myself that I can do it. Right now I really don't have a lot of faith in myself that I will do it but that's another area where determination comes in. I will be determined to have faith in myself.

I will be making the world and my surroundings better, just by being an intelligent Black woman. Helping people get to know their rights and telling them exactly what they are entitled to. And how to go about getting what they deserve and not always what the government thinks they should get.

As for Campbell's cycle, I'm in the middle of my departure now. I'm finishing school and making plans for what I want to do after high school. My entrance into the belly of the beast is enrolling in Catherine College and finishing the program. Then I handicap the dragon by getting my paralegal degree. And I slay the dragon when I go to the Bar Association. And with that I return to the world and get cases to work on. My gift is when I start to teach seminars and discuss about the law and peoples rights.

I believe in doing this I will be a tragic hero. I was born strong but the environment is stronger than me. I don't really have any special powers to help me. Only my mind and those who support me.

How Will You Be a Hero in Your Own Life?

by Anonymous, 16 years old

I took my Departure once I realized I can't afford to mess up anymore. Like when I was a kid I could do something wrong and there were my parents, and my problems would disappear. But then real problems arose like the law, fights, and everything that went along with that. Lots of major things followed these problems, like court and more fights.

Entrance into the Belly of the Beast is everything I went through after my Departure. I mean problems with gangs, because where I was at, "if you soft, you lost." That's why I had to ride with force. I later realized I was wrong, and got away from all of that.

Slaying of the Dragon was when I finally got away from all that gangbanging shit. Getting out was a major decision, because you can really get hurt and you have to take it. And I took it.

My helper was my girlfriend, Jasmine. Because she also talked me into getting out and to get away from all that because it wasn't worth it.

Return to the world was when I started school again, because I had to keep myself busy so I could stay away from all the gangbanging. So I started school and now I'm heading toward graduation.

My Elixir will someday be my poetry. Someday I will be discovered and my fame will transform me into a poetic architect.

I would say I have two outta three ingredients of heroism. I have commitment because I've been with my girlfriend for almost four years, and once I start something I must finish it.

I have compassion because I care about my fellow man and women. I don't think they should be treated like some people treat animals (cruel and unusual). That's how I describe some people in this world.

I would like to believe I have a social conscience because I care about how my people and other "minorities" are being treated. I'd like to make a drastic change in the way society works. I would like to make life easier, less complicated, and more equal, more fair. At least I believe that there's hope for the next generation, which would be our children. But it's not gonna happen until we get some kind of equality established among all of us. There are no simple answers for this. I feel it messing with my head every day in day out. In ten years, I'd like to be stable, in a job that I would be happy and proud of doing. Something I love like writing. Will this make me a hero? What do you think?

☷ References

These references are divided into two parts. The first part is a general listing of all works cited for instructors' use or reference. The second part contains listings of all works cited in instructional units. These works are organized by genre. Some works may be included in more than one section.

GENERAL REFERENCES

American Association of School Administrators. (1989). *Students at risk: Problems and solutions* [Critical issues report prepared by B. Brodinsky with K. Keough]. Arlington, VA: Author.

American Me. (1992). Universal Studios.

Atwell, N. (1987). *In the middle: Writing, reading and learning with adolescents.* Upper Montclair, NJ: Boynton/Cook.

Boyz N the Hood. (1992). Columbia Pictures.

Campbell, J., with B. Moyers. (1988). *The power of myth* (B. S. Flowers, Ed.). New York: Doubleday.

Chaucer, G. (1985). *The Canterbury tales: A verse translation* (with introduction and notes by D. Wright). Oxford, UK, & New York: Oxford University Press.

Collins, R. L. (1992). Teachers' conceptions of ability. In J. H. Johnston & K. M. Borman (Eds.), *Effective schooling for economically disadvantaged students: School-based strategies for diverse student populations*. Norwood, NJ: University of Cincinnati Series, Ablex.

de Saint-Exupery, A. (1971). *The little prince*. New York: Harcourt Brace Jovanovich.

Deal, B. (1983). Antaeus. In J. W. Johnson & M. G. Forst (Eds.), *MacDougal, Littell literature: Orange level* (p. 24). Evanston, IL: MacDougal, Littell. (Original work published 1962)

Duska, R. F. (1975). *Moral development: A guide to Piaget and Kohlberg*. New York: Paulist Press.

Fly Jones, B. (1988). Toward redefining models of curriculum and instruction for students at risk. In B. Z. Presseisen (Ed.), *At-risk students and thinking: Perspectives from research*. Washington, DC: National Education Association/Research for Better Schools.

Foucault, M. (1980). *Power/Knowledge: Selected interviews and other writings, 1971-1977* (C. Gordon, Ed. & Trans.). New York: Pantheon.

Freire, P. (1971). To the coordinator of a cultural circle. *Convergence, 4*(1), 111-116.

Frye, N. (1957). *The anatomy of criticism: Four essays*. Princeton, NJ: Princeton University Press.

Gabriel, P. (1986). In your eyes. *So*. Geffen Records.

Giovanni, N. (1983). My house. In N. Giovanni, *My house: Poems by Nikki Giovanni*. New York: Quill.

Golding, W. (1959. *Lord of the flies*. New York: Capricorn.

Hawthorne, R. K. (1992). *Curriculum in the making: Teacher choice and the classroom experience*. New York: Teachers College Press.

Hayden, L. (1967). Let's put grammar back in the "grammar schools." *English Journal, 56*(7), 1030-1031.

Hillocks, G. (1971). *The dynamics of English instruction: 7-12*. New York: Random House.

Hillocks, G. (1980). Toward a hierarchy of skills in the comprehension of literature. *English Journal, 69*(3), 54-59.

Hillocks, G., & Ludlow, L. (1984). A taxonomy of skills in reading and interpreting fiction. *American Education Research Journal, 21*(1), 7-24.

Ice T. (1988). Power. *Power*. Sire Records.

Illich, I. (1970). *Deschooling society*. New York: Harper & Row.

Johannessen, L. R., Kahn, E. A., & Walter, C. C. (1982). *Designing and sequencing prewriting activities*. Urbana, IL: ERIC Clearinghouse on Reading and Communication Skills and the National Council of Teachers of English.

Johnston, J. H., & Borman, K. M. (1992). Preface. In J. H. Johnston & K. M. Borman (Eds.), *Effective schooling for economically disadvantaged students: School-based strategies for diverse student populations*. Norwood, NJ: University of Cincinnati Series, Ablex.

Kohl, H. (1967). *36 children*. New York: New American Library.

Kuhmerker, L. (1991). *The Kohlberg legacy for the helping professions*. Birmingham, AL: R.E.P. Books.

Merimee, P. (1961). The pearl of Toledo. In R. G. Goodman (Ed.), *75 short masterpieces: Stories from the world's literature* (p. 195). New York: Bantam.

Mulcrone, P. (Ed.). (1990). *The new GED: How to prepare for the high school equivalency exam.* Chicago: Contemporary Books.

Natrillo, G., McDill, E. L., & Pallas, A. M. (1990). *Schooling disadvantaged children: Racing against catastrophe.* New York: Teachers College Press.

Orwell, G. (1946). *Animal farm.* New York: Harcourt, Brace, & World.

Pauly, E. (1991). *The classroom crucible: What really works, what doesn't, and why.* New York: Basic Books.

Price, R. (1992). *Clockers.* New York: Houghton Mifflin.

Richter, C. (1966). *The light in the forest.* New York: Knopf.

Rifas, L., & Campos, M. (1988). *AIDS news* [Comic book]. Seattle, WA: People of Color Against Aids Network.

Romanek, E. (1987). *GED: Preparing for the high school equivalency examination: Literature and the arts: New GED test 4.* Chicago: Contemporary Books.

Shor, I., & Freire, P. (1987). *A pedagogy for liberation: Dialogues on transforming education.* South Hadley, MA: Bergen.

Southern Poverty Law Center. *Teaching Tolerance* [SPLC magazine available from Teaching Tolerance, 400 Washington Avenue, Montgomery, AL 36014].

Steinbeck, J. (1947). *The pearl.* New York: Viking.

Stern, D. (1992). Structure and spontaneity: Teaching with the student at risk. *English Journal, 81*(6), 49-55.

Thomas, P. (1991). *Down these mean streets.* New York: Vintage. (Original work published 1967)

Warriner, J. E., & Graham, S. L. (1977). *English grammar and composition.* New York: Harcourt Brace Jovanovich.

WORKS CITED IN INSTRUCTIONAL UNITS

Major Works (novels, nonfiction, full-length dramas)

Angelou, M. (1969). *I know why the caged bird sings.* New York: Random House.

Arnow, H. (1954). *The dollmaker.* New York: Macmillan.

Bennet, J. (1991). *Skinhead.* New York: Ballantine.

Chernin, K. (1983). *In my mother's house.* New Haven, CT: Ticknor & Fields.

de Jesús, C. M. (1962). *Child of the dark: The diary of Carolina María de Jesús* (D. St. Clair, Trans.). New York: E. P. Dutton.

de Saint-Exupery, A. (1971). *The little prince.* New York: Harcourt Brace Jovanovich.

Dorris, M. (1987). *Yellow raft in blue water.* New York: Henry Holt.

Duska, R. F. (1975). *Moral development: A guide to Piaget and Kohlberg.* New York: Paulist Press.

Ellison, R. (1952). *The invisible man.* New York: Random House.

Foucault, M. (1980). *Power/Knowledge: Selected interviews and other writings, 1971-1977* (C. Gordon, Ed. & Trans.). New York: Pantheon.

Frye, N. (1957). *The anatomy of criticism: Four essays.* Princeton, NJ: Princeton University Press.

Gibbons, K. (1987). *Ellen Foster.* New York: Vintage.

Gibson, W. (1984). *Neuromancer.* New York: Ace.

Golding, W. (1959). *Lord of the flies.* New York: Capricorn.

Greenburg, J. (1964). *I never promised you a rose garden.* New York: Holt, Rinehart & Winston.

Guthrie, W. (1968). *Bound for glory.* New York: E. P. Dutton.

Haley, A., with Malcolm X. (1965). *The autobiography of Malcolm X.* New York: Grove.

Heinlein, R. A. (1961). *Stranger in a strange land.* New York: Ace.

Hesse, H. (1951). *Siddhartha.* New York: New Directions Publishing.

Hinton, S. E. (1967). *The outsiders.* New York: Vintage.

Irving, J. (1989). *A prayer for Owen Meany.* New York: Ballantine.

Keyes, D. (1966). *Flowers for Algernon.* Harcourt, Brace, & World.

Kingsolver, B. (1988). *The bean trees.* New York: Harper & Row.

Kuhmerker, L. (1991). *The Kohlberg legacy for the helping professions.* Birmingham, AL: R.E.P. Books.

Least Heat Moon, W. (1983). *Blue highways: A journey into America.* Boston: Little, Brown.

MacInerney, J. (1985). *Ransom.* New York: Vintage.

Miller, S. (1986). *The good mother.* New York: Harper & Row.

Moody, A. (1968). *Coming of age in Mississippi.* New York: Dial.

Mukherjee, B. (1989). *Jasmine.* New York: Grove Weidenfeld.

Pirsig, R. M. (1974). *Zen and the art of motorcycle maintenance.* New York: William Morrow.

Price, R. (1986). *Kate Vaiden.* New York: Atheneum.

Rodríguez, L. J. (1993). *Always running: La vida loca: Gang days in L.A.* Willamantic, CT: Curbstone.

Salinger, J. D. (1951). *Catcher in the rye.* Boston: Little, Brown.

Shakespeare, W. (1970). *Romeo and Juliet.* Baltimore, MD: Penguin. (Original work c. 1595)

Spiegelman, A. (1986). *MAUS: A survivor's tale.* New York: Pantheon.

Steinbeck, J. (1947). *The pearl.* New York: Viking.

Tan, A. (1991). *The kitchen god's wife.* New York: Ivy.

Taylor, M. D. (1976). *Roll of thunder, hear my cry.* New York: Dial.

Terkel, S. (1992). *Race: How Blacks and Whites think and feel about the American obsession.* New York: New Press.

Thomas, P. (1991). *Down these mean streets.* New York: Vintage. (Original work published 1967)

Trumbo, D. (1967). *Johnny got his gun.* New York: Bantam. (Original work published 1939)

Vonnegut, K. (1969). *Slaughterhouse five.* New York: Delacorte.

Walker, A. (1982). *The color purple.* New York: Pocket Books.

White, E. (1982). *A boy's own story.* New York: E. P. Dutton.

Wiesel, E. (1960). *Night.* New York: Bantam.

Yezierska, A. (1925). *Bread givers.* New York: Doubleday.

Chapters and Excerpts From Longer Works

Bing, L. (1992). Gang class. In L. Bing, *Do or die* (pp. 120-127). New York: HarperPerennial.

Fausto-Sterling, A. (1985). The biological connection: An introduction. In A. Fausto-Sterling, *Myths of gender: Biological theories of men and women* (pp. 3-5). New York: HarperCollins.

Hamilton, E. (1940). Theseus. In E. Hamilton, *Mythology* (pp. 149-157). Boston: Little, Brown.

Hayton-Keeva, S. (1987). Karla Ramirez. In S. Hayton-Keeva (Ed.), *Valiant women in war and exile: Thirty-eight true stories* (pp. 1-6). San Francisco: City Lights Books.

Illich, I. (1970). *Deschooling society*. New York: Harper & Row. [Abstract provided in Chapter 7]

Kozol, J. (1969). Stephen. In J. Kozol, *Death at an early age* (pp. 40-45). Tucson, AZ: Motivational Programming Corporation.

Kozol, J. (1991). *Savage inequalities* (pp. 51-74). New York: Crown.

Price, R. (1992). *Clockers* (pp. 345-349). New York: Houghton Mifflin.

Rodríguez, L. J. (1993). *Always running: La vida loca: Gang days in L.A.* (chap. 6, pp. 132-159; chap. 7, pp. 160-188). Willamantic, CT: Curbstone.

Sabo, D. (1987). Pigskin, patriarchy, and pain. In F. Abbott (Ed.), *New men, new minds: Breaking male tradition*. Freedom, CA: Crossing Press.

Sheffield, A., & Frankel, B. (Eds.). (1988). *When I was young I loved school: Dropping out and hanging in by Children's Express*. New York: Children's Express Foundation.

Terkel, S. (1974). Herb Goro: A fireman. In S. Terkel, *Working: People talk about what they do all day and how they feel about what they do* (pp. 446-449). New York: Pantheon.

Articles

Bing, L. (1988, August). Reflections of a gangbanger. *Harper's*, pp. 26, 28. (Original work published May 1988 in *LA Weekly*)

Carlozo, L. (1993, November 7). High school drama students give legislators a tip: Act. *Chicago Tribune*, "Chicagoland" section, pp. 1-2.

Dreyfuss, J. (1992, November). White men on Black power. *Essence*, pp. 66-70, 124, 126, 128.

Gelman, D. (1993, August 2). The violence in our heads. *Newsweek*, p. 48.

Jarrett, V. (1985, December 22). The beast in "Purple." *Chicago Sun-Times*, p. 55.

LeBlanc, A. N. (1991, April 23). Girlfriends: Three lives in the drug trade. *Village Voice*, pp. 30-35.

Levi Strauss, D. (1991, June 1). The youngest homeless: A threnody for street kids. *The Nation*, p. 752.

Malone, B. (1991, July, September-December; 1992, January-March, June-August). Radio graffiti [columns]. *Spin*.

Marriott, M. (1993, January 24). Rap's embrace of "nigger" fires bitter debate. *New York Times*, sec. 1, p. 1.

Nichols, L. M. (1991). Reducing economic inequality can stop racism. In *Racism in America: Opposing viewpoints* (pp. 240-246). San Diego: Greenhaven. (Original work published 1990)

The roots of economic violence: Dim economic prospects for young men. (1987, November). *Dollars and Sense*, p. 84. (As excerpted in *Utne Reader*, 1989, May/June)

Sagan, C. (1985). Twelve things I wish they taught me in school. *Literary Cavalcade, 37*(6), pp. 3-5.

Smith, D. (1994, January). Dreaming America: Hip hop culture. *Spin*, p. 83.

Short Stories

Deal, B. (1983). Antaeus. In J. W. Johnson & M. G. Forst (Eds.), *MacDougal, Littell literature: Orange level* (p. 24). Evanston, IL: MacDougal, Littell. (Original work published 1962)

Gibbs, A. (1961). The test. In R. G. Goodman (Ed.), *75 short masterpieces: Stories from the world's literature* (p. 90). New York: Bantam. (Original work published 1940)

Merimee, P. (1961). The pearl of Toledo. In R. G. Goodman (Ed.), *75 short masterpieces: Stories from the world's literature* (p. 195). New York: Bantam.

Poems

Bishop, M. (1973). The perforated spirit. In A. Daigon & R. T. LaConte (Eds.), *The good life U.S.A.: A book about the pursuit of happiness* (p. 11). New York: Bantam. (Original work published 1955)

Chou, N. (1990). You have to live in somebody else's country to understand [Student poem]. First appeared in *Locked in/locked out: Tracking and placement practices in Boston public schools*. Boston: Massachusetts Advocacy Center.

Dugan, A. (1983). Prayer. In A. Dugan, *New and collected poems, 1961-1983*. Hopewell, NJ: Ecco Press. (Poem also found in A. Poulin, Jr., Ed., 1985, *Contemporary American poetry*, pp. 117-118, New York: Houghton Mifflin.)

Giovanni, N. (1983). My house. In N. Giovanni, *My house: Poems by Nikki Giovanni* (p. 67). New York: Quill.

Henley, W. E. (1973). Invictus. In A. Daigon & R. T. LaConte (Eds.), *The good life U.S.A.: A book about the pursuit of happiness* (p. 10). New York: Bantam. (Original work published 1908)

Hughes, L. (1970). Let America be America again. In L. Hughes & A. Rontemps (Eds.), *Poetry of the Negro, 1746-1970* (p. 193). Garden City, NY: Doubleday.

Levertov, D. (1985). The altars in the street. In A. Poulin, Jr. (Ed.), *Contemporary American poetry* (p. 310). New York: Houghton Mifflin.

Mora, P. (1984). Elena. In P. Mora, *Chants* (p. 50). Houston: Arte Publico Press-University of Houston.

Parker, P. (1978). For the white person who wants to be my friend. In P. Parker, *Movement in black*. Ithaca, NY: Firebrand.

Piercy, M. (1971, 1973, 1982). Barbie doll. In M. Piercy, *Circles on the water*. New York: Knopf. (Poem also found in A. Poulin, Jr., Ed., 1985, *Contemporary American poetry*, p. 409, New York: Houghton Mifflin.)

Piercy, M. (1971, 1973, 1982). A work of artifice. In M. Piercy, *Circles on the water*. New York: Knopf. (Poem also found in A. Poulin, Jr., Ed., 1985, *Contemporary American poetry*, p. 407, New York: Houghton Mifflin.)

Rilke, R. M. (1981). Sometimes a man stands up during supper . . . In R. Bly (Ed.), *Selected poems of Rainer Maria Rilke* (p. 49). New York: HarperCollins.

Rodríguez, L. J. (1989). *Poems across the pavement*. Chicago: Tia Chucha Press.

Rodríguez, L. J. (1991). *The concrete river*. Willamantic, CT: Curbstone.

Updike, J. (1984). Ex-basketball player. In D. W. Foote & B. P. Perkins (Eds.), *MacDougal, Littell literature: Blue level* (p. 442). Evanston, IL: MacDougal, Littell. (Original work published 1957)

Yevtushenko, Y. (1966). Conversation with an American writer. In H. Marshall (Trans.), *Yevtushenko Poems*. New York: E. P. Dutton.

Yevtushenko, Y. (1991). Lies. In R. Milner-Gulland & P. Levi, Trans., *Yevgeny Yevtushenko: The collected poems 1952-1990* (p. 3). New York: Henry Holt.

Songs

Anthrax. (1987). Indians. *Among the living*. Island Records.

Arrested Development. (1993). People everyday. *3 years, 5 months, and 2 days in the life of . . .* Chrysalis Records.

The Cure. (1979). Boys don't cry. *Boys don't cry*. Elektra/Asylum Records.

The Disposable Heroes of Hiphoprisy. (1992). The language of violence. *Hypocrisy is the greatest luxury*. Island Records.

Gabriel, Peter. (1986). In your eyes. *So*. Geffen Records.

Ice T. (1988). Power. *Power*. Sire Records.

Joel, Billy. (1977). She's always a woman. *The stranger*. CBS Records.

Lennon, John. (1970). Working class hero. *Plastic Ono Band*. Capitol Records.

Lisa Lisa and Cult Jam/Full Force. (1985). I wonder if I take you home. *Lisa Lisa and Cult Jam/Full Force*. Columbia Records.

LL Cool J. (1987). I need love. *Bigger and deffer*. Columbia Records.

NWA. (1988). I ain't tha one. *Straight outta Compton*. Ruthless/Priority Records.

Paris. (1989/1990). The hate that hate made. *The devil made me do it*. Tommy Boy Records.

Paxton, Tom. (1962). What did you learn in school today? Cherry Lane Music Publishing Company. [Performed by Pete Seeger: *Pete Seeger: The complete Carnegie Hall Concert June 8, 1963*, Columbia Records]

Sister Souljah. (1992). Brainteasers and doubtbusters. *360 degrees of power*. Epic Records.

Slayer. (1989). Kill again. *Hell awaits*. Metalblade Records.

Springsteen, Bruce. (1980). Pointblank; Glory days. *The river*. Columbia Records.

Sweet Honey in the Rock. (1980). Oughta be a woman. *Good News*. Flying Fish Records.

2Pac. (1990). Violent. *2Pacalypse now*. Interscope Records.

Was/Not Was. (1983). Out come the freaks. *Born to laugh at tornadoes*. Geffen Records.

Films

American Me. (1992). Universal Studios.

Boyz N the Hood. (1992). Columbia Pictures.

The Color Purple. (1985). Warner Brothers.

Coming Home. (1978). United Artists.

Do the Right Thing. (1989). Universal Studios.

Just Another Girl on the IRT. (1993). Truth Productions.

Malcolm X. (1992). Warner Brothers.

Norma Rae. (1979). Twentieth Century Fox.

Rebel Without a Cause. (1955). Warner Brothers.

Say Anything. (1989). CBS/Fox Pictures.

Sid and Nancy. (1986). Zenith Productions Ltd.

Silkwood. (1983). ABC Motion Pictures.

Straight Out of Brooklyn. (1991). Samuel Goldwyn Company.

Taxi Driver. (1976). Columbia Pictures.

The Terminator. (1984). Cinema 84, a Greenberg Brothers Partnership.

Other Materials

Copies of blank schedules used in your school.

Discipline policies or official list of rules from a local institution.

Groening, M. (1987). *School is hell.* New York: Pantheon.

Lauro, S. (1984, October). Open admissions [Play]. *Literary Cavalcade, 37*(1), pp. 9-14. (Original work published 1979; copyright 1979, 1980, 1981, 1984 by Shirley Lauro)

Room 222 [Transcribed scene from television show]. (1973). In A. Daigon & R. T. LaConte (Eds.), *The good life U.S.A.: A book about the pursuit of happiness* (pp. 17-19). New York: Bantam.

Southern Poverty Law Center. *Teaching Tolerance* [SPLC magazine available from Teaching Tolerance, 400 Washington Avenue, Montgomery, AL 36014].

Williams, R. L. (1972). *The Black intelligence test of cultural homogeneity* (BITCH test).

⊞ Index